THE GULF ECONOMIES IN TRANSITION

THE GULF ECONOMIES IN TRANSITION

Henry T. Azzam

St. Martin's Press   New York

© Henry T. Azzam, 1988

All rights reserved. For information, write:
Scholarly & Reference Division,
St. Martin's Press, Inc., 175 Fifth Avenue, New York, NY 10010

First published in the United States of America in 1988

Printed in Hong Kong

ISBN 0-312-00079-0

Library of Congress Cataloging-in-Publication Data
Azzam, Henry T., 1949–
The Gulf economies in transition.
Bibliography: p.
Includes index.
1. Arabian Peninsula—Economic conditions.
2. Arabian Peninsula—Economic policy.   3. Monetary
policy—Arabian Peninsula.   4. Economic forecasting—
Arabian Peninsula.   I. Title.
HC415.3.A95   1987   330.953′053   86–21957
ISBN 0-312-00079-0

To My Wife and Friend Reem
Whose Joyful Character Makes Life
More Exciting
and My Sons Suhail and Ramzi
May They Grow to Share Our Affection for the
Region

Contents

1	Characteristics of the Transitional Stage	1
2	The Oil Market: A Gulf Perspective	20
3	Investment Climate in the Gulf	33
4	Gulf Consumer Markets	45
5	Financial Development and Capital Markets in the Gulf	66
6	A New Era for Gulf Banking	88
7	The Declining Construction Sector	106
8	The Industrial Challenge in the GCC Region	121
9	Gulf Currencies, Foreign Investments and External Balances	159
10	Other Economic Sectors	182
11	Country Credit Analysis in the GCC Region	205
	Statistical Appendix	225
	Index	257

The views expressed in this book are those of the author and do not necessarily reflect those of his present or previous employers.

1 Characteristics of the Transitional Stage

THE REGION EXPERIENCING STRUCTURAL CHANGES

It appears that the states of the Gulf Co-operation Council (GCC): Saudi Arabia, Kuwait, United Arab Emirates, Oman, Bahrain and Qatar will continue to adjust to a slower pace of growth and development in the coming few years. The slowdown in the GCC states, in contrast with that of the industrialized countries, is not foreseen as a cyclical phenomenon, rather, it is the outcome of external and structural changes that started in 1981–82. The decline in the region's oil revenues, the lingering Iran–Iraq war and the rising toll of Al-Manakh stock market crisis in Kuwait are at the root of the present downswing in overall economic activities.

The annualized double digit growth rates of the 70s have given way to much lower growth rates in 1983, 1984 and 1985. Saudi Arabia for example recorded a negative growth in its GDP in these years (Table 1.1). Non-oil GDP for the six countries is estimated to have increased by around 3% during the fiscal year 1984/85 (4.5% in Saudi Arabia), the lowest rate in the 80s. The 1986–87 growth rates are projected to be even lower and the trough of the cycle is forecasted to be reached in 1988. By late 80s early 90s growth in the region would start to pick up momentum fuelled by the forecasted increase in world demand of OPEC oil.

Table 1.1 Growth rates in nominal GDP (%)

	1981	1982	1983	1984	1985
Saudi Arabia	34.90	0.79	−20.87	−10.60	−8.60
UAE	7.00	−7.32	−7.07	1.60	−6.60
Oman	20.69	4.94	4.83	10.50	13.00
Qatar	10.11	−12.29	−15.50	5.02	−9.00
Kuwait	−9.50	−10.98	6.95	4.50	−9.60
Bahrain	13.25	8.09	4.36	5.50	1.00

Source
Various National Sources, 1981–85.

The region's well-being is closely associated with future outlook in the world oil market. The GCC countries are preparing themselves to cope with lower oil revenues for sometime to come. The world oil market continues to be basically weak with little or no increase projected in the coming few years for world demand of OPEC oil. On the contrary, with the rising output of non-OPEC producers, demand for Middle East oil is expected to continue to be depressed in the foreseeable future.

The GCC countries are currently restructuring their economies to bring forth a more diversified economic base where crude oil revenues would constitute a declining source of income, while exports of petrochemicals, fertilizers and oil refining products will continue to be on the rise. Exports of crude oil and refined products contributed about 68% of total revenues of Saudi Arabia in 1985 compared to a much higher percentage few years ago.

Demographic changes have been noticeable aspect of the adjustment process. In 1982 there were a total of around 6 million expatriates in the GCC countries, representing approximately 45% of the countries' combined population of around 13 million. For the first time in recent history the total population of the GCC countries did not increase in 1984 and it is expected to actually decline in 1985–90, with more than 2 million expatriates projected to leave the region in the coming few years.

When all the economic structural adjustments are completed, and the world demand for OPEC oil reverses its present decline, and when the de-stabilizing external variables are replaced by an assuring geo-political atmosphere, then the economies of the region will be able to position themselves on a more stable growth path. The present period of structural adjustment could continue for a few more years to come with an upturn projected to start in the late 80s early 90s.

Notwithstanding these changes, the Gulf region still provides the single largest concentration of commercial opportunities in the developing world. Per capita income is among the highest in the world, even after taking into consideration declining oil revenues. The Gulf states have been a consistently stable region and given their sizeable oil reserves and development plans, the present economic slowdown would eventually give way to a new phase of growth and development, characterised by a more realistic pace than was witnessed in the 70s.

A NEW DEVELOPMENT STRATEGY

The Gulf states are basically at comparable stages of development, they have similar resource and structural base and share a common strategic outlook. They are all moving from public sector led growth and overdependence on oil to private sector initiatives and diversified production base. The general objectives of the evolving development strategy in the region include:

1 diversifying the region's economic structure in order to minimize its exposure to external factors and allow a bigger share of the industrial sectors;
2 the development and optimal utilization of the region's human resources, increasing human productivity and enhancing the relation between reward and productivity;
3 increasing the value added of local natural resources through downstream processing;
4 meeting the local market demand in as much as possible with an outlook toward increasing exports by capitalizing on the region's relative advantage in certain products;
5 creating an industrial and technological base that is self sustaining and is reasonably independent from the oil sector; and
6 working toward a geographically balanced development of the region in order to enhance regional cooperation.

The first stage of economic development in the region is almost completed, the stage lasted from the early 70s till the early 80s and made use of increasing oil revenues to help build the basic infrastructure both physical, human and financial – airports, sports, roads, schools, housing, universities, hospitals, telecommunications and financial institutions. The second development phase has actually started. It involves a larger participation of the private sector and relies more on attracting foreign investors as joint venture partners, including the transfer of appropriate technology, management skills and international distribution system. In other words, the existing infrastructure will be used to build new industries that have a clear commercial viability.

The sectors that are expected to continue to do well include capital intensive products, high technology items, maintenance and various services, especially health, human resources development and communications.

Gulf economies, are in a way unique. While the institutions and the nomenclature are the same as in the developed countries, they function somewhat differently and must be interpreted with skill. Those foreign enterprises which are able to understand the region and position themselves for a long-term commitment in this part of the world would find the Gulf countries to be quite rewarding.

GREATER INVOLVEMENT OF THE PRIVATE SECTOR

Governments of the region expect their private sectors to take more of a lead in the region's development. They point out that private business in the last 10 years has accumulated enormous amounts of assets in the region and abroad. An enormous pool of private capital has accumulated abroad and in the Gulf countries that has not yet been productively mobilized. There are substantial funds deposited with banks in the region that have been invested abroad. According to IMF statistics, net foreign assets of Gulf commercial banks exceeded $45 billion by the end of 1985. Although the private sector's own financial assets are substantial, new private sector activities will continue to be supported by a sizeable flow of long term credit from specialized institutions in the region especially Industrial Development Banks and Funds. Saudi Arabia, for example, has over the past 15 years provided close to $60 billion of low interest loans to industry.

However, after around three years of economic slowdown, expectations of the private sectors in the region are still running low, and a further consolidation of activities is to be expected. Many small and inefficient businesses would continue to face financial difficulties and some of them could find it increasingly difficult to operate. The chances of a few bankruptcies producing a chain reaction cannot be ruled out.

Perhaps what had most affected the financial positions of merchants in the Gulf was the drop in real estate and stock values. Prime property in Jeddah, for example, had fallen by up to 40% in value during the 1983–85 period. In Kuwait the decline in certain cases was even higher. A good number of commercial and residential buildings in the region continued to be empty by mid-1986. It was no longer possible to finance new projects or bail out for all troubled operations with a quick sale of land.

Stock prices have also been on the decline. The all share price index of officially traded Kuwaiti shares plummeted in 1984 by 50%.

Characteristics of the Transitional Stage

In the first six months of 1985, the price index declined still further by around 39%. The drop is believed to be much larger as there were no transactions recorded in the stocks of 18 out of the 47 listed companies. In Saudi Arabia, bank shares have fallen by half compared to the levels attained in 1981–82. SABIC shares which were offered at 680 riyals when first floated in 1984 were trading at around 550 riyals by the end of 1985.

Rents in the region declined as well and the downfall in some cases reached 30–50%. Lower prices and slower rates of economic activities forced traders and contractors to accept lower profit margins. The high profit margin rates of up to 200% in the 70s were scaled down towards the mark up levels normally applied elsewhere in the world.

A new set of problems are therefore facing the private sector reflecting the overall tighter business environments:

1 falling demand, increased competition on domestic markets emphasized the need for and value of effective selling and marketing strategies, and generally increased business risks;
2 profit margins narrowed and the need for sound financial discipline increased;
3 high expertise in management became a precondition for corporate survival; poor decision-making could no longer be cushioned by high margins; and
4 substantial excess capacity now exists throught the private sector of the region which had been installed in anticipation of continued high levels of economic activity.

Gulf Governments were quick to take action in support of the private sector. In Saudi Arabia for example, open tendering on all Government contracts had been introduced to provide an equal opportunity for all Saudi companies. Greater attention was given to the 30% regulation, which required at least 30% of the value of Government contracts awarded to foreign companies to be provided by Saudi companies.

In 1970, around 38% of the region's GDP was generated by the private sector, this percentage is estimated to have increased to more than 55% in 1984 and is expected to further increase in the foreseeable future as the economies of the region gear towards greater involvement of their private sectors. In Saudi Arabia, for example, private business is increasing at the rate of 13% annually. Apart from incentives to keep funds at home, including tax holidays and cheap loans, governments are starting to sell state owned industries and to create channels to attract larger private sector investments.

The implications for future private-sector development are clear. The previously experienced high rates of growth cannot be expected to continue throughout the 80s. Even if oil revenues picked up substantially, with most of the infrastructure in place there will be no return to the high rates of activity in the construction sector, as Government expenditures will be channelled to new sectors. There is likely to be a further continuation in this adjustment, as firms ill-equipped for the tougher trading environment fail to keep pace. An increasing demand for outside finance will be generated which will place growing demands on the region's financial structure.

COMMERCIAL BANKS FEEL THE PINCH

The main subject of concern among the banks in the region is the potential default of private borrowers and the difficulty of obtaining the repayment of loans. The number of non-performing loans have been on the rise, and the depressed property and stock prices have undermined some of the best collateral that banks hold.

A combination of non-performing loans and slower lending activities is pulling down earnings of Gulf banks. The 1984 and 1985 bank results show an overall trend of declining profits. For example, bad loan provisions were estimated at $2.2 billion in the UAE, or close to 23% of the $9.2 billion of outstanding loans to the private sector by the end of 1985. In Kuwait, close to $4.7 billion of loans outstanding, out of total loans of $16 billion by the end of 1985, were considered non-performing and banks had to take provisions ranging between 15% and 100% depending on the length of the non-payment period. Whereas in Qatar, around 10% of all credit facilities extended by the commercial banks were classified as non-performing by the end of last year. Provisions against bad loans totalled around $338 million.

In Bahrain, the OBUs saw the income from their traditional profit centers sharply eroded by the continued economic downturn in the region and the shift in the international market away from syndicated lending. The consolidated assets of the 77 offshore units seem to have settled by the end of 1985 at around $57 billion. Assets denominated in regional currencies declined 10% to $9.9 billion or 16% of the total in 1985, its lowest level since OBUs started operations in Bahrain a decade ago. About 67.7% of total assets continued to be in interbank

Table 1.2 Saudi Arabia joint venture banks results, 1985

	(SR MILLIONS) Assets (% change)	Loans (% change)	Provisions (% change)	Net earnings (% change)
Saudi French	14.3(+5.4%)	6.6(+4.4%)	84.6(+104.3%)	53.3(−15.6%)
Saudi American	14.1(+3.5%)	4.5(−12%)	70.3(+135.6%)	85.8(−37.5%)
Arab National	10.8(+9.5%)	2.8(+2.9%)	36.6(+40.5%)	80.2(−31.6%)
Saudi Hollandi	9.7(+8.9%)	4.2(−1%)	25.0(−13.7%)	11.0(−56%)
Saudi British	7.9(−5.4%)	3.1(−8.1%)	n.a.	n.a.
Saudi Cairo	n.n	n.n	−	−
Al Jazira	4.6(−9.8%)	1.8(−4.5%)	−	−
United Saudi	3.7(+35.2%)	0.7(+11.6%)	19(+90%)	−5.9(+55%)
Saudi Inv.	3.5(−9.1%)	1.12(−10.7%)	20(0%)	1.1(−178.2%)

funds. In 1984 and 1985, only few banks on the island were able to record major asset growth while income growth for many of them was modest at best.

A sharp drop in profits was also recorded by most Saudi banks between 1984–85. The bad loan position is by far the most important issue facing Saudi banks: Up to 40% of many institutions' loan portfolios were considered non-performing. The nine bank's provisions for loan losses between 1984–85 rose by an average 61.3%, compared with growth of just 5.6% by all institutions between 1983–84 (Table 1.2). This surge in provisions had a direct impact on net earnings, already hard hit by the lower interest payments resulting from the high level of non-interest bearing deposits.

The problem of non-performing loans is not going to be solved easily, and has serious implications for the whole banking sector. The situation is still deteriorating, and further large provisions will have to be made in 1986 and 1987. The biggest headache for banks has to do with use of collateral and the payment of interest. The inability of the courts to enforce interest payments on loans may be in line with the sharia law, but it is having a disastrous effect on banks and general business confidence. If borrowers can ignore their obligations, the banks have little choice but to cease lending and turn more towards the international market for their operations.

The depressionary trends in the region had profoundly affected the consumers market products and led to problems of overstocking by importers and retail sellers. With the rising number of expatriates leaving the Gulf countries and the overall decline in income levels, at least in real terms, local demand for electronic products, cars, air conditioners, foodstuffs and household equipment in general, among others, continued to decline. Retail sales have fallen to near breakeven point and stocks in 1985 were high reflecting negatively on the financial status of importers and retail sellers.

Many companies operating in the Gulf had already gone bankrupt, and several others are facing difficulties. Some of the known merchant companies in the region may experience as well liquidity problems. The firms who did not specialize and who branched into various economic sectors and expanded too fast are the ones being affected most. Also affected were importers and retail sellers of cars, electronics, furniture, consumer products, construction materials and equipment in general. In the rest of this decade, the major areas of expansion will be non-durable consumer goods, operation and maintenance services directed mainly to the public sector, computers and communications equipment, and manufacturing of intermediate chemical products.

A TRANSITION FROM SURPLUSES TO DEFICITS

Government expenditures in 1985 were reduced compared with 1984. The 1985/86 Saudi budget calls for a balance between government revenues and expenditures at SR200 bilion (US$55.4 billion), following two years in which lower oil revenues have forced the government to run down foreign reserves to finance deficits. The forthcoming budgets are also expected to be basically deflationary with cuts of up to 30% in government expenditures.

In the other GCC countries governments were looking at ways and means to cut down on their budgetary expenditures. Kuwait's 1985/86 budget included the first planned spending cut in the country's recent history. General expenditures were 4.4% down on the year before to $12.5 billion, and the budget had a nominal deficit of $2145 million down by 8.3% from that of the previous year. The reduction in the 1985/86 budget was an indication that the government was not willing to use public funds to further stimulate the economy.

Qatar's 1985/86 budget was its second consecutive austerity budget, projecting a deficit of $2 billion compared with $1.4 billion the year before. Total revenues declined by 18.7% while total expenditures were marginally above those of the previous year. UAE had also come up with another austerity budget in 1985/86.

Table 1.3 GCC current account balances
(US$ million)

	1981	1982	1983	1984	1985	1986*
Saudi Arabia	38 360	−1 040	−16 066	−19 043	−17 500	−20 000
Kuwait	14 680	5 010	5 120	5 570	4 400	2 759
UAE	9 210	7 000	5 620	7 130	7 080	3 808
Qatar	2 380	1 130	310	1 200	1 000	−192
Oman	1 360	550	359	107	110	−64
Bahrain	550	640	117	−104	609	50
Total	66 540	13 290	−4 540	−5 140	−4 301	−13 639

Sources: IMF *International Financial Statistics*, April, 86; GCC: *Central Banks and Monetary Agencies Annual Reports*, 1983, 1984, 1985.
* Projections.

In the last few years the region witnessed a transition from surpluses in the balance of payment and government budgets into corresponding deficits. The GCC countries recorded an aggregate current account deficit of around $5.14 billion in 1984 and a deficit of $4.30 billion in 1985, a sharp decline from surpluses of more than $66.54 billion in 1981 and $13.29 billion in 1982 (Table 1.3). The 1984 and 1985 deficits would have been much greater had the GCC countries not slashed imports and public spending programs, or had the dollar not strengthened thereby improving the GCC's terms of trade with Europe and Japan.

Merchandise imports which grew at the rates of 50% in 1973–78 period, then at around 17% in 1979–81 period have recorded negative growth in 1984 and 1985(Table 1.4). Total GCC imports from the EEC declined by 23% in 1983–85 whereas total imports from Japan were down by 30% for the same period. Total GCC imports from the US dropped by 40% in 1983–85 to $5953 million compared to $9928 million in 1983.

Saudi Arabia, which constitutes by far the largest consumer market in the region, recorded a drop of 40% in its imports from major trading partners over the 1983–85 period, down to $14.8 billion in 1985 compared to $24.6 billion in 1983.

In 1985, Japan replaced USA as the major exporter to the region capturing around 30% of the total GCC imports from major trading partners. USA share declined to around 23%, followed by UK, West Germany, Italy and France with share market estimates of 15%, 12%, 11% and 8% respectively.

Table 1.4 GCC Imports from main trading partners (US$ million)

	Japan 1983	1984	1985	% 83–85	U.S.A. 1983	1984	1985	% 83–85	U.K. 1983	1984	1985	% 83–85	Germany 1983	1984	1985	% 83–85	Italy 1983	1984	1985	% 83–85	France 1983	1984	1985	% 83–85
S. Arabia	6 683	5 623	3 922	–41	7 903	5 564	4 474	–43	2 242	1 858	1 609	–28	2 989	2 238	1 778	–40.5	3 008	2 402	1 826	–39	1 813	2 311	1 226	–32
Kuwait	1 763	1 429	1 548	–12	741	636	551	–26	505	402	447	–11.5	693	635	507	–27	592	529	427	–28	442	716	259	–41
UAE	1 357	1 125	1 173	–14	864	695	597	–31	861	723	798	–7	515	431	429	–17	507	591	456	–10	394	283	384	–2.5
Oman	469	507	559	+19	175	168	160	–9	679	519	638	–6	169	214	198	+17	57	62	80	+40	54	73	110	+104
Qatar	233	174	166	–29	109	84	64	–41	329	178	182	–45	116	83	104	–10	60	55	62	+3	107	100	109	+2
Bahrain	329	273	193	–41	136	145	107	–21	229	185	209	–9	150	118	101	–33	115	158	82	–29	54	39	36	–33
Total	10 834	9 131	7 561	–30	9 928	7 292	5 953	–40	4 845	3 965	3 883	–20	4 632	3 719	3 117	–33	4 339	3 797	2 933	–32	2 844	3 522	2 124	–25

Sources: 1986 Direction of trade statistics yearbook: International Monetary Fund Central Banks Reports of various Gulf Countries, 1983–1985.

Over the past decade, oil revenues had far exceeded budgetary expenditure allocations in the GCC region and substantial surpluses were accumulated over the years. The governments were the main propellors of economic and business activities with the private sector playing a secondary role in the overall development process. However, with the decline in the region's oil revenues, the GCC countries started operating under deficit budgets. In fiscal 1984/85, budget deficits ranged from $12 911 million for Saudi Arabia to $591 million for Oman. Whereas the 1985/86 budget of Saudi Arabia was heuristically forecasted to be in balance, the budgets of Kuwait, UAE, Qatar and Oman were projected to have another large deficit (Table 1.5).

The main theme of the 1985/86 GCC budgets was rationalization of government expenditures, increasing non-oil sources of revenues and minimizing the drawdown on foreign assets estimated in 1985 at around $205 billion for the 6 member states. The 1985/86 budgets aimed at bringing forth a slower and more normal pace of economic growth. The private sector was called upon to shoulder an increasing responsibility in the overall development process.

FINANCING GCC BUDGETS

Countries of the region had started looking more seriously into non-oil sources of revenues to help finance their current and future budgets. The world oil market continued to be depressed and short-to medium-term prospects did not look encouraging. Investment income, especially in Saudi Arabia will be on the decline as the Kingdom continues to draw on its foreign assets to help finance its current account and budget deficits. Besides, only part of the region's total foreign assets is considered to be liquid or could be liquidated without major losses. This source therefore, does not provide a viable option for additionl revenues.

Taxation is a plausible alternative and governments of the region may have considered levying personal or corporate taxes. However, taxes would prove politically difficult to impose during periods of economic slowdown as they tend to accentuate the depressionary trends in the region. Besides, the tax base is rather small and the percentage would have to be so low that it might not justify the cost of introducing an elaborate tax machinery.

Imposing fees and reducing subsidies on specialized services and goods provided by various corporations of the public sectors could be a better alternative. Fees are easier to administer and they usually have less damaging effect on economy. At the present time several specialized institutions, e.g. universities and hospitals, among others in the region, supply expensive services free of charge. A lot of the goods and services normally provided by the public sector such as water, electricity, telephone, gasoline, wheat, etc. continue to be highly subsidized. Governments' subsidies could gradually be reduced so that people in the middle- and higher-income brackets end up paying the full value of the services and goods they are receiving, while those in the lower-income brackets could be compensated directly by giving them rebates to boost their income. Citizens and expatriates in the region would start shouldering an increasing responsibility to ensure rational utilization of resources.

Another plausible alternative would be to increase customs tariffs. This would not only generate additional revenues for the governments but would also bring forth more rational consumption habits, better allocation of financial resources and a declining import bill. Saudi Arabia, for example, had raised recently custom tariffs from 4 to 7% on imported goods not considered to be necessary, e.g. automobiles, jewellery, furniture, perfumes, electrical appliances, footwear, etc. Goods for which similar products are made locally are subject to a duty of 20%. A big cut was also announced in the price that the government will pay wheat farmers for their annual harvest.

Efforts have already been made in various countries of the region to reduce administrative spending. In Bahrain, the government called on its ministries to reduce expenditures by 13% during the 1985–87 period. In Saudi Arabia, the government requested all spending departments to fix expenditure appropriation submissions for the 1986/87 budget 15% to 30% lower than in the 1985/86 budget. A limit was set on the amount of overtime government officials may work and foreign travel was curtailed and several pay cuts for government employees, teachers and hospital workers, among others, were also announced. During fiscal 1984/85, subsidies on water, electricity, petrol and certain foodstuffs have been invariably reduced as well.

Government expenditures could also be reduced by abandoning the ownership of some of the public commercial corporations and transforming them to joint stock companies to be run more efficiently, on profit and loss basis, by the private sector. By doing so, governments would be able to reduce the burden of administering

Table 1.5 GCC budgets for the years
1981/82–1985/86
(US$ million)

	1981/82	1982/83	1983/84	1984/85	1985/86
Saudi Arabia					
Total revenues	107 761	71 690	64 378	60 225	55 400
Total expenditure	83 352	70 974	74 392	73 136	55 400
Surplus or (deficit)	24 409	716	(10 014)	(12 911)	–
Kuwait					
Total revenues*	15 454	11 074	10 359	10 646	10 352
Total expenditure	13 464	10 752	12 681	12 969	12 497
Surplus or (deficit)	2 011	322	(2 322)	(2 323)	(2 145)
UAE					
Total revenues	6 318	4 372	3 526	3 502	3 537
Total expenditure	5 621	5 245	5 014	4 696	4 531
Surplus or (deficit)	697	(873)	(1 488)	(1 194)	(994)
Qatar					
Total revenues	5 170	4 514	2 400	3 280	2 650
Total expenditure	4 069	4 166	3 900	4 644	4 694
Surplus or (deficit)	1 101	348	(1 500)	(1 364)	(2 044)
Oman					
Total revenues	3 654	3 402	4 178	4 519	5 105
Total expenditure	3 258	3 061	4 777	5 110	5 695
Surplus or (deficit)	396	341	(599)	(591)	(590)
Bahrain					
Total revenues	1 427	1 512	1 663	1 449	1 463
Total expenditure	1 132	1 389	1 681	1 449	1 463
Surplus or (deficit)	295	123	(18)	–	–

Notes
* Does not include income from foreign investments.

Source
Economic Report Issue No. 1. GCC Secretariate (Riyadh, 1986).

these institutions and cut down on the 'recurrent expenditure' item of the budgets. The process had already started in Saudi Arabia when stocks of Saudi Arabia Basic Industries Company (SABIC) and those of National Industrial Company (NIC) were floated in the market in 1984 and 1985. The same may be applicable to such public and semi-public companies as National Airways, Petroleum companies, PTT, Railways, Petrochemical Complexes, etc.

Other sources of non-oil revenues include issuing public debt instruments and developing money market activities to motivate domestic savings and enable financial institutions to channel these savings into productive investments. The advantages of issuing public debt instruments are not only limited to opening new domestic investment opportunities and generating additional revenues for the Government, but equally important, the debt instruments could serve as an effective tool of monetary policy and help the monetary authorities to better control liquidity in their respective economies. If well priced, these instruments could help repatriate foreign assets from abroad and prevent more financial resources from leaving the country in search of profitable investment opportunities abroad.

Another source of revenues that countries of the region could revert to is the orderly devaluation of their currencies against the US dollar. Because most of the region's foreign exchange revenues are received in dollars – devaluation will boost the local currency value of oil proceeds and would provide governments with a windfall increase in revenues to finance internal expenditures. Devaluation would also raise prices of imports and curtail spending on foreign commodities and services. This in effect would be a form of indirect taxation that would spread the impact of the fall in oil prices to the population as a whole. It is also an easy way of administering higher revenues without introducing an elaborate tax machinery.

Few countries in the region had borrowed internationally. A limited form of long-term borrowing would be another way of stemming the drain on the region's foreign reserves and could help cushion declining oil revenues. Loans would be repaid in instalments over an extended period of time when hopefully world demand for Middle East oil will be on the rise again. External debt of the GCC countries in 1985 was either non-existent or very low, this would allow countries of the region to borrow internationally at very fine rate.

Borrowing whether from domestic markets or internationally would expose governments of the region to criticism from the powerful religious establishments who object to any form of usury. One way to handle the situation is to design ingenious methods of borrowing that would hide interest costs inside instalment payments, e.g. long term letters of credit to finance direct government purchases from abroad.

CAPITAL OUTFLOW

A large drop in foreign liabilities of Gulf commercial banks and a noticeable increase in foreign assets of these banks was recorded in 1984 and 1985. This, together with the increase in foreign investment outside the region accounted for a massive outflow of funds estimated at around $25 billion annually. The outflow of funds has been fostered by slower economic activities and the lingering Iran–Iraq war. Capital outflow from the UAE, for example, has more than doubled in fiscal 1984/85. It rose to $5.6 billion from $2.8 billion in the year before. On the other hand, Gulf governments turned to their foreign assets and reserves to cover whatever budget gaps their spending rollbacks could not close. All told, Gulf governments repatriated an estimated $35 billion in 1984–85, most of it in high yielding dollar dominated assets. A new era of reversed recycling had actually prevailed.

Over the past decade the Gulf states were compelled to invest $338 billion overseas because local economies could not absorb profitably the sudden accumulation of capital. In 1985, direct investment was estimated to have represented less than 20% of official public sector investments, but more than 50% of the private sector's investments. There was also a difference in the objectives behind investment abroad by different countries in the region. Saudi Arabia, with a potentially large economic base, has tended to look at overseas investments as a temporary placement of surplus funds to be repatriated home at a later date. Whereas Kuwait considered such investment as a way of diversifying its economy and developing a new source of income. As a result, Saudi investment was concentrated in liquid assets while Kuwait capital favoured more direct investment in energy, real estate and manufacturing. The other Gulf states have a varying combination of these two policies to provide stability to their economies and cushion their dependence on a single export commodity.

SOCIO-POLITICAL STABILITY

The international banking community has been over-alarmed by what they perceived as potentially destabilizing elements threatening the internal stability of the GCC countries. Doing business in the region is now considered to be more risky. The business climate is already charged with distress, regional risks are considered high and the appetite for new business ventures in the area has been on the decline.

The present economic slowdown did not reflect negatively on the internal socio-political stability of the region. Nevertheless, as the present recession becomes well entrenched, and as subsidies are slashed and taxes gradually raised, the high standard of living that people have been accustomed to would prove harder to maintain. There is a growing fear that unfulfilled economic expectations could fuel feelings of resentment that have been subdued by economic prosperity up till now. The strains of the recession could gradually hit a wider spectrum of the social circles and with the revival of Islamic fundamentalism, outside powers could find certain sectors of the region's population a fertile soil for instigating internal trouble and disorder.

After more than a decade of booming business conditions, businessmen may find working in a 'normal' economy less pleasant than they expected. It may also be that young people just leaving university will be dissatisfied when they realize that they cannot earn the incomes that they had expected to get, or that their predecessors who left in the 70s used to earn.

The Iran–Iraq war remains a critical destabilizing element and its effect on the region could be serious if other countries were drawn into the conflict or if Iran succeeded in placing a halt on the flow of oil through the strait of Hormuz. Such developments are still unlikely to happen in the foreseeable future, however, even the fact that events like these are plausible is adversely affecting the international confidence in the region.

Nevertheless, a fairly large segment of the population was not at all unhappy with the slowdown in economic activities of the region. Both the conservative sector of population and an increasing number of liberal intellectuals perceived the rapid pace of industrialization and modernization of recent years as being wasteful and has undermined the region's traditional Islamic values. Increasing competition is one way where weak companies which depended mainly on personal connections to win business will fade away and the economy would gradually become more efficient. This could also be an opportunity to introduce a more rigorous work ethic and develop a more productive indigenous work force. Accordingly, lower oil revenues and slower economic growth were believed to give GCC governments the time needed to carry out reassessment of their economic, social and political development goals.

THE OTHER SIDE OF THE BOOM YEARS

In the early years of the 70s an era of prosperity began. But unlike the different phases of developments that other nations went through, the region had to pay a special price. The sudden boom brought along the sudden wave of new conceptions and ideas affecting societies that had long preserved many of their traditions for centuries.

The boom caught the people in the region unprepared. Bouts of unexpected wealth found its way to some, forcing the character-face that the West like to portray of the Arab Sheikh, and allowed the secretions of some negative attitudes to infiltrate society and be accepted by it.

People have depended heavily on the Government to do everything for them. They used the high income to live a comfortable way of life but they did not help themselves as individuals to undertake long-range planning. A good part of the region's youth chose to be unproductive. Instead of taking interest in the development of their countries they became lazy, expecting others to do all the work for them. This of course, neccessitated the import of hundreds of thousands of skilled and unskilled labour just to cope with the growth needs. The influx of so many foreigners into the region had its effect. New values and ideas were injected into the Gulf's society.

It was like a viscious circle: the more the number of foreign workers the less work nationals wanted to do. This increased the demand for more foreign labour and pushed the youth more towards laziness and unproductivity.

The impact of the sudden boom and the rapid development that the region have witnessed has caused great deal of mess in the social structure and distorted many of the values the region used to cherish. Families were too busy to take care of their children who were left to be catered for by nannies from the Philippines, Sri Lanka, Thailand, etc. Children were raised to speak English first rather than Arabic and were influenced by habits and attitudes alien to them.

Also parents depended entirely on schools for their children's growth and ignored the rule of co-ordination between the home and educational institutes.

The phenomenon of extravagance was overwhelming. It became an accepted ailment in the society. Women did not mind paying $2000 for a metre of cloth and young men simply had to change their cars every six months. A holiday spent abroad every summer and mid-year vacation became a routine event. People did not travel to neighbouring countries like Egypt and Syria but to Europe and the US. The high income produced a higher tendency to spend.

The root cause of the problem was money. This became the sole objective in people's lives and controlled their habits, attitudes and their social principles. Money totally overruled the age-old Arab traditions, values and family unity, even national interests became of secondary importance.

Consumer spending became almost like a contagious disease spreading from home to home. To the point that even those who could not afford it, borrowed to keep up appearances. The young people who were supposed to form the backbone of future societies were also effected. Money could be acquired without effort and the aspect of a fair day's work for a fair day's pay was forgotten.

The boom years created a supposedly élite, who had the wealth without education, work or even cultural values. They rose to positions of influence, because their names were recognised both inside and outside their own country. This created an adverse image of Arab society to the outside world.

With all these points in mind one can understand the adverse effect that the sudden boom of the 70s and early 80s has had on various aspects of life in this part of the world. This is why the economic slowdown was welcomed by many in the region as a blessing in disguise. It would help policy markers to scale down development strategies and people to reconsider their overall outlook to life.

MEDIUM TO LONG TERM OUTLOOK

Despite the ongoing retrenchment effort in the GCC region the medium-term outlook is not discouraging. The present stage of transition would eventually bring forth a more stable growth path without assuming the skyrocketing growth rates of the 70s. The huge financial resources (estimated at around $200 billion), amassed during periods of successive budgetary surpluses in the 70s will continue to provide a useful cushion in time of retrenchment and consolidation.

Demand for oil in the OECD region has reversed its decline recently and world oil glut is expected to disappear by the late 80s. A higher percentage of oil from the GCC countries will be exported in product form, and sales of petrochemical products would further boost the region's revenues. The emerging industrial sectors of the GCC countries are expected to become more viable in the coming few years, with the private sector contributing a large proportion of the region's non-oil GDP.

The expansion is further expected to be fostered by a more stable geo-political atmosphere. By the late 80s the Manakh débâcle will be completely unfolded and the Iran–Iraq war would have consumed itself to an end. The process of reconstruction and development of the two warring countries could well boost business activities in the region as a whole.

In the 90s the region may witness another high growth period. The world will once again become heavily dependent on oil from Saudi Arabia and the other Gulf countries. Within 10 years from now the Gulf region is projected to account for more than 75% of world oil exports. Revenues from oil and from sales of petrochemical products could again bring forth a major upswing in the GCC region.

2 The Oil Market: a Gulf Perspective

INTRODUCTION

OPEC production of crude oil fell from a peak of 31.3 mb/d in 1979 to around 16 mb/d in 1985. The Gulf countries and especially Saudi Arabia bore the brunt of the decline in output. Before picking up in the fourth quarter of 1985, the Kingdom's daily oil production dropped to around 2.5 million in the second and third quarters of that year, well below its OPEC quota level of 4.35 mb/d (Table 2.1). The decline in the region's oil revenues had accentuated the financial squeeze in the Gulf and prolonged the economic slowdown started in mid-1983.

Table 2.1 OPEC crude oil production (mb/d)

Country	1984 Quotas	1985 Av. production	Estimated 1986 capacity
Ecuador	0.18	0.27	0.30
Gabon	0.14	0.15	0.15
Algeria	0.66	0.65	0.70
Qatar	0.28	0.30	0.40
Libya	0.99	1.20	1.60
Venezuela	1.56	1.60	2.00
Nigeria[a]	1.30	1.50	2.00
Indonesia	1.19	1.20	1.70
Iran	2.30	2.10	3.00[d]
Iraq	1.20	1.30	2.00[d]
UAE	0.95	1.20	2.00
Kuwait[b]	0.90	1.02	1.70[e]
Saudi Arabia[b]	4.35	3.50	8.70[e]
Total	16.00	16.00	26.25

Notes
[a] Quota temporarily increased to 1.45.
[b] Including neutral zone.
[c] Calculated at an average price at $27/8.
[d] Restricted by export constraints.
[e] Not physical but policy constraint.

The Oil Market: a Gulf Perspective

The same was, to a large extent, true for the other GCC countries who were experiencing declining oil revenues and slower growth prospects. It was perhaps not in the Gulf countries' best interest to have continuously reduced their production levels throughout 1984 and 1985 in an effort to support the benchmark price of OPEC, while other oil producers increased theirs. By allowing oil production to fall to the low levels recorded in summer 1985, the GCC countries had made a tactical error from which they were trying hard to recover. It was logical, therefore, to see countries of the region attempting later on to revert to previous production quotas agreed upon by OPEC.

OPEC had difficulties within the organization because the member countries were continually forced to try and share out an ever smaller volume among themselves. They started in 1982 with something like 19 mb/d. In 1983 and 1984 they were asked to distribute among themselves something like 17.5 mb/d, then 16 mb/d, and if they wanted to maintain higher oil prices in 1986 they should share out much less. OPEC was pushed in terms of market share much to the point where it had become impossible for the organization to produce only what the market requires.

By 1986, Saudi Arabia was able to increase its production to its OPEC quota level of 4.35 through its 'net-back' contract deals. These deals linked the price of crude oil to the free market value of the refined products it yields. The Kingdom's oil revenues were therefore based on the realized price of the product less the cost to the oil companies of transport and refining. Net back deals were becoming a standard practice in 1986 marking an end to OPEC's efforts to control world oil prices. Most trading in the future will probably be done through net-back agreements, with relatively little on the spot market.

It has become evident that OPEC as a whole can only increase its market share in the short and medium runs at the expense of the non-OPEC producers and in view of the determination of these producers to continue to maximize output, the intended supply of both OPEC and non-OPEC will exceed expected demand for several years. The only possible outcomes of such a situation are either a continued price decline or a change of heart on the part of producers (either non-OPEC or OPEC or preferably both) about their supply policies. As long as this change does not occur (and even if it does, it will take some time), the price competition will continue among all exporters.

An end to the Gulf war could further destabilize the oil market. However, even if there were a complete cessation of hostilities soon, it should not be assumed that the two countries would raise oil production to full capacity. The realities for the oil market would be instrumental in dampening the two countries' expectations. They do realize that the goal to maximize oil revenues cannot necessarily be achieved by maximizing export volumes. Iraq may well be satisfied by an increase in its production of 500 000 b/d to 800 000 b/d while Iran would raise its production by 500 000 b/d. OPEC members would then have to reduce their quota allocation to accommodate the 0.8 mb/d increase in their total production. This together with the 350 000 b/d Saudi Arabia and Kuwait have been producing on Iraq's behalf and the projected increase in world demand for OPEC oil, will ease the transition to lower post-war oil production levels.

Declining oil prices will have a positive effect on the world economy and will eventually translate into a higher demand for OPEC oil. Accordingly, countries of the region would be able to gradually boost their oil exports and this would become more evident in the late 80s early 90s. Export revenues would furthermore be complemented by higher exports of refined products, petrochemicals and natural gas liquid and would reflect positively on current account balances of the various GCC countries.

STRUCTURAL CHANGES IN THE OIL MARKET

It appears that OPEC's difficulties are likely to last throughout the 80s. The main reason is that the rebound in oil demand is proving lower than generally anticipated. Evidence is growing that oil prices will remain under pressure in the foreseeable future, and the group of oil exporting countries will continue to face the dilemma of how to parcel out a small increase in demand during a period in which many of its members expect and need increased revenues. Since 1981 official OPEC prices had lagged behind spot market prices reflecting conditions of excess supply in world oil markets (Figure 2.1).

The structural changes in the world oil market were brought on by changes in the oil industry, market fundamentals, conservation, and geo-political factors. These changes have shifted the balance of power away from OPEC.

OPEC produced over 30 mb/d in 1979. In 1985 it produced just over 16 mb/d, while its total production capacity was about 26 mb/d, mostly

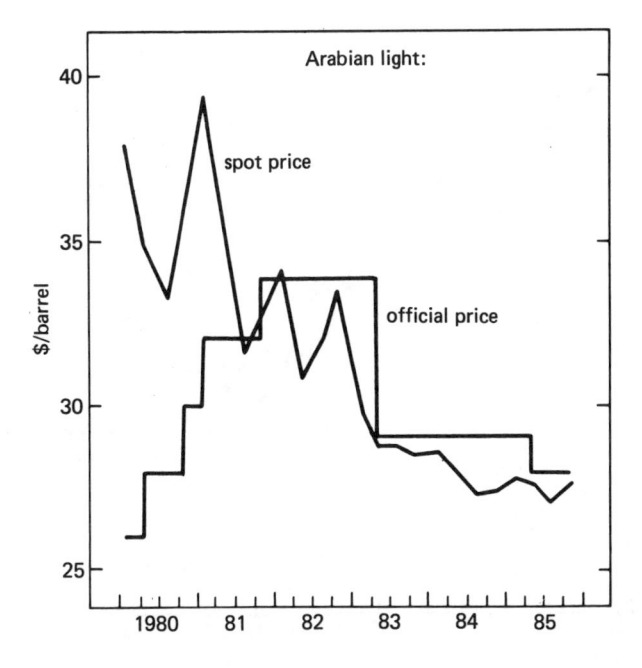

Figure 2.1 *Crude oil prices and production*

of low marginal production cost oil. On the other hand, non-OPEC oil producers were already producing in 1985 very close to their capacity limits and their capacity is generally estimated (by the IEA, for instance) to decline slightly over the next 5 to 10 years.

The argument for a gradual drop in oil prices might prove acceptable for the Gulf countries on economic and financial grounds. The region's wealth is divided between oil and financial assets, with much invested in US government securities. In the 70s, the real return to US Treasury securities was low, often negative. In contrast, oil in the ground was appreciating, and expectations were that it would continue to do so. The decision to lift less oil made sense not only because it pushed prices up, because it was a sound portfolio choice. Now the real return on the US Treasury securities is higher than in the 70s, and the outlook is for oil prices to fall rather than rise. Prudence therefore dictates another portfolio shift – this time liquidating oil rather than financial assets.

In the OECD region, which accounts for two-thirds of total world oil demand, the ratio of oil consumption to GDP dropped by over 25% between 1978 and 1984. An international comparison of petroleum

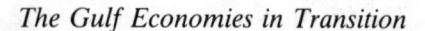

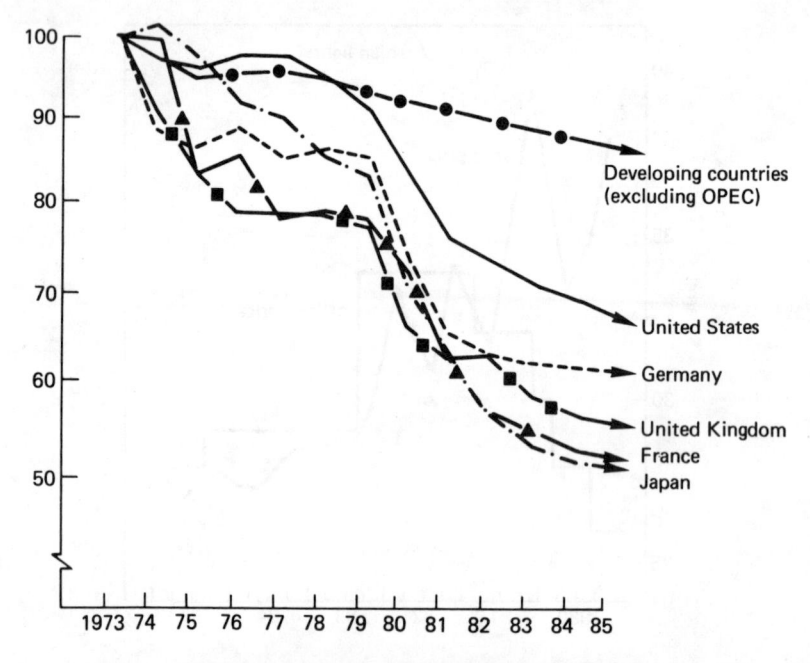

Figure 2.2 *International comparison of petroleum consumption per unit of GNP (1973 = 100)*

consumption per unit of GNP is given in Figure 2.2. The trend is clearly downward and more so for the developed countries than for the developing ones. In 1982 a 5% rise in GDP of the OECD region brought about a 7% increase in oil consumption. In 1984, a 4.9% growth in GDP brought a corresponding growth in oil demand of 2% only.

The industrial countries were successful in utilizing alternative energy resources to reduce their dependence on oil imports from OPEC. In 1979, oil was supplying 50% of the OECD's primary energy requirements. During the first six months of 1985, oil supplied 40%. This loss of market shares relative to nuclear energy, gas and coal as a group may be effectively irreversible, despite the relative price changes in oil's favour witnessed in late 1985 early 1986.

International consumption of nuclear energy, for example, has jumped from 6.5% in 1973 to 10.7% in 1984. While international consumption of coal had increased from 26.2% to 30.3% over the same period, and the corresponding increase in gas consumption was from 18.1% to 19.6%.

The Oil Market: a Gulf Perspective

The number of nuclear reactors which were under operation worldwide by the end of 1984 were 317 with a total capacity of 190 gigawatt, while 209 were under construction in 1985 with a total capacity of 194 gigawatt, and most of them in the industrialized countries.

The structural changes include as well the shrinking role of the heavy manufacturing industry in the Western economies and the effectiveness of energy-saving investments over the past ten years. Even at the peak of the current upswing OECD oil demand was more than 4 mb/d lower than in 1978, the previous consumption peak. The pattern varies from one country to another, but the trend seems well established, and future GDP growth rates are expected to be accompanied by a smaller rise in oil needs. In 1985, oil provided only about 40% of OECD's area primary energy requirements against 50% in 1979.

In 1985, a 2.3% drop in the demand for oil in the OECD region was recorded. Only in the Third World countries and especially countries of South East Asia, did demand for oil rise at around 1% which is the same growth level attained in the previous two years. Total world demand for oil was, therefore, around 45.7 mb/d in 1985.

Fortunately for oil suppliers, the developing countries were to some extent offsetting the drop in OECD oil demand. As they develop, these countries will find it more efficient to substitute oil for wood and other energy sources.

There have been structural changes on the supply side as well. At least part of the increase in the world demand for oil in 1986 and 1987 is expected to be picked up by non-OPEC producers. Additional non-OPEC capacity outside the communist countries is being developed, especially in Egypt, North Sea, Brazil and Mexico. The 20 or 50 non-OPEC countries increased their production by 0.4 mb/d in 1984 and by an additional 1 mb/d in 1985 to a peak of 28 mb/d.

During the 1975–85 period, non-OPEC producers raised their total production by 75%, while the OPEC countries reduced theirs by over 33% to provide not more than 15% of the world's crude consumption. Western Europe (almost entirely Britain and Norway) and North America continued to increase their production. Between them they accounted for 30% of world output in 1985 (Figure 2.3).

Some of the largest non-OPEC producers include China, Egypt, India, Australia, Brazil, Oman, Argentina and Malaysia had an average production of over 400 000 barrels a day each in 1985. Others were small in extraction but high in expectation, and were

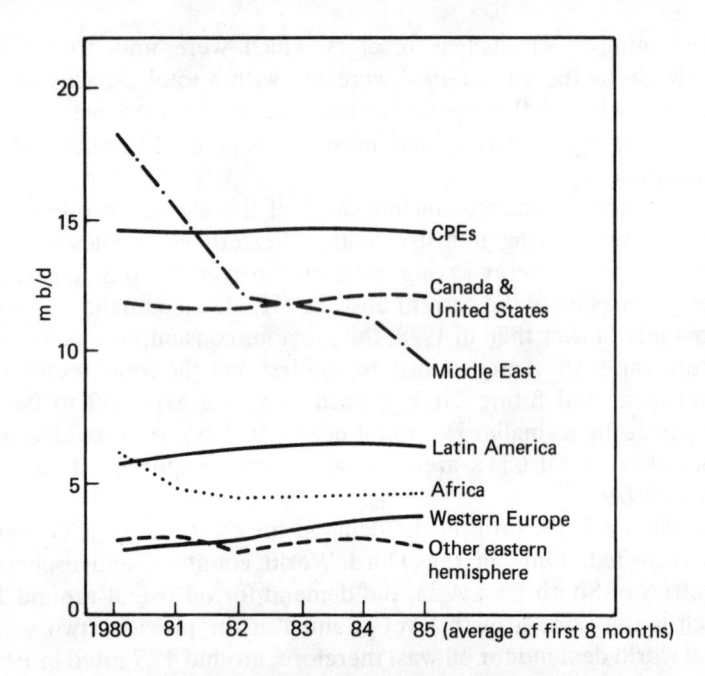

Figure 2.3 *World crude oil production*

mostly Arab countries such as the North Yemen, Syria and Sudan.

Others still were considered respectable exporters, notably Australia, Brunei, Bahrain and Colombia. Add to that the major non-OPEC oil producers such as the Soviet Union, Britain, Mexico, Norway, the US and Canada, to be followed on the far side of the scale, by small producers such as Peru, Tunisia, Cameron, Trinidad and Tobago, Angola and Pakistan, would explain the big increase in non-OPEC oil production during the late 70s and the early 80s.

Net exports from the communist countries dropped to 1.8 mb/d in 1985 down from the levels attained in 1984 of around 1.9 mb/d. Growing domestic gas use in the Soviet Union is seen counter balancing at least partially declining oil production and releasing oil for exports. However, net oil exports from the communist countries are projected to continue their downward trend.

A BRIGHTER LONGER TERM OIL OUTLOOK

Looking ahead for the years to come, world demand for oil is expected to continue to climb very slowly, but steadily. The long run demand for oil is influenced more by structural changes and not merely by fluctuations in economic variables. There are an additional 100 million people on earth each year. A reverse in the trend towards greater conservation of energy resources should be expected. Conservation and substitution are difficult and expensive processes, they really occur when oil prices are very high, not when they are on the decline as it has been the case. Besides, many developing countries would need to expand their oil consumption to facilitate their drive to growth and industrial development.

Non-OPEC oil producing nations are gradually approaching their production limits and without a noticeable increase in oil prices, production from the more expensive oil field of Alaska and the North-Sea becomes uneconomical (production cost per barrel in these areas ranges between $5 and $20). Beyond 1990, only two non-OPEC oil exporters, Norway and Mexico will be able to increase their oil production. By contrast, a 15 to 20% decline in production is expected in the US and Britain, while net exports from the Communist countries will drop to very low levels.

Much of the high-risk exploration undertaken in frontier areas of the world in the past few years already looked uneconomical in 1985, and that was when prices were in the mid to high 20s. Plans to develop known reserves in the US and Canadian Arctic have been scrapped because of the low profit potential. In the US, 25% fewer rigs were drilled in 1985 compared to a year before.

With the decline in oil prices, development of alternative energy resources in the OECD region would either be suspended or indefinitely delayed. Gas liquefaction has proved too expensive, shale oil is in a shambles, and coal and nuclear energy have alarming ecological problems. Even if some of these programmes are reconsidered, they will not prove to be cost efficient given the comparatively lower price of oil fuelled energy.

A 1985 UN report reflected a generally gloomy picture of the development of alternate energy resources worldwide. According to this report, projects for the production of coal, nuclear power and other new and renewable sources of energy – such as oil shale, tar sands and synthetic crude oil – have slowed down significantly in comparison to the 70s and early 80s. Moreover, the report saw a change in this trend unlikely in the near future because of the general weakness of energy prices.

The report also noted that there has been a widespread sense of disappointment with the pace of development of coal resources and the rate of growth in coal production in the market economy. It added that expectations formed in the mid-1970s to the effect that coal exploration and development would boom virtually everywhere over the next two decades, have been borne out by events.

Although the report (prepared by the Secretary-General Javier Perez de Cuellar, and presented to the ninth session of the Committee on Natural Resources, an Economic and Social Council Group, April 1985) described the expansion of nuclear power in the present decade as 'impressive', it said that 'when the focus shifts from past accomplishments to new development prospects, the nuclear picture appears less bright'.

The outlook for major new oil discoveries is not encouraging. A recent study by a US Geological survey estimated that two-thirds of the oil in the world has already been discovered and most of it is concentrated in the Gulf and further discoveries are not likely to change the situation. Furthermore, because of the general ease in the oil prices, oil companies are going heavily into debt to buy their own stocks. As they roll back exploration and production efforts to cut cost, they are foregoing the chance of developing new sources of oil.

Total crude oil reserves of the OPEC countries rose by 3.8 billion barrels to 470.5 billion barrels by the end of 1983, representing 67.9% of total world reserves and sufficient to last for 76 years at current levels of production.

Iraq, Saudi Arabia and Ecuador contributed around 0.8% of the increase to the OPEC's total reserves in 1984. Iraq which discovered an additional 6 billion barrels of oil, was rivalling Kuwait for second place after Saudi Arabia. The Saudis added 3.5 billion barrels to reserves and Ecuador, which has seen its reserves almost double in the 1980's boosted its total to 1.7 billion. Exploration drilling increased in Indonesia, Kuwait, the UAE and Venezuela, with a total of 3128 wells drilled during 1984 compared with 2927 in 1982 (Table 2.2).

Since OPEC's thirteen member states control around 68% of the free world's proven oil reserves, their economic power is self-evident. And since GCC member states also possess some of the world's choicest exploration prospects, their economic influence – in a world heavily dependent on liquid fuels – seems likely to grow. However, OPEC's power will continue to be limited so long as current demand for its exports falls short of the governments' preferred level of production. Excess crude production capacity could keep oil prices under pressure for the remainder of this decade.

The Oil Market: a Gulf Perspective

Table 2.2 OPEC: crude oil reserves
(billion barrels)

	End 1983	End 1984	% Change 1983/84	Crude oil reserves/ production ratio (years) 1983	1984
Algeria	9.4	9.2	−2.1	37	38
Ecuador	1.4	1.7	21.4	18	19
Gabon	0.5	0.5	−	9	10
Indonesia	9.6	9.1	−5.2	20	20
Iran	55.3	51.0	−7.8	63	57
Iraq	59.0	65.0	10.2	160	162
Kuwait	67.2	67.0	−0.3	223	174
Libya	21.5	21.3	−0.9	52	53
Nigeria	16.8	16.6	−1.2	36	37
Qatar	3.4	3.3	−2.9	28	34
Saudi Arabia	165.3	168.8	2.1	70	102
UAE	32.4	32.3	−0.3	71	77
Venezuela	24.9	24.7	−0.8	36	38
Total OPEC	466.7	470.5	0.8	67	76
Total world	690.4	693.3	0.4	35	36
OPEC percentage	67.6%	67.9%			

Notes
Neutral Zone Reserves are Equally Shared between Kuwait and Saudi Arabia.

Source
OPEC Annual Report, 1984.

The world demand for oil is seen as slowly rising for the rest of this century. It is forecasted by the International Energy Agency to recover to around 50 mb/d by 1990 up from 45.7 mb/d in 1985, and to reach 55 mb/d by the end of the century (Table 2.3). Demand for oil in the developing countries is expected to continue to be on the rise until the end of the decade. The average daily consumption could reach 14 mb/d in 1990, going up to 17 mb/d by the end of the century.

Conservation and efficiency utilization would continue to dampen growth rates of oil consumption in the industrialized countries. Total consumption there would rise to 36.0 mb/d in 1990 and up to 38 mb/d in year 2000. These estimates are on the conservative side and

Table 2.3 Long term oil outlook (mb/d)

	1985	1990[a]	2000[a]
Consumption	45.7	50.0	55.0
Industrial countries	34.0	36.0	38.0
Developing countries	11.7	14.0	17.0
Non-OPEC production	27.2	24.4	24.0
Communists net exports	1.8	1.5	0.5
OPEC production[b]	15.9	24.1	29.5
Preferred production[c]	25.0	28.5	30.5
Export availability[d]	21.0	24.3	25.0

Notes
[a] Projections.
[b] Crude oil plus natural gas liquids.
[c] Taking account of technical limitation and Government ceilings.
[d] Allowing for home consumption.

correspond to low economic growth rates scenarios. However, if higher economic growth rates were postulated then world demand for oil could reach as high as 62 mb/d by the year 2000.

For crude oil demand to remain constant under a growing economy, requires new capital investments to be increasingly oil efficient. Eventually, falling oil prices are going to reduce the incentives for such efficiency improvements and total oil demand will begin to rise again.

OECD figures suggest that in the long-run a 30% fall in real oil prices might raise demand for oil by around 15–25%. For OPEC, which in 1985 produced about 45% of the world's oil, the potential gain is much greater. Because non-OPEC producers were already pumping at about their maximum output, OPEC could hope to gain nearly the whole of any increment in oil demand. A 15% increase in world oil demand could translate into a 33% gain for the organization. Those OPEC members, notably the Gulf countries, who made much greater efforts to restrain production than others, could hope to gain even more.

On the supply side, non-OPEC production is expected to reach a peak in 1987 before starting to decline thereafter. Most of the non-OPEC producers are already close to their production limits. Total non-OPEC supply – including net exports from the communist countries – is forecasted to decline to 24.4 mb/d in 1990, down from 29.0 in 1985. By the year 2000, net exports from the communist countries are expected to drop to 0.5 mb/d while the other non-OPEC producers would witness a decline in their production level to 24 mb/d. As a result, demand for OPEC oil is expected to rise from 15.9 mb/d in 1985 to perhaps 24.1 mb/d in 1990 and by the end of the century it is modestly projected to reach 29.5 mb/d.

In sum, the scope for substantial gains in non-OPEC output is virtually non-existent until 1990, and there is little evidence to suggest a major change thereafter. Non-OPEC production is close to its peak, and accelerated production there will not suffice to offset the inevitable decline of US production. In 1985, the USA was still accounting for 22% of world's oil and gas production. However, its reserves then did not exceed 10 years compared to 90 years for the Mid-East OPEC members.

OPEC's expected or preferred production – taking account of known resources, possible new discoveries, technical factors, official ceilings, etc. – is seen as rising from a potential 25 mb/d in 1984 to 28.5 mb/d in 1990 and perhaps to just over 30 mb/d in the year 2000. Allowing also for the exporters' home consumption, OPEC's export availability (21 mb/d in 1985) is expected to be little more than 24 mb/d for the rest of this century. This estimate is clearly of crucial importance.

The projections suggest that OPEC's export availability in the second half of the 80s will be ample to cover requirements even at the top end of the demand estimates. Thus some production controls will need to be retained, implying that there will be little scope for a price surge in this period unless there is an unforeseen interruption in supplies.

A 1985 study by Texaco attempting to forecast the free world demand for the four main types of energy, found that this demand would rise by nearly 40% between 1984 and the year 2000, with oil's share falling from 49% to 42%, coal's rising from 21% to 26%, gas and hydro power showing little change, and nuclear power moving up from 4% to 7%. Figures for these four categories are shown in Table 2.4.

Depending on one's view of economic growth prospects, it seems likely that a reasonable balance between supply and demand for OPEC oil will persist into the 90s. By the end of the century,

Table 2.4 Free world energy demand

	million b/d oil equivalent			% Shares	
	1984	1990	2000	1984	2000
Oil	46.3	49.5	54.7	49	42
Natural gas	16.7	20.5	22.9	18	18
Coal	19.6	24.9	33.1	21	26
Nuclear energy	4.1	7.1	9.1	4	7
Other	7.6	8.7	10.2	8	8
Total	94.3	110.7	130.0	100	100

Source
Texaco, *Free World Energy Review* (Oct. 1985).

however, that period will almost certainly have passed. The growth of free-world demand could by then have equalled and overtaken OPEC's export availability. Accordingly, OPEC's economic power would be strengthened, and there would be strong upward pressure on prices.

The positive impact of lower oil prices and higher demand for OPEC oil on the GCC countries would be more pronounced. By 1995, Saudi Arabia, Kuwait, UAE, Iraq, Iran and Mexico would account for around 85%, of world oil exports. Countries like Indonesia, Venezuela, Nigeria, Algeria, Libya, and Britain are projected to become by then, either self sufficient or net importers of oil.

By 1995 the world may become once again heavily dependent on oil from the Gulf. Crude oil revenues and revenues from sales of petrochemicals, fertilizers and refined oil products will finance high growth prospects in the GCC countries, and the 90s could very well see the region experiencing boom conditions reminiscent of the 70s.

3 Investment Climate in the Gulf

INTRODUCTION

The Gulf countries are at the threshold of a new economic era characterized by reduced dependence on oil revenues, diversification of the economic structure, rationalization of public expenditures, wider involvement of the private sector, enhancement of local skills and products and greater emphasis of regional co-operation. While Gulf countries may differ in their overall economic performance, they are basically at comparable stages of development. They also have similar resource and structural base and share common future strategic outlook.

If we adopt Rostow's stages of economic development, then the Gulf countries are in the state of transition from the 'take-off' stage to that of maturity. The 'take-off' stage is almost completed, it lasted from the early 70s till the mid-80s and made use of increasing oil revenues to help build the basic infrastructure of the region. In non-economic terms, the 'take-off' witnessed social, political and cultural changes that influenced all aspects of life and recorded a huge step forward toward modernization.

The 'drive to maturity' stage had actually started and is expected to prevail for several years to come. During this stage, the economies of the Gulf will shift gradually away from oil to a more diversified production base. The existing infrastructure will facilitate the diversification and growth process. More emphasis will be placed on the commercial viability of the new projects and foreign investors will be attracted as joint venture partners to provide the transfer of appropriate technology, management skills and international distribution systems.

In 1985, Governments' expenditures in the region accounted for 90% of all domestic liquidity creation, more than half of all gross capital formation and nearly half of all consumption spending. However, public sectors are expected to retract while a larger participation of the private sector is planned for.

The economic outlook for the region hinges on future development in the oil market. Conditions in this market are expected to be depressed for some time to come and this will have adverse effects on the region's oil revenues. It would make it extremely difficult for the GCC governments to attain the growth rates projected in the present 1986–90 development plans. Saudi Arabia's plan for example is based on a projected oil production level of 3.8 mb/d and a postulated price per barrel of $26–8. Such price and production levels are considered to be far too optimistic at least for 1986 and 1987.

Austerity measures introduced in 1984–85 would continue to be implemented, and imports of both capital and consumer goods would assume their declining trends. Several projects specified in the new development plans may have to be dropped out, others will be scaled down or implemented over a longer period of time. Projected growth rates of 4% in the 1986–90 development plans for Saudi Arabia and Kuwait are clearly on the high side. Growth rates in most of the GCC countries would be far below these levels.

A NEW DEVELOPMENT STRATEGY

At the heart of the new development strategy of the various GCC countries, as reflected in their respective 1986–90 development plans, is the expanding role of the private sectors. An enormous pool of private capital has accumulated abroad and in the region that has not yet been productively mobilized. The Gulf governments will in the future concentrate on regulatory and promotional functions and allow the private sector, through the market system, to meet the region's demand for goods and services. The private sector is therefore expected to acquire and manage projects currently operated by the governments and to spearhead this stage of economic development.

Gulf governments are also emphasizing the role that leading trading partners can play in establishing joint ventures. Foreign companies are encouraged to establish ventures capable of producing goods valued at 30% of this exports to the region.

Associated with this goal is the development of more appropriate financial system that would facilitate channelling private capital to productive projects. This would involve the creation of new financial intermediaries and new investment instruments and companies. Commercial banks will be called upon to extend credit facilities to production projects instead of concentrating on import finance and declining construction sector activities. The incorporation of more joint stock companies would be encouraged and viable systems for the exchange of company shares would be established.

A particular aspect of the new development strategy concerns human resources development and planning. Measures to change the region's employment pattern will be introduced, including the reduction of expatriate labour force, investment in labour saving technologies and a commitment to upgrade the skills of nationals through on-the-job training. The education system would be made more efficient and more responsive to development requirements.

The enforcement of stricter measures on the employment of foreigners throughout the Gulf will become more evident in the coming few years, and the composition of the expatriate labour force will also change. With the completion of the major infrastructural projects, the demand for unskilled and semi-skilled labour will be less. On the other hand, professionals and higher skilled workers will be required more to man the services and maintenance sectors and to manage the emerging industrial sectors and train the national labour force.

Industrialization is at the heart of the new development strategy. It has become a national objective and a vital instrument of socio-economic development across the Gulf countries. During the 1986–90 development plans, the industrial sectors are targeted to grow at average annual rates ranging from 5.8% for Kuwait (Table 3.1), to 15.5% for Saudi Arabia (Table 3.2). The total contribution of manufacturing sectors to the region's non-oil GDP is projected to increase to 20% by 1990 from a low of 12% in 1984.

Although individual Gulf countries have adopted different programs of industrial development, a comprehensive approach taking into consideration the collective Gulf resources in the context of economic co-operation is being pursued. The general objectives of the industrial strategy include:

1 the development of the second generation industrial ventures founded on the basic chemical and metal industries that are now almost completed;
2 the development of associated support industries which can cater for the maintenance and repair requirements of many basic industrial and infrastructural activities;
3 increased import substitution in combination wherever possible with the transfer of technology from abroad;

Table 3.1 Kuwait's 1985–90 development plan
GDP by type of economic activity
(KD million)

	First Year 1984/1985	Last Year 1989/1990	Average Annual Growth (%)
1. Oil Sector (crude oil, nat. gas & explor.)	3 154	3 748	3.5
2. Non-oil sectors	3 549	4 360	4.2
Agricultural & fisheries	38	47	4.3
Mining & quarrying	8	10	4.6
Petroleum refineries	221	300	6.3
Manufacturing	261	346	5.8
Electricity & water	45	59	5.6
Construction	325	377	3.0
Trade, restaur., & hotels	711	846	3.5
Transport, stor. & commun.	217	278	5.1
Finance, insur., real est., & bus.	712	919	5.2
Public adm. and social services	914	1 065	3.1
Personal services.	97	113	3.1
3. Import Duties	83	104	–
4. GDP (1+2+3)	6 786	8 212	3.9

Source
Economic & Financial Bulletin, No. 9 (Kuwait, National Bank of Kuwait, Nov. 1985).

4 increasing exports by capitalizing on the region's comparative advantage in certain products (basically oil and gas related);
5 the development of intersectoral linkages to exploit the industrial opportunities provided by mineral resources, agriculture and new technology;
6 working towards a geographically balanced development of the region by enhancing regionally based industries; and
7 industries in the region would address the collective Gulf market and avoid in as much as possible duplication of projects that result in over capacity.

Table 3.2 *Saudi Arabia's 1986–90 development plan GDP by type of economic activity* (SR million)

	First Year 1985/1986	Last Year 1989/1990	Average annual growth (%)
Production sectors	62 328.0	73 152.3	3.3
Agriculture & forestry	7 056.3	9 442.9	6.0
Mining & quarrying[a]	1 795.0	2 081.0	3.0
Other manufacturing	12 511.4	20 612.0	10.5[b]
Petrochemicals	–	5 149.2	–[b]
Electricity, gas and water	794.7	1 014.3	5.0
Construction	40 170.6	34 852.9	−2.8
Service sectors	77 552.8	93 239.6	3.8
Trade, catering and hotels	27 069.1	30 626.2	2.5
Transport, storage and Communications	22 177.6	28 304.9	5.0
Real estate	12 171.0	12 171.0	0
Finance, insurance and business[c]	8 460.3	13 017.3	9.0
Community & personal affairs	7 674.8	9 120.2	3.5
Government	30 944.2	30 944.2	0
Total non-oil sectors	170 825.0	197 336.1	2.9
Total oil sectors	113 289.9	148 562.2	5.9
Total GDP[d]	284 114.9	345 898.3	4.0

Notes
[a] Excluding oil and gas.
[b] The combined annual growth rate for both sub-sectors is projected at 15%.
[c] Excluding bank service charges.
[d] Excluding import duties.

Source
Compiled from *Fourth Development Plan 1405–1410 AH* (1985–90 AD), (Ministry of Planning, Riyadh, Sept. 1985).

As can be seen from these objectives there is a shift from encouraging one-shot investment and establishing production units on a turn-key basis to the promotion of the transfer and adaptation of technology to offset the region's shortages in certain labour skills. Such an approach will require further development of services, engineering, consultancy and research and development facilities.

INVESTMENT OPPORTUNITIES IN THE REGION

Private sectors in the various Gulf countries have become increasingly important over the years contributing to over 25% of GDP in 1984/85. During the first half of the 80s, the region witnessed a significant numerical growth in manufacturing enterprises. By 1985, and according to the Gulf Organization for Industrial Consulting, there were about 3600 licensed companies operating in the region, with total investment of $75 billion. The majority of which where engaged in import substitution products and depended mostly on imported skills and raw materials for their operation. The production–consumption gap in a large number of products remains very wide in the region, with excessive reliance on imports for certain critical products.

Despite the present economic slowdown there are still ample opportunities for investors from inside the region as well as from abroad. Perhaps the most important factor in the list of benefits which the Gulf countries can offer is their stability and high credit worthiness. The various countries of the region are considered to be good risk both economically and politically. They enjoy one of the highest per capita income in the world and have foreign assets exceeding $200 billion. External debt is either very low or non-existent and there are no serious disorders threatening the internal stability of these countries. The Gulf countries still represent the single largest concentration of commercial opportunities outside the OECD region.

The second factor in the Gulf's appeal to investors is the firm commitment of the various governments in the region to the economic philosophy of free enterprise and to a development policy based on private sector participation. The free convertibility of regional currencies, the freedom to repatriate profits and fees and the relative simplicity of the tax systems in the various Gulf countries all add to the attractiveness of investing in the region. Besides, Gulf governments continue to offer generous incentives to private investors. These include low cost land, tax holidays, subsidized utilities, appropriate industrial infrastructure and easy credit facilities. The objective of creating a competitive industrial environment is forcing governments of the region to stream line their bureaucratic procedures and consider additional incentives. Saudi Arabia, for example, has over the past 15 years extended $58 billion of low interest loans to industry.

Private sector investment is also encouraged through procurement practices and promotion campaigns that emphasize sales of locally produced commodities, coupled with numerous market research and feasibility studies to help identify investment opportunities. In special cases, modest tariff protection is also introduced. While there are no tariffs on imported raw materials, those on manufactured goods are around 4–7% and tariffs can go up to 20%, where there is a local industry to compete with the imports.

With the implementation of the Unified Economic Agreement among the six GCC states, a large number of manufacturing projects would become viable on a regional basis. The Agreement specifies that local manufacturing within the GCC will be protected by a common tariff applied by all the member states once reasonable capacity has been reached. Investment decisions should therefore capitalize on the opportunies provided by the existing co-operative schemes among the GCC states and reap the benefits of a Gulf wide market. Further more, return to investment in the region should not be measured only by the return on capital invested, but also by the related trade arising from the investment.

Locally manufactured goods will also be favoured in government contracts. The rule that requires all foreign companies winning government contracts to subcontract 30% of it to a wholly owned domestic contractors and suppliers will be more strictly applied.

Looking more specifically at industrial investment opportunities, the field of petrochemical products leads the way. The availability of low priced local feedstock in reliable supplies is an important incentive for companies planning to manufacture plastic goods or other derivatives of petrochemicals. Most of the cheap plastic household goods on the local markets normally imported from abroad could definitely be produced locally. Household detergents, automobile tyres, PVC pipes, polyester fibres, paints, among many other downstream products provides potential opportunities for investments in the Gulf region.

Besides providing the feedstock for industry, the hydrocarbons became a major source of fuel supply to energy-intensive aluminium and copper smelters, steel plants, cement, water desalination and electricity generation. Any capital intensive investment proposition aimed at adding value to hydrocarbons in the region is therefore likely to have a head start. Similarly, any investment in environmental control in the Gulf – air-conditioning, desalination, even power generation has natural market advantages.

Outside the oil sector, industrial production in the region is still in a developing stage. Food processing industry has mushroomed wherever raw materials are available, either from agriculture or from milk farms, poultry farms and fishing. However, more than half of market demand for food and beverages is still met by imports, and the gap between local production and domestic demand may widen still further.

Industries catering for other consumer products especially durables, are comparatively less active either because upstream production functions are non-existent or for lack of suitable manpower and absence of adequate local research and development base. Industrial establishments, when they exist are by and large service and repair shops with some skills to make occasional alterations on customer specifications.

Another category of activity relates to small and medium industries including wooden/metallic furniture, hollow glass products, paper and paper tissue products, plastic bags, household utensils, toys, fibreglass products, toiletries, and detergents. There are still at their early stages of development and continue to be imported on a large scale. There is therefore much scope for the establishment of factories to manufacture all sorts of consumer products catering first and foremost one word toward satisfying the domestic Gulf markets.

The mineral sector exploitation is only just beginning to provide another opportunity for investments. Preliminary exploration has been encouraging, with interesting quantities of a variety of commercially valuable minerals being discovered mostly in Saudi Arabia and Oman.

Engineering industries are noticeably absent from the industrial base. A lot of emphasis is placed in the 1986–90 development plans on maintenance of infrastructure and industrial projects in the region. Machining and light engineering industries which can cater for the repair requirements of many of these activities would be much in demand.

Moreover, new technologies that can be introduced into established activities, such as cement production, conventional air conditioners, etc., that would bring several of the region's plants into the ranks of the most advanced factories of the world would prove to be a sound and profitable investment.

To conclude this section, the opportunities for industrial investment in the Gulf region are reasonably abundant. The prospect for the future looks even much brighter considering the vast increase in the younger population and the needs to create jobs for an increasing number of highly trained labour force.

In order to capitalize on the opportunities offered by the Gulf market, and to insure a sound and profitable investment decisions, private investors, especially those from abroad should try to understand the development strategy of region. What the Gulf countries are after is not simply the establishment of production units but the transfer, adaptation and acquisition of know how and technology.

A good understanding of the nature of the local market is also needed, with the realization that it is becoming more durability rather than luxury-oriented market. Moreover, a thorough market and cost research should be carried out in order to insure the rationality of an investment decision. It also should be noted that factors influencing the viability of a project in the Gulf are of a relatively dynamic nature and should be looked upon from that perspective.

RISKS AND INVESTMENT CONSTRAINTS

Declining oil revenues, the fear of a spillover in the Iran–Iraq war and the anxiety over the political future of the area had undermined, to a certain extent, the confidence of the private sectors in the prosperity and stability of the region.

The recession had produced over capacity in many areas of business which militates strongly against future investments. The lack of investment opportunities of the sort that businessmen normally found in the 70s, the greater complexity of the next generation of projects and the fact that investors wanted to assess the performance of the industrial plants already built, all contributed to a lull in private investment in the region in the past few years.

Industries in the Gulf do not have, overall, a tempting track record. Many have closed down and many more would certainly have done so but for direct government support with a 'buy local goods' policy. Several firms, especially the small ones have gone under due to the lack of good management, insufficient study of the market, undercapitalization and poor quality control.

The region is in the midst of a period of transition that is likely to continue for the remainder of the decade and will be marked by fierce competition, which only the most efficient producers agents and contractors will survive. Profit margins have been reduced substantially and there is expected to be an increase in the complexity of market conditions as new regulations of commercial practices are introduced.

There are several constraints that hinder private sector investment in the Gulf. At the head of the list is lack of highly skilled manpower. The transition from foreign to local labour may prove expensive and difficult to implement. Governments in the region are understandably insisting on replacing expatriates by nationals. In Saudi Arabia for example, companies are supposed to employ Saudis up to 75% of their labour force or up to 51% of their payroll. With at least 100 000 university graduates and a much larger number of school leavers entering Gulf labour markets over the next five years, the emphasis on employing nationals will grow.

Unfortunately, nationals may prove to be high cost labour for several years to come. The number of those who are well qualified and hard working will continue to be on the rise, nevertheless many lack the experience needed and the will to man an expanding industrial sector. Training may be the answer, however it is an expensive and time consuming process that the private sector may not be willing to undertake during a crunch period.

The education system in the Gulf is partly to be blamed. Countries who are industrializing need more technical colleges producing skilled labour and less lavish universities pouring out many graduates with degrees in economically less useful subjects.

Nevertheless, the trend toward technical education and vocational training is spreading throughout the region. The normalization of the region's economy is also introducing stricter discipline to Gulf labour markets, encouraging nationals to accept lower wages and directing them towards blue collar jobs that they used to discard before.

Another limitation to private sector investment, whether from the region or abroad is the less developed financial and legal environment. In certain Gulf countries, it is not clear whether Islamic or western legal principles apply to business and banking activities. Resolution of investment disputes remains local and even though it is improving it is still procedurally cumbersome. Patent laws do not exist and copyrights are virtually unenforceable. In general, the legal system has not evolved at the same pace as the modernization process. The absence of a well-defined legal infrastructure to fall back on may have discouraged banks and private business from taking a longer term exposure in certain countries of the region.

Financial development in the Gulf has been lagging behind economic development. At present there are limited opportunities for the recycling of private sector financial surpluses into productive domestic investments. Outside Kuwait, there are no official stockmarkets and most industrial projects have been financed through equity contribution by partners, commercial bank lending and Industrial Development Fund lending, all relatively short-term. Debt and financial instruments are not common with most of the domestic savings channelled to commercial bank deposits. To attract private capital into the development process, a more sophisticated financial market need to be developed, including the creation of new financial intermediaries, new investment instruments, public efficient stock markets, investment funds and venture capital companies.

Declining oil and gas prices have not only axed the region's oil revenues but have also undermined the Gulf countries' comparative advantage in producing petrochemical products. The main advantage was to be natural gas feedstock that cost only a fraction of world prices which made it possible for countries of the region to produce and sell petrochemicals at competitive prices. As world oil and gas prices fall, that advantage shrink, and Gulf disadvantages like high transport costs loom larger.

The difficulty to penetrate world markets constitutes another constraint to private sector investments in the region. To reap the benefits of economies of scale, Gulf industries, especially petrochemicals, cement, aluminum, steel and fertilizers have to expand beyond their domestic market comprising only around 14 million people. However, in the world market with big vested interests involved, the new comers like the Gulf countries, have a little chance to break through.

It is becoming of widespread disappointment to find the traditionally defenders of free trade in Europe and America threatening to use trade controls and commercial barriers against manufactured imports. Deliberate actions to limit Gulf manufactured exports to these markets will definitely dampen the future prospects of industrialization in this part of the world and possibly lead to retaliation to offset the trade imbalance that exists between the Gulf countries and the OECD region.

Finally, declining government subsidies may discourage private sector investment and could make it difficult for several existing ventures to continue operating profitably. In the past, Gulf government were quite generous in extending subsidized loans to offset the normally high cost of establishing industries in the region. All material except oil and gas have to be imported, and so did most of the labour force. Capital equipment proved often expensive to maintain in the touch climate. The high cost of production when added to the costs of transport made Gulf industries relatively expensive. A wide range of financial and tax incentives might, therefore, still be needed to encourage prospective entrepreneurs and to promote larger private sector participation.

CONCLUSION

The current depressionary mood of Gulf investors together with the various constraints to profitable private sector investments constitute major challenges to the new development cycle. Nevertheless, these constraints are not unsurmountable and investors need to take a long-term view of opportunities in the region.

The continuing strength and stability of Gulf countries' political systems have proved earlier doubters wrong, and these systems show every indication of their ability to cope with the current transitory period. Few years from now the Iran–Iraq war would have consumed itself to an end and the oil market would have stabilized allowing the Gulf countries to position themselves on a more normal growth path.

The prospects of such developments would boost overall business confidence in the region, which together with the significant advantages that exist for investment in the various Gulf countries, would lead to a larger private sector involvement. The returns far exceed the risks for investments in light manufacturing, supplies of downstream petrochemicals, avionics, manpower development, operations and maintenance services, computers and data processing, telecommunications and various consulting services among others.

4 Gulf Consumer Markets

CHANGING STRUCTURE OF GULF CONSUMER MARKETS

Slower economic growth, declining business opportunities, expanding local manufacturing base, modernized infrastructure for distribution and retailing, changing population structure, consumption habits, literacy rates and life styles in the region are expected to have a noticeable impact on Gulf consumer markets over the near to medium term.

At the macro-level, the slowdown in Gulf economic activities that started in 1982 has not yet bottomed out. The Gulf countries continue to face soft world oil markets and lower than anticipated oil revenues. This would further accentuate depressionary trends in the region and force governments to implement higher spending cuts in their 1986/87 budgets and to scale down their (1986–90) five year development plans. All economic sectors are expected to be affected with possibly education, electronic communication and health suffering less than other sectors. Commercial vehicles, electronics, appliances and consumer durables in general will feel the brunt of the overall decline.

The effect of declining oil revenues are already evident in trade statistics. Merchandise imports which grew at rates reaching up to 50% in the 1973–78 period, then at around 17% in 1979–81 period, recorded negative growth in 1984 and 1985. Total GCC imports from the EEC declined by 23%. Japan's exports to the Gulf countries for example, dropped by around 30% for the same period, down to $7561 million from $10 834 million. Whereas total GCC imports from the US dropped by 40% to $5953 in 1985 million compared to $9928 million in 1983.

Saudi Arabia, which constitutes by far the largest consumer market in the region, recorded a drop of 40% in its imports from major trading partners over the 1983–85 period, down to $14.8 billion in 1985 compared to $24.6 billion in 1983. Consumer demand has also decelerated, and the high growth rates of real private consumption expenditures recorded in the 70s are giving way to declines in the range of 4% to 8%.

In 1985, Japan replaced USA as the major exporter to the region capturing around 36% of the total GCC imports from major trading partners (US, Japan, UK, Germany, France and Italy). USA share declined to around 23%, followed by UK, West Germany, Italy and France with share market estimates of 15%, 12%, 11% and 8% respectively. However, as the US dollar continues to decline on foreign exchange markets, Gulf countries, whose currencies have been closely tied to the dollar, will find their purchasing power hurt outside the US and may turn to the American markets for a higher percentage of their import needs of goods and services.

Throughout the Gulf, the number of expatriates leaving is steadily rising and countries of the region are enforcing stricter measures on the employment of foreigners. It is estimated that up to 2 million expatriates will leave in the coming five years. Many companies, especially construction firms, have cut staff and reduced salaries and employees' benefits. Others have practically frozen new appointments. Several companies operating in the region are renewing contracts of expatriate workers only if they accept pay cuts as high as 30%. The decline in consumers' purchasing power is expected to have more of a dampening effect on demand of consumer durables (e.g. cars, electrical appliances and luxury items) than on what consumers consider to be necessities basically food, health, education and housing.

Saudi Arabia has decided over the next five years to relieve 600 000 expatriates working for the government. The figure does not include dismissals by private Saudi companies which could match or even exceed those laid off by the government.

In Kuwait a draft law has been submitted to reduce the number of non-Kuwaitis to 45% of the population over the next 20 years. In 1985, non-Kuwaitis constituted around 60% of the 1.7 million population. In the Emirates, the Federal National Council submitted a recommendation to the cabinet to take immediate steps to reduce the inflow of expatriate workers. Currently, a 'six month rule' requires that any expatriate finishing employment in the UAE must leave the country and stay away for at least six months before returning to new employment.

Elsewhere in the Gulf, employment of expatriates is becoming increasingly difficult. Even in Oman, where the number of new work permits issued showed a net increase of 26.1% in 1984 compared to 1983, an outflow of expatriates, now comprising more than three-

Table 4.1 Ownership of consumer durables in the Gulf countries

% of Households	1970[a]	1985[a]	1995[b]
Car	60	65	85
Deep freezer	30	50	70
Washing machine	75	80	90
Refrigerator	90	95	98
Colour television	30	65	80
Video	6	45	70
Food processor	40	60	80

Notes
[a] Estimates.
[b] Projections.

quarters of the private sector labour force of 300 000 is expected this year as economic growth in the sultanate stabilizes.

With the completion of the major infrastructural projects in the region, the demand for unskilled and semi-skilled labour will be less. On the other hand, professionals and higher skilled workers would be required more, to man the services and maintenance sectors, and to manage the emerging industrial sectors. The changing character, composition and size of the expatriate labour force in the Gulf is of major significance to companies supplying consumer goods to the region where expatriates constitute a vital part of the markets.

At the micro-level, the structure of the typical family in the region has been changing. Multiple households belonging to one man and the extended family structure are gradually being replaced by smaller cellular family units. Children tend to become economically independent at a much earlier age than before. The region is also witnessing changes in the time-use, attitudes, life styles, social values, literacy rates, education and income levels. All these factors will have a clear impact on the micro-aspect of Gulf consumer markets and should be taken into account when forecasting the type of product that will appeal to the consumers in this part of the world.

Analysing the ownership levels of consumer durables yields some conclusions about the development of Gulf consumer markets. Table 4.1 shows Gulf ownership levels for a range of household items, and projections of market penetration in 1970, 1985, and 1995 (the so-called Gulf average is an index weighted by the number of households in each country).

CHARACTERISTICS OF GULF CONSUMER MARKETS

The six GCC countries have a combined population of some 13 million people, with Saudi Arabia (9 million) being by far the largest individual country. In the last two decades, the region's population has been increasing rapidly due to high birth rates as well as high immigration rates. According to the International Labour Organization, there was an estimated total of around 6 million expatriates living in the region in 1982 representing approximately 46% of the total population and a much higher percentage of the labour force. Non-nationals were estimated to constitute 85% of the labour force in the UAE, 82% in Qatar, 77% in Kuwait, 70% in Oman, 58% in Bahrain, and 46% in Saudi Arabia.

The Gulf region has also a higher percentage of males than females. The ratio differs from one country to another but it could reach the high level, of 2 to 1 as in the UAE. Such a population structure together with the fact that a high percentage of the national population (40% to 50% in each country) is aged below 15 years have major implications on Gulf consumer markets.

Consumer markets in the Gulf are basically fragmented. Retailers must deal with a wide spectrum of consumers of various nationalities with different tastes and buying habits. The difference between locals and expatriates as well as between expatriates themselves is evident in the buying of everything from food to automobiles. Lower paid Asian workers and their families buy different products from western expatriates, while expatriate Arabs have different buying habits from those of the Gulf nationals. For example, western expatriates tend to buy goods that last for their average two-year stays. Third World expatriates buy the smaller stereos, colour televisions and cars, because they want to take as many goods back home with them as possible.

Gulf consumer markets are also very competitive and dynamic. They are the most open and the most easily accessible markets in the world. Not only because as a rule there are no significant tariff barriers, but also custom duties are either non-existent or low compared to other markets of the world. In addition there is an excellent distribution system and an oversupply of potential agents. Unlike most Western consumers' product markets, where there may be one or two foreign and several local competitors, competition in the Gulf markets is truly international. Brands are from the United States, Europe, Japan, India, Pakistan, North Korea, Taiwan and other

Arab and North African countries – and in many cases, there are local competitors as well.

The openness of Gulf consumer markets is exemplified by the low custom duties levied on imported commodities to Saudi Arabia. There are three categories of duties: the first category is that of exempted goods, and covers foodstuffs, agricultural and industrial materials and items related to education and health. The second category taxed at the rate of 7%, group of items which are not necessary and are considered almost a luxury such as electrical appliances, certain furniture, clothing, shoes, perfumes and others. The third applied to goods for which similar products are made locally in the Kingdom and these are subject to a duty of 20%.

CARVING A NICHE IN THE GULF MARKETS

Successful companies in the region have certain characteristics in common. They have the right technologies and products, they have recognized brands and consumer awareness and enjoy a very good image among their users, they have as well an effective marketing, advertising and distribution system.

The brand image is an important variable in the markets of the Gulf. Sales depend, to a certain extent, on how the customer perceives the brand. Certain brands dominate most markets, just to give a few examples – Nescafé, Tide, Mercedes, Lux, Pepsi, Brylcreem, Eveready, Lipton, Sony, National, Vicks, etc. All these have a much bigger share of their respective market in the Gulf than they have in most other countries of the world. In times of economic slowdown people become more brand conscious, they want more of what they perceive as dependent items and they tend to shift accordingly to the well-known brands.

Because the customers in this part of the world are so brand-conscious, those firms that entered the market early and made good reputation will be affected least. Imports of the less-known brand images are expected to feel the pinch more. South Korean, European and new Japanese products that have not yet been well entrenched in the market will take the brunt in the expected overall slowdown of sales unless they boost the image of their product by a strong advertising campaign and compete more on lower prices.

Innovative technology, back-up service and advertisement are very important for sales of consumer products. Superior technology guarantees sales and thus market share. It seems that the GCC markets are saturated with new models, and as long as the major manufacturing companies continue to introduce innovative products their market share will not be affected.

The back-up service provided by dealers is also important. During times of recession, consumers become more conscious of the durability of the product and the quality of the after sales service provided by the dealers. Many cannot afford anymore to just replace a malfunctioning machine or piece of equipment, instead, appliances are considered to have a longer life-span now. Good back-up service is, therefore, expected to reflect positively on sales of consumer products.

EFFECTIVE MARKETING IN THE REGION

Suppliers and distributors must adapt to the changing character of Gulf consumer markets. Above all they must sharpen their competitive edge by recognizing evolving market needs. In order to survive many will have to reduce prices and increase volume through effective and informed marketing. Quantitative market research could be very useful and more emphasis should be made on specific advertising and promotion campaigns. Sales' forecasts based on projections from previous years can be rather deceiving in the light of declining overall activities.

Here are a few suggestions that could prove useful when designing a marketing campaign or undertaking quantitative research in the Gulf countries. Gulf nationals are generally extremely polite and courteous, they may therefore politely answer questions about a product with the response they think you want to hear. And if they were not pleased with the product, they may withhold negative remarks. Besides, interviews with women can cause difficulties particularly in Saudi Arabia. To tackle these issues it would be helpful to use known yardstick brands and close ended questions and when the need arises use the telephone to conduct interviews.

With the variety of ethnic consumer differences in the Gulf region, the researcher should carefully consider to whom he really wants to appeal, and then research accordingly. For example, local Arab and Asian tastes differ considerably, but both groups are potentially important customers. The researcher should be aware that among expatriate workers, men outnumber women by up to ten to one, depending on nationality and country.

Gulf Consumer Markets 51

There are five main racial groups in the Gulf market. First, there are local citizens of each nation. In some of the countries, local citizens can be a small percentage of the total population. In the UAE, for instance, it is likely that only 10–12% of the total population are local nationals. The second group is other Arabs. This group consists of Palestinians, Lebanese, Egyptians and nationals from other Arab countries. In Kuwait, as much as a third of the population is made up of other Arabs. The other three major groups are Europeans and Americans; Asians from India, Pakistan and Bangladesh (in the UAE, nearly 50% of the population is from this group); and Far Easterners such as Filipinos and Koreans. Most of the expatriate populations have historically been connected with projects to build the infrastructure of the countries. Their presence has also resulted in a need for extra infrastructure, which suggests a surplus of facilities should they all leave.

The key to marketing in this region is understanding the consumer. All good marketing is based on this concept, but it is surprising how many companies that operate on this principle in their home countries lose sight of it in foreign markets. They attempt to manufacture and market goods for the Middle East based on their understanding of their home-country domestic consumer rather than of their potential Middle Eastern consumer.

Getting to know the consumer in the Gulf region requires visiting the markets, observing and listening to as much of the people in the area as possible, and trying to understand the salient characteristics of these markets.

In many of the region's markets, advertising especially on radio and television is highly restricted or generally unavailable to most consumers, and the package and its graphics serve as the major source of communication to the consumer.

Brands are frequently referred to by illustrations rather than brand name because of the consumers' inability to pronounce the foreign name or to read it at all. Redesigning a pack can clearly have pitfalls if this factor is not recognized.

Consumers in the area – more so than elsewhere – often like to handle, fiddle with and sniff products before purchasing. An attempt to market in one of the countries of the region an air freshener that could not be smelled without significantly destroying the outer packaging failed because consumers wanted to actually smell it rather than rely on the fragrance description.

Consumers in the Arab world, like consumers elsewhere, tend to believe that imported products are somehow better than local ones. So while there should ideally be enough Arabic on the package for the consumer to understand the brand and how to use it, there should also be enough of the foreign language to show that it is an international brand.

Packaging has to cope with ravages of climate. Imagine what a temperature of 130°F in the shade means to a steel shipping container left in the sun at dockside! Many packaging forms cannot withstand the temperature without modification.

A large number of consumers in the area do not speak English. A company which has an English brand name also has instructions on the package in Arabic as well. It is essential for a company to be aware that its brand name is likely to mean at best nothing at all in Arabic, and at worst something derogatory. The Arabic language has an alphabet that differs from English without, for example, the letters "p" or "v" (Pepsi Cola for example is commonly known as 'Bebsi').

The Muslim religion which is predominant in the Gulf countries is very specific on how one should behave and conduct one's life. In marketing terms, these specifics can affect a company's decisions on what to call a brand, how to package it, and certainly how to advertise it.

Traditionally, a good part of the shopping by nationals in the region has been done either by the man in the household or by the servant. Clearly brands aimed at women may suffer under these circumstances, since the brand name must be communicated to a husband or brother or possibly an illiterate servant, as a shopping instruction.

The food-trade structure in the area is changing rapidly. Nevertheless, the traditional souk outlets, small shops in a populated area, are still common. The number of supermarkets is increasing rapidly, and in some areas they are very popular. But much of everyday shopping is still done in the small stores. In terms of marketing for example, these small shops need smaller case sizes than would be used in multiple outlets or larger supermarkets.

The few differences discussed above – there are many more – should not be daunting. Peter Whitaker elaborated on these differences in the *Middle East Executive Report*, September 1985. These differences should rather be seen as factors to be recognized in efforts to understand consumers in a region that has enormous potential because of the high disposable incomes. There are several product markets in the Middle East – fragrances and soft drinks are two

Table 4.2 Estimated number of televisions sets in the GCC countries (1984)

	Number of TV sets	Whether commercial
Bahrain	100 000	yes
Kuwait	600 000	yes
Oman	100 000	no
Qatar	707 000	yes
Saudi Arabia	1 300 000	yes
UAE	250 000	yes

Source:
Arab British Commerce Journal (London, Nov–Dec 1983).

examples – where the per capita consumption is the highest in the world. Because of this potential, the market place is highly competitive.

Unlike most Western consumer product markets, where there may be one or two foreign and several competitors, competition in the Gulf market is truly international. Brands are from the United States, Europe (the United Kingdom, France, Germany, Italy and Spain), the Far East, Japan, India and Pakistan, other Arab and North African countries and in certain cases, there are local competitors as well.

Advertisement whether in newspaper, radio, television, video or on bill boards has played a significant role in promoting a specific brand image, achieving market penetration and sales of consumer products in this part of the world. Arab customers appear to be more vulnerable than others to promotions. The advertising expenditures in the Gulf were estimated at $175 million in 1984. The per capita national advertising budget in Saudi Arabia stood at $15, in Kuwait it was around $36 and between $22 and $26 in Qatar, Bahrain and the UAE.

Television is probably the most important medium for commercial advertisement in UAE, Kuwait, Qatar and Bahrain (see Table 4.2). It is picking up in Saudi Arabia where only recently international TV advertisement was allowed on both the Arabic and English channels. Whereas, no commercial advertising is allowed in Oman.

An important advertising medium in Saudi Arabia in the last two years have been home videos. Videos have immediate appeal to the Kingdom's style of life, where home entertainment is preferred to outdoor activities. The popularity of video entertainment is evident in the region as a whole. Saudi Arabia and other Gulf countries are rated to have the world's highest percentage of video cassette recorders per urban home.

In the region where literacy rates have been rising as a result of extensive educational programmes, and where many locally-based newspapers and magazines have been set up, opportunities for advertising in the 'print' media have become both greater and more appealing. There are now daily newspapers, in Arabic and English, in every Gulf country, as well as a wide range of locally published magazines including women's magazines and those catering for general interests, industry, construction, sports and technical reviews.

Exporters to this part of the world have for a long time appreciated the value of national, regional and international trade fairs and exhibitions. Such events are regularly held in major Gulf cities and often attract many visitors including businessmen and representatives of purchasing organisations. They provide useful venues for market testing, creating and developing business contracts and for introducing new products to the region.

THE MARKET FOR ELECTRONICS AND ELECTRICAL APPLIANCES

Japanese products are estimated to constitute around 70% of the electronics and electrical appliances market in the GCC region. USA captured by South Korea, Taiwan and the other far Eastern countries.

After increasing at rates ranging from 20% to 50% in the late 70s/early 80s. Gulf imports of electronics and electrical appliances recorded a small increase of 3% in 1983 compared to 1982. In 1984 to 1985 unusual declines of around 10% in imports were recorded and a further drop of 15% was projected for 1986. The fall in demand during this period has been accompanied by a sharp price reduction, averaging around 25% leading to a massive drop in dealers' margins.

The Gulf region, despite shrinking demand remains a vital market for electronics, and there is no doubt that clients in the region have developed a taste for Japanese technology. However, consumers are not limiting themselves to the myopic approach of getting the best price possible and are taking into account a host of other concerns including quality, types of guarantees associated with the product, the service record of the shop selling the merchandise, and how the item is marketed. In addition, the consumer electronics market as a whole is marked by improved ordering systems, and more aggressive sales campaigns.

Promotion is playing an increasingly significant role in how well a specific consumers' durable item performs in the market. Manufacturers are coming up with inducements for consumers particularly in the form of improved warranties. As recently as two years ago, the warranty was of little concern to the Gulf consumer, particularly in light of the competitive aspect of the market that forced many prices down. But the service warranty has become a standard incentive in today's market and many manufacturers are boosting their sales back-up force by increasing the number of workshops. Sony, which together with National accounts for some 60% of electronics sales in the region, has come up with a 'worldwide guarantee', which illustrates how a manufacturer responds to the demands of a particular international market. The worldwide guarantee is targeted at the expatriate segment of the market, extending the company's standard three-year warranty to include a one-year period when the merchandise is taken to the expatriate's home country.

The electronics and electrical appliances market in the Gulf has changed from a seller's market to a buyer's market. Sales are expected to continue to decline in the coming few years. With an estimated 2 million expatriates projected to leave the region by the end of this decade and given the declining levels of income, the overall size of the market could shrink by 50% from the levels assumed in the hey days of 1981/82. However, as the exodus of labour continues, more electronic products will be sold to the departing labour. This one time surge in demand may temporarily disguise the huge drop in the market base for electronics in the Gulf.

THE MARKET FOR COMPUTERS AND COMMUNICATION PRODUCTS

A clear exception to the overall decline in the Sales of electronics in the region are computers and communication products. The growth of the information technology market in the Gulf has been explosive in the last few years with annual growth rates estimated at between 50–70%.

In 1984, it was estimated that over $500 million worth of computer hardware was imported by the GCC countries, approximately 70% of which came to Saudi Arabia. Taking software sales into account, and the cost of training and support, the value of information technology bought up by the governments and private sectors is likely to have reached $800 million in 1985.

The purchase of computer systems by government ministries and public authorities will continue to form the core of sales in the region. While networks of minicomputers are being installed by the public sectors, mainframe computers still account for about 65% of sales in the market.

Large and medium level business firms, airlines, banks, hospitals and educational institutions are major constituents of the personal and home computers market. A lost of local companies would like to go for computers but are delaying their decisions in view of cash flow difficulties.

The development of an industrial sector in the region has given ample emphasis in the current five year development plans (1986-90) being implemented in the various Gulf countries. The projected growth in this sector is around 20%. Utilities are also expected to grow around 25% over the same period. Both these sectors are prime candidates for computerization.

The growth in sales of hardware equipment has been more than matched by the growth in the demand for software, specifically Arabic software. Several firms have been established in the region with the resources to take on complete projects from feasibility study to facility management and training. Given the growth of computing in the private and public sectors, the demand for companies to develop applications software specially tailored for the respective needs of the end users would continue to be on the rise. There is urgent need for Arabic operating systems and application packages written in Arabic. As the Arabization of computer applications become widespread, whole new markets for computers are expected to open up.

American exports continue to dominate the lucrative Gulf markets for computers with Japanese products lagging a distant second followed by European products. IBM corporation of New York, stands out, particularly in Saudi Arabia, where it reportedly commands 50% of the fast growing market for personal computers (PC). IBM is so strong throughout the region that a key selling point for competing equipment is that it is 'IBM compatible'.

NCR Corporation, however, boasts of being No. 1 in the five other Gulf Cooperation Council (GCC) states outside of Saudi Arabia.

The Ohio-based computer hardware company has carved out for itself a firm position in supplying computerised cash registers to retail outlets and automated teller machines (ATM) to banks. The company claims to be the supplier for eight of the region's top 10 banks.

Apple Computer has been less successful in penetrating the Gulf market than its larger American competitors, but is gearing up for a major assault in the PC area, when an Arabic-language version of the Macintosh computer is introduced in the Middle East. This could change the microcomputer market in the region from exclusively English-speaking users to one that embraces the population at large.

THE MARKET FOR COMMERCIAL VEHICLES

Japanese, European and American manufacturers of commercial vehicles are facing a declining market in the Gulf area, where falling oil revenues have brought an end to the demand boom of the 70s. In 1985, car sales fell by up to 50% in some parts of the Gulf. In Saudi Arabia, the largest market in the region, car imports dropped by 32.7% to $2.2 billion with 298 000 cars imported in 1984 compared to 421 285 in 1983. Total sales of cars in the six GCC countries dropped to around 430 000 in 1984 from 575 000 in 1983. The position is certain to have deteriorated still further in 1985 and 1986.

In 1985, Japanese makers supplied some 77% of the cars bought in the Gulf. The US ranked a distant second supplying around 10% of the market with General Motors accounting for 90% of the US share. The remainder of the car market was divided among medium to expensive European models and inexpensive Asian Cars. In the light trucks sector, Japan has an overwhelming 95% of the Gulf market, while the US holds 4%. However, in the medium to heavy truck category, the US held 8%, the Japanese 23% while West Germany accounted for an impressive 50% of imports.

Estimates are that over 80% of all vehicles on GCC roads are of Japanese origin.

The 1985 figures, collated by the Japanese Car Manufacturers' Association, show the 'big two' of Toyota and Nissan far out in front with 53% and 33% of Japanese imports respectively. A long way behind come Mazda (3.7%), Daihatsu (3.2%), Isuzu (3.1%), and Mitsubishi (2.7%), with Suzuki and truck manufacturer Hino still further behind.

Even though the exchange rate has been a plus for the Japanese

Table 4.3 Japan's Gulf car markets
(000 sold)

	1984	% Change	1983	% Change	1982
Saudi Arabia	275	−33%	365	−6%	388
Kuwait	36	−30%	47	−24%	62
Oman	42	2%	43	−3%	44
UAE	23	−35%	31	−18%	37

exporters up until 1985, nevertheless, the declining number of expatriates in the region, and the fact that buyers are servicing their cars better and are retaining them for a longer period of time have reflected negatively on sales of Japanese cars (Table 4.3). Dealers of Japanese cars in the region especially those in the Kingdom were reported in 1985 to have been holding enough inventory of cars to cover 1986 demands without having to import new models. Dealers acted as if the boom conditions in the region would continue forever and did not control costs or examine the market closely. Until market conditions pick up momentum, several dealers may continue to face liquidity problems and a lot of the smaller ones may go out of business.

Sales of American cars have also been hurt, however, the market for luxury cars is still going strong. West Germany's Mercedes-Benz, for example, have even increased sales in countries such as Saudi Arabia, Bahrain and the UAE. In Bahrain, sales of Mercedes-Benz cars in 1985 were at least 5% over the 750 vehicles sold the year before. On the other hand, big American cars have lost the appeal they used to have in the 60s and 70s. They have been replaced in prestige by German cars and in number by Japanese cars.

There is also a qualitative change in the market. A few years ago, the average life of a new car in the Gulf was two years. In 1985, vehicles are kept for 3.5 years on average, and sales of used cars were much more frequent. Owners tend to be more conscientious about having their cars maintained, so that the repair business is brisk. Whereas the initial price of a car used to be the only cost factor involved in the choice of model for most buyers, now they also want to find out about the terms and length of the warranty, the cost of spare parts and the availability and quality of workshop facilities.

The latter point greatly favours the large-scale importers who can afford to establish good service facilities. For smaller importers, the difficulties of winning a substantial share of the market at this slow time are compounded by fears among customers that it will be hard to obtain parts and service, a fear that particularly affects some of the European manufacturers.

The slump in the region's construction industry and over capacity and increased competition in both the short haul (urban) and the long haul (national) trucking sectors have dampened the demand for such vehicles. Purchases have slackened off in the 1983–86 period especially the small pick up trucks which had traditionally accounted for a major share of the commercial vehicle market. Tractor sales dropped as well, and in the Kingdom only 600 tractors were sold in 1984 compared to more than 1100 in 1983. Many customers upgraded their fleets using larger vehicles and consolidating loads. Buyers started planning to have their heavy chassis vehicles to last from 7 to 10 years.

The Gulf markets for used construction related vehicles and equipment (cranes, bulldozers, and heavy trucks) dropped considerably in recent years with prices declining by 50% or more in 1984–85. The oversupply of used equipment has become a flood in recent years as large contractors finished up sizeable infrastructural projects and attempted to liquidate activities. With new construction contracts at their lowest point since the early 70s there is expected to be little demand for construction vehicles and equipment especially larger ones in the foreseeable future.

Leaner municipal budgets have greatly dampened as well the demand for specialty vehicles such as street cleaners, but opportunities are believed to be good in the area of port handling equipment particularly equipment suitable for the smaller Red Sea ports which have been experiencing a substantial increase in demand recently.

The market for commercial vehicles in the Gulf has become acutely price sensitive. Exporters and dealers who can afford to play the long-term strategy giving discounts and selling at or below cost now, in the expectation of retaining their present share when the market normalises, would be able to maintain their normal market shares. Dealers will have to revert more to leasing and/or offering credit facilities to finance an increasing portion of commercial vehicle demand. This will force the large dealers to become financing firms with all the intricacies associated with such activities. In a period of economic slowdown, leasing and financing of commercial vehicles become important complementary business to sales of vehicles. However, the risk associated with such a business is relatively high and it could turn out to be quite tricky.

In June 1985, the dealers of GM cars in Saudi Arabia, introduced an instalment scheme that enabled customers to purchase vehicles on a down payment of 50% of their price and the balance to be spread out over a year. Another lease programme was introduced on 1 January 1986 where there is no down payment. The cars leased on a monthly basis will still be in the dealer's name, but the customer will have a contract for servicing insurance and the right to purchase at the end of the lease. It was reported that the sale of the GM cars in general in the Kingdom has gained some momentum as the result of the new instalment scheme.

THE MARKET FOR FURNITURE

Domestic furniture demand has also been affected by the current economic slowdown in the region albeit less than many other consumer products. In the majority of cases, government housing development programmes have slowed down and fewer projects have continued at the previous large scales. While there has been a lessening of demand in relation to expatriate housing, demand amongst the national population has continued to be strong fuelled not least by the number of young people reaching adulthood and moving into their own dwellings.

Total imports of furniture for the 6 GCC countries, were estimated at around $1.5 billion in 1985. Saudi Arabia was by far the largest individual market, accounting for some 64% of imports, followed by Kuwait (approx 14%) and the UAE (10%). The total represents a major increase on the 1980 figure of $592 million. Moreover, these exclude carpets, floor coverings and lighting as well as bathroom and kitchen equipment.

Separate estimates for GCC imports of carpets and 'floor coverings' suggest an increase from $675 million in 1984 to $780 million in 1985. This despite that fact that Saudi Arabia already has the capacity to produce 9 million square metres of carpet a year. An important element in the coming few years will be the market for replacement furniture which was insignificant in the 70s and 80s. In addition to refurbishment of family homes built during the 1970s construction boom, there is a continuing demand for prestige furniture in hotels competing to maximize occupancy rates as well as in hospitals and clinics which are still being expanded and built.

Italian suppliers dominate the market for domestic furniture in the

Gulf, taking some 35% of total import demand. Their share of the market has remained relatively constant in recent years and they have a strong presence in each of the individual countries except Oman where they come second place after the UK. Italy's success is generally attributed to a combination of popular styles, favourable credit terms and sustained marketing.

US suppliers were able to increase their share of supply from 12.4% in 1980 to 17.5% in 1982, however, because of the appreciating exchange rate of the dollar in recent years, the share dropped to 15% in 1985. The success of the American suppliers is concentrated in the Saudi market, which accounted for 87% of their sales in 1985 compared to 9% and 12% in Kuwait and Bahrain respectively.

West German suppliers occupy third place in furniture sales in the region, although their share has fallen from 12% in 1980 to 9% in 1985. This was mainly due to the loss of sales in Saudi Arabia possibly to US suppliers with whom they share a similar image/profile. French and Japanese suppliers have largely maintained their overall share of supply although in different sectors of the market. The Japanese suppliers mainly operating in the middle to lower end of the market, while French furniture suppliers are associated with the higher-priced area of the market and the interior design sector.

Danish manufacturers, although accounting for only 3% of the supply in 1985, have been steadily increasing sales to the region and have developed a good reputation for both product and marketing. There is also a successful Danish/Kuwaiti joint venture – KUFUMA – manufacturing domestic furniture in Kuwait and exporting to other Gulf countries.

Although enjoying a very strong market position in the mid-70s, UK suppliers have performed badly in recent years and their share has fallen to about 5% in 1985. UK companies are still the leading suppliers in Oman and have a reasonable presence in the other lower Gulf States, but even in those countries their share is declining.

Japan does not have a particularly strong position as a furniture supplier in the Gulf. Nevertheless, many express the view, largely based on the supply situation in electronics, cars and air-conditioners, that Japanese manufacturers will inevitably begin to dominate the furniture market. Predictably, they are expected to do this with inexpensive, but well constructed furniture, copied from European designs.

Local manufacture is a significant feature of the domestic furniture market in Kuwait, but does not feature strongly – by comparison with import value – in the other markets. This situation is changing quite rapidly, however, and there are a considerable number of furniture factories approaching or in production (a number of them being joint venture operations). The degree of support provided by a number of the individual countries to domestic manufacturers is considerable (the Saudi Government for example, has a 20% tariff on imports, gives preference to local manufacturers on its own contracts, and insists that contractors employed on government contracts also give preference to local sub-contractors and suppliers). These factors together with the GCC proposals for similarly supportive tariff structures, are likely to result in an expansion of domestic share in the middle and lower ranges of the market.

Furniture retailers stress the importance of design content in domestic furniture and many of them point to the Italian manufacturers as examples of flexibility in producing designs applicable to the market. Italian manufacturers are praised for their ability to produce very attractive/impressive furniture at a competitive price. It is generally accepted that much of this furniture is not particularly well constructed, however, the frequency with which local consumers change their furniture reduces the need for long-term durability, and increases the importance of price.

There is a definite trend towards appreciation of furniture quality and durability – a trend which US suppliers appear to have exploited in Saudi Arabia – which is likely to be furthered by the more conservative mood associated with the current economic slowdown in the region and the recent decline in the exchange rate of the US dollar.

THE MARKET FOR FOODSTUFFS

Like other consumer products the size of the market for foodstuff has been on the decline mostly due to the rising number of expatriates leaving the region. The trend is expected to continue in the foreseeable future.

Most of the fresh food items (vegetables, grain crops, fruits, meat, eggs, etc.) are imported to the region from neighbouring Arab countries as well as Turkey and Pakistan. Increasingly more agricultural crops are being produced locally, especially in Saudi Arabia, UAE and Oman. Canned foods are imported mostly from Europe while more meat is being imported from Australia and New Zealand.

Saudi Arabia is clearly the largest market for foodstuffs in the region constituting around 70% of total imports.

China, New Zealand and Australia are the main contenders in an intense struggle for the lucrative live sheep market in the Gulf. Increasing demand for fresh, lean meat and for sacrificial animals for the Hajj (pilgrimage) season has boosted imports in the Arab Gulf states to 8–10 million head a year.

In the past, livestock came from a variety of sources, including Sudan, Turkey, Eastern Europe and Argentina. Australia currently dominates the market, but is now facing a sharp challenge on both prices and quality from China and New Zealand.

In a significant move, New Zealand has recently lifted its ban on the sale of live sheep to the Middle East imposed to protect the local meat-freezing industry. The decision was prompted by the slump in New Zealand lamb sales to the EEC.

The old freewheeling days of the Gulf food business, when a merchant could make his fortune by monopolizing the market are over. In most states the market is now subject to varying degrees of government control. The sole exception is the UAE, where control is unnecessary, according to importers, because market forces ensure that prices are among the lowest in the Gulf.

In Bahrain, Kuwait and Qatar some or all of the basic commodities – rice, sugar, locally milled flour, meat and cooking oil – are either subsidised or controlled to maintain constant prices, and lists of maximum permitted prices for fruit and vegetables are posted daily by municipalities. Bahrain's Ministry of Commerce plays an active role in the bulk food trade, handling purchases either directly or through two public shareholding companies in which the state has a 10% investment.

In Qatar the government body responsible for essential foodstuffs is the supply department of the Ministry of Petroleum. While in Kuwait the Government's purchasing area for wheat, barley, sugar and rice is the Kuwait Supply Company, and co-operative stores in the country are required to display subsidised commodities on separate shelves.

A new force in the Gulf food trade is the co-operatives, of which there are 32 in Kuwait. They have formed a union to import their supplies directly. Dubai co-operatives are increasing as well and importing their own foodstuffs. While in Qatar the co-ops still depend on local wholesalers but account for 75% of the retail market.

Brand loyalty has always been a feature of the Gulf food market.

Lipton's teabags for example, probably outsell all competitors put together. Buying habits, however, are changing with new affluence and exposure to modern marketing techniques. The practice of selling loose rice and sugar from the sack in small shops is fast declining, and supermarkets are using plastic bags to make up their own packages.

Generally people in the region have now a much more varied diet than before. They are eating more bread and fruit and vegetables are served with every meal. Desserts are no longer a luxury and there is a growing taste for sweets and confectionery. Most of the foods imported for the expatriate population of the Gulf are now just are regularly eaten by the national population.

The strict application of regulations governing production and expiry dates has forced traders to improve both stock control and distribution. Stricter labelling requirements were also introduced, and a list of ingredients of canned food in both English and Arabic is becoming a prerequisite for all preserved food imported to the region.

It seems that the Gulf countries especially Saudi Arabia are strongly committed to develop their agricultural sector and reduce their dependancy on imported food. The Kingdom is now more or less self-sufficient in wheat. The other GCC countries are investing in the agricultural sector and have achieved varying degrees of success in cultivating grain crops, fruit and vegetables.

CONCLUSION

The depressionary trends in the region had adversely affected Gulf consumer markets and invariably led to problems of overstocking by importers and retailers. The markets are expected to continue to contract in the foreseeable future, with demand becoming increasingly price sensitive.

Notwithstanding these changes, the Gulf region continues to provide the single largest concentration of commercial opportunities in the developing world. Per capita income is still among the highest in the world, even after taking into consideration declining oil revenues. The Gulf states have been a consistently stable region and given their sizeable oil reserves and development plans, the present economic slowdown would eventually give way to a new phase of growth and development, characterized by a more realistic pace than was witnessed in the 70s.

Exporter and retail sellers need therefore to design a long-term strategy that would see them through the 90s. Meanwhile as Gulf consumer markets become increasingly price sensitive, producers may find themselves compelled to sell at break-even levels in the expectation of retaining their share when the market normalizes.

Japanese and European exporters, many of whom are well entrenched in the Gulf markets, are facing a compounded problem. Not only have their sales to the region been on the decline due to the lingering economic slowdown, but also their market shares are threatened because of the appreciation of the yen and the European currencies *vis-à-vis* the Gulf currencies. Prices of Japanese and European consumer products have already recorded an increase of up to 30% compared to 1985's prices. This together with the overall decline in consumers' purchasing power point to perhaps more difficult conditions ahead. Quantitative market research could prove useful to design a long-term strategy for sales and promotions. It would also help exporters to better understand the changing structure of the Gulf's consumer markets.

It is important to point here to the Unified Economic Agreement of the Gulf Co-operation Council which covers a wide range of commercial and social areas, that should be studied by all companies concerned with the Gulf markets. The essence of the objective relating to trade and local manufacture, are that local manufacturing within the GCC – once reasonable capacity has been reached – will be protected by a common import tariff applied by all GCC states. Locally manufactured goods will also be favoured in government contracts and the rule that calls for local contractors and suppliers to get 30% of the value of the contract will be more strictly applied.

The overall direction is therefore clear, it points to the future importance of joint venture manufacturing/assembly operations in the Gulf. Exporters to the region are accordingly advised to start considering this prospect more seriously.

5 Financial Development and Capital Markets in the Gulf

INTRODUCTION

The Gulf Co-operation Council has been successful in introducing co-operative measures among its member states in economic, social, political, cultural, and military spheres. The challenge it faces today is to extend the spirit and practice of co-operation to the financial sphere as well. More than ever before, the Gulf countries need now to develop their financial and capital markets in order to mobilize private savings and open up new domestic investment channels. They need as well to co-ordinate their efforts in order to better mobilize the resources they have at the regional level and to channel these resources into financing their target growth rates.

Money markets have grown well during the past decade in line with the overall economic development of the region. Gulf commercial banks are coming of age and gradually maturing. Many of them are emerging as truly international institutions capable of competing, in both capital and services, with the well-established banks of the world. Unfortunately, capital markets have lagged behind. Most of the debt in the region is still raised through syndicated loans and bank facilities. Very few private companies and government institutions have up till now resorted to the issuance of debt and capital instruments and Gulf banks have played only a negligible role in the underwriting of Eurobond issues. Activities in the Kuwait stockmarket continues to be depressed and stock-markets elsewhere in the Gulf have yet to be formally established. Bahrain is planning to have an official stock exchange in 1987. There are only a few opportunities available now for investing and trading in local long- and medium-term paper.

Financial development is characterized by having a higher degree of monetization of the economy, the spread of the 'banking habit', the availability of diversified financial instruments widely acceptable at the individual and corporate levels, and ultimately, the presence of active primary and secondary capital markets where financial instruments (bonds and stocks) can be issued and traded providing an infrastructure for the efficient utilization of resources. Financial development can be indexed by the increase over time in the ratio of total financial assets to total assets in a particular country.

The financial system acts as a filter of information about available resources, and as such could significantly affect the use of these resources. Financial underdevelopment may lead to the inefficient utilization of savings, suppress entrepreneurial development, accentuate speculation, increase inflationary pressure on real assets (e.g. real estate), and can influence adversely the real rate of growth of the economy, especially the growth of the private sector.

Over the past decade GCC countries were able to attain high growth rates and made impressive strides in socio-economic development. However, financial development lagged behind, there was no need then to develop capital and financial markets and no sophisticated financial instruments were introduced, at least not on a wide scale. The abundance of capital reflected in the low cost of funds made it possible for investors, whether private or public, to accept lower rates of return on domestic investments. Efficient utilization of savings was not perceived as a prime policy goal at times when countries of the region were facing problems of limited absorptive capacity and excess financial resources.

With the dwindling financial surplusses and the gloomy outlook for oil revenues in the coming few years, the efficient utilization of savings is undoubtedly becoming a priority goal for the Gulf countries. Accepting low rate of return on domestic investment in the early stages of development could be justified on nationalistic grounds and may be reconciled with the fact that infrastructural projects normally have lower rates of return than commercial projects. The possibility of increasing the supply of the co-operant factors (availability of labour with higher skills, management and entrepreneurial experience, building the country's infrastructure, absence of cultural and social constraints on development, etc.) which would eventually increase rates of return on future investments is another adequate reason for accepting lower rates of return initially.

Today as the region's economies are maturing with most of the infrastructural projects being completed, and the drive towards industrialization is taking off, more emphasis will be placed on selecting investments with higher rates of return and on projects that are commercially viable. Capital resources are less abundant and the opportunity cost of capital is much higher than what it used to be in the 70s. Unless national resources (land, labour, capital and mineral resources) are priced according to their true economic value, they will continue to be utilized inefficiently. Financial development will not only help channel direct investments towards the highest yielding projects but also would enlarge the pool of investible resources and attract part of the region's savings from abroad.

THE NEED TO DEVELOP GULF FINANCIAL MARKETS

Financial development and the mobilization of domestic financial resources are *sine qua non* of privatization and industrialization in the region. For the past 10 years the GCC governments were the main propellors of growth. Massive government expenditures fuelled the expansion in all sectors of the economies and laid down the needed physical, social and financial infrastructure. Private sectors played only a secondary role in the overall development process. Governments expect their private sectors to take gradually more of a lead in the overall economic growth process. Privatization is one of the hallmarks of the region's 1985–90 development plans.

If the private sector is to be mobilized, and for it to spearhead the industrialization drive, the risk assessment process should be drastically improved. Reporting standards in the region are improving, however, they still lack the depth found elsewhere. The less attention is paid to financial data, the more investment will be driven by speculation. The first step therefore, would be to pursue more stringent financial reporting practices and put in place a better control system. This would be followed by the creation of appropriate financial environment, whereby every effort would be made to enhance the financial consciousness of the population and increase awareness towards new channels of savings and investments.

During the early take-off stage, Government and large private and public corporations start issuing their own debt and equity instruments and sell it at competitive prices or on discount basis to the private sector. These institutions command the trust and confidence of the public at large and should expect to see good response to the flotation of their public issues.

With time, as debt and equity instruments become more widely accepted commercial banks, insurance companies, and industrial and commercial institutions among others, would start floating their own issues. This would create a range of financial products differentiated by credit and quality risk. Eventually, capital markets will be established with primary markets developing first followed at a latter stage by secondary markets.

However, for such a development to take place specialized financial institutions are needed to undertake the role of underwriting new issues, wholesaling and investing in them and making markets for these products. The Gulf Investment Corporation (GIC) of Kuwait which is backed by the six GCC countries together with the emerging investment banks and companies in the region could co-operate to create the nucleus of a Gulf capital market.

The process of selling debt and equity instruments could also help restrict capital outflows. The existence of good quality names in the domestic markets would limit the need of investors to venture into foreign capital markets seeking diversified investment opportunities there. A local investor whose revenues are dominated mostly in local currencies will initially look into the range of investment products available in the domestic market rather than introduce a foreign exchange risk element when investing abroad.

The eventual yield of the domestic issues will depend upon the number of sellers or buyers for such issues. Therefore, the investor who may not be interested to place his money in local bank deposits because of the relatively low yield on these deposits may be enticed to keep his funds in the country but invested in higher yielding quality issues.

It is often pointed out that commercial banks in the last 10 years have accumulated enormous amounts of assets in the region and abroad. According to IMF statistics, net foreign assets of Gulf commercial banks exceeded $45 billion by the end of 1985. These figures are supported by data from 1985 SAMA publication and UAE central bank statistics. While UAE commercial banks increased their foreign assets 129% in 1984 to $6.6 billion, the amount of foreign assets held by local banks in Saudi Arabia totalled SR73.4 billion ($20.11 billion) at the end of fiscal 1984/85. At the same time, foreign liabilities of Saudi banks amounted to only SR8.9 billion ($2.44 billion). Thus Saudi banks held a net balance of about SR64.5 billion ($17.67 billion). The question is will banks enter into long- and medium-term financing of industrial projects, and will they repatriate funds from abroad to be invested locally?[1]

It is evident that the first responsibility of bankers is toward their shareholders and depositors. Bankers work with someone else's deposits, and thus must maintain liquidity and not take high risks. Commercial banks in the region lack medium- and long-term resources of funds. It would not be logical for them to acquire longer-term assets, nor are they expected to do so. Mismatching assets and liabilities is a clear deviation from sound banking practices. If conditions abroad offers them better risk/returns ratios and meet the requirements of their depositors and shareholders, then no one expects them to forego such opportunities. Only if domestic and regional conditions offer better alternatives then the banks themselves would be the first to make use of these opportunities.

The real impediment, therefore, to larger private sector participation and further involvement of commercial banks in long-term industrial ventures is the under-developed financial and capital markets in the region. If commercial banks were able to issue their own long- and medium-term debt instruments, then banks would be able to channel funds towards long-term investments. Equally important, savers will not shy away from acquiring these debt instruments as long as the institutions issuing them are solid and professionally managed, and the instruments are considered liquid, i.e. there exists secondary markets for trading in these instruments.

FINANCIAL DEVELOPMENT INSTRUMENTAL FOR FISCAL AND MONETARY POLICY

Over the past decade, oil revenues had far exceeded budgetary expenditure allocations in the GCC region and substantial surplusses were accumulated. However, with the decline in the region's oil revenues the GCC countries started operating under deficit budgets. In fiscal 1984/85, budget deficits ranged from US$10 200 million for Saudi Arabia to US$691 million for Oman. Whereas the 1985/86 budget of Saudi Arabia was heuristically forecasted to be in balance, the budgets of Kuwait, Qatar and Oman were projected to have a larger deficit than the year before, and the UAE projected a marginally smaller deficit.

Governments of the region are looking at ways and means to reduce government expenditures, bring forth greater private sectors' involvement and beef up non-oil revenues. One way of achieving that is to abandon the ownership of some of the public commercial corporations and transfer them to joint stock companies to be run more efficiently on profit and loss basis by the private sector. By doing so the Governments would be able to reduce the burden of administering these institutions and cut down on the 'recurrent expenditure' item of the budget. The process had already started last year when stocks of such Saudi public companies as Saudi Basic International Corporation (SABIC) and National Industrial Corporation (NIC) were floated in the market.

Non-oil sources of revenues include introducing taxation, imposing fees, reducing subsidies on specialized goods and services provided by the public sector, and issuing debt instruments. Taxes would not be welcomed during a period of economic slowdown because of their depressionary effect on the economy. Imposing fees and cutting subsidies could only be introduced gradually otherwise they would have a political back-lash. The advantages of issuing debt instruments are not only limited to generating additional revenues for the governments, but equally important, they could serve as a tool for better implementing effective monetary policy and simultaneously providing new domestic investment channels for the private sector.

The introduction in 1985 of certificate of deposits (CDs) by UAE Central Bank and the 90 days Banking Security Deposit Accounts (BSDA) introduced by Saudi Arabia Monetary Agency in 1984 were steps forward towards affecting better monetary policy in the region. By varying the amounts of funds held in the BSDA, SAMA was able to influence the amount of money in the banking system and increase control over monetary variables in the Kingdom. However, the response to the two financial instruments was not very favourable because of the associated unattractive yields.

SAMA took another tentative step at the end of April, 1985 towards setting up a full tradeable instrument. A new 180-day BSDA was introduced by was not made compulsory for the banks to participate. The aim was to add flexibility to the existing system, enhance the role of the BSDA in the domestic money market, and help banks relieve unexpected shortages which may occur in their clearing transactions. By 1985, banks in the Kingdom were 'contributing' some SR500 million (US$137 million) a week into the central bank's 90-day bankers security deposit account. With these two instruments running side by side, SAMA could haul around SR1000 million (US$274 million) a week out of the banking system.

It appeared that SAMA was slowly but surely transforming the BSDA into a money instrument. By late 1985, the instrument could already be traded and used for short-term clearing with SAMA; and the Monetary Agency was also ready to buy it back to help out with any liquidity crisis. SAMA clearly needed a monetary instrument which is based on some form of interest. To do so, it has had to move slowly to accustom the public, and some government elements as well, to the idea of a zero-coupon bond, which is what the BSDA effectively is.[2]

CAPITAL MARKETS IN THE GULF

Capital markets in the Gulf remained to a large extent fragmented and underdeveloped. By 1985, the acceptability of government debt instruments, and of course corporate bonds, was rather limited and modern debt markets had yet to be established. Only Kuwait had an official stock market then while the other Gulf states were at various stages of developing their own stock markets.

The history of Gulf trading has been that of families. Since the oil boom, many of those families have come to preside over fortunes and commercial empires. It was hard to imagine such families readily relinquishing control over the companies they have. Nevertheless, if those companies are to keep on growing, the owners have to accept the fact that the companies cannot be one man operations for ever, and they have got to share growth potentials with the public.

The economic recession from which the region was suffering in the first half of the 80s had had a negative impact on the development of capital markets in the various Gulf countries. There were other factors as well that had adversely affected such a development. These include the following:

1. The acute drop in share prices, in general, (with the exception of few companies) during the 1983–85 period has led many shareholders in the Gulf to hold on to their shares, hoping for higher prices in the future, instead of selling them at the depressed market prices. People who did sell their shares ended up incurring heavy losses.
2. The general drop in share prices discouraged as well many potential investors. The problem was further aggravated by the fall in real estate values and rentals, as well as, by a noticeable drop in governments' expenditures.
3. The lack of understanding of accepted investment criteria and the scarcity of readily available information and investment analysis were major constraints to the growth of share markets in the Gulf.
4. Liquidity and individual savings constitute important factors in the

decision of investors to buy shares. The declines in the growth of liquidity and the drop in savings that were associated with the overall economic slowdown in the region had had their negative impact on demand for shares despite the shares' low prices.
5. Abstention of most banks to provide facilities or loans to citizens against buying shares, according to the prevailing policy.
6. The internal regulations (statutes) of most companies whose shares were offered for circulation do not allow the sale of their shares to non-nationals whether individuals or institutions. Consequently, offshore provident funds, regional banks or financial establishments as well as expatriates living in the Gulf were prohibited from buying shares. This represented a further limitation of price and volume of shares traded in the Gulf.
7. The Souk Al-Manakh, the stock-market in Kuwait was psychologically damaging and had seriously constrained further investments in Gulf shares. The Iraq–Iran war continued to have as well similar adverse psychological and direct effects on share markets in the region.
8. Investors in the Gulf normally concentrated on companies of high annual yields. Capital, growth prospects, and rights of shareholders did not weigh heavily in their investment decisions. Consequently the demand was higher on a limited number of shares in anticipation of distribution of high profits. The contrary was true regarding companies who distributed lower dividends but had strong growth potentials.

The classical function of a stock market is to mobilize national savings and allocate financial resources among various domestic investment opportunities. However, because the Gulf region was experiencing boom economic conditions in the 70s and domestic investment opportunities were scarce compared to the amount of capital available, there was actually no inherent need for a stock market at that point in time. Where a stock market did exist, e.g. Kuwait, the limited domestic absorptive capacity led to periodic bouts of overspeculation with stock prices skyrocketing then collapsing. This had had serious social and economic repercussions on the country.

However, the situation in the second half of the 80s would be completely different. The efficient utilization of savings has undoubtedly become a priority goal, and various rules and regulations to establish indigenous stock markets and make sure they are well managed and controlled have been studied and enacted.

Issues of government treasury bills in local currencies have invariably been used in several Gulf countries. The form of this debt ranged from deposits with the central banks and short-term treasury notes and certificates of deposits, to long-term development bonds. Only few Gulf banks used the international credit markets to raise long-term funds through the issue of floating rates notes and certificate of deposits in foreign currencies.

Here is a brief review of capital markets in the various GCC countries.

Kuwait

By 1985, Kuwait capital and financial markets were at a more advanced state than the other GCC countries. Confidence in the markets has been shaken by the Manakh crisis. However, the successful implementation of the various regularity measures introduced by the government, and the listing on the official stock market of 27 bonds denominated in Kuwaiti dinars alongside shares of Kuwaiti and Gulf companies had helped widening the market's base and reduced speculative pressures. Unlisted Gulf companies who wished to have their shares traded in the new stock exchange were allowed to do so if they had at least three years of proven financial record, and could stand the test of the new market supervision committee.

In April 1985 there were 47 Kuwaiti companies eligible for trading on the official stock exchange and eight non-Kuwaiti companies. The former consisted of eight banks, six investment companies, four insurance firms, six real estate companies, 12 industrial concerns, six service companies and five food companies (Figure 5.1). In October 1985, Kuwaiti authorities suspended trading in shares of Gulf companies presumably until a comprehensive review of their financial status is completed.

The all share price index of officially traded Kuwaiti share plummeted in 1984 by around 47% form the artificial price support level prevailing at the start of the year (Table 5.1). In the first six months of 1985, the price index declined still further by around 39% (see Figure 5.2). Gulf prices fell by a similar amount in 1984, and the decline in the first half of 1985 was around 24%. The most affected were shares on banks, real estate and industrial companies. Since no transactions were recorded in the shares of 18 out of the 47 listed companies subsequent to the withdrawal of the support operation, the actual decline in realisable value was certainly much higher.

Figure 5.1 Companies listed on Kuwait's official Stock Exchange[a]

Banks
National Bank of Kuwait
Gulf Bank
Commercial Bank of Kuwait
Alahli Bank of Kuwait
Bank of Kuwait & the Middle East
Burgan Bank
Kuwait Finance House
Kuwait Real Estate Bank

Investment
Kuwait Investment Company
Kuwait Foreign Trading Contracting & Investment Company
Kuwait International Investment Company
Commercial Facilities Company
Al-Ahlia Investment Company
Kuwait Financial Centre[b]

Insurance
Kuwait Insurance Company
Gulf Insurance Company
Al-Ahleia Insurance Company
Warba Insurance Company

Real Estate
Kuwait Real Estate Company
United Realty Company
National Real Estate Company
Salhia Real Estate Company
Kuwait Project Company
Kuwait Real Estate Investment Consortium

Industrial
National Industries Company
Kuwait Metal Pipe Industries
Kuwait Cement Company
Refrigeration Industry & Cold Storage Company
National Automotive Manufacturing & Trading Company
Gulf Cable & Electrical Industries Company
Kuwait Melamine Industries Company
Kuwait Tyres Company
Kuwait Pharmaceutical Industries Company
Kuwait International Petroleum Investment Company
Kuwait Shipbuilding & Repairyard Company
Contracting & Marine Services

Services
Overland Transport Company
Kuwait National Cinema Company
Kuwait Hotel Company
The Public Ware House
Kuwait Commercial Markets Complexes Company
Mobile Telephone Systems Company

Food
Livestock Transport & Trading Company
United Fisheries of Kuwait
Kuwait United Poultry Company
Kuwait Food Company (Americana)
Agriculture Food Product Company

Non-Kuwaiti
First Gulf Bank
Bahrain International Bank
Bahrain Middle East Bank
United Gulf Bank
Coast Investment & Development Company
Arabian General Investment Company
Arab Iron & Steel Company
Gulf Petroleum Products Company

Notes
[a] As at 1 Apr. 1985.
[b] Suspended until further notice.
Source
Stock Exchange Bulletin (May 1985).

Table 5.1 Market valuation of Kuwaiti listed companies – by sector (KD million)

End of period	1982	1983		1984	
Sector	Value	Value	% Change	Value	% Change
Banks	3831	3314	−13.5	1731	−47.8
Investment	1320	1254	−5.0	536	−56.3
Insurance	589	562	−4.6	229	−59.3
Industry	1027	978	−5.8	674	−31.1
Transport & services	486	440	−9.5	767	−45.1
Real estate	1558	1397	−10.3	767	−45.1
Total	881	7945	−9.8	4192	−47.2

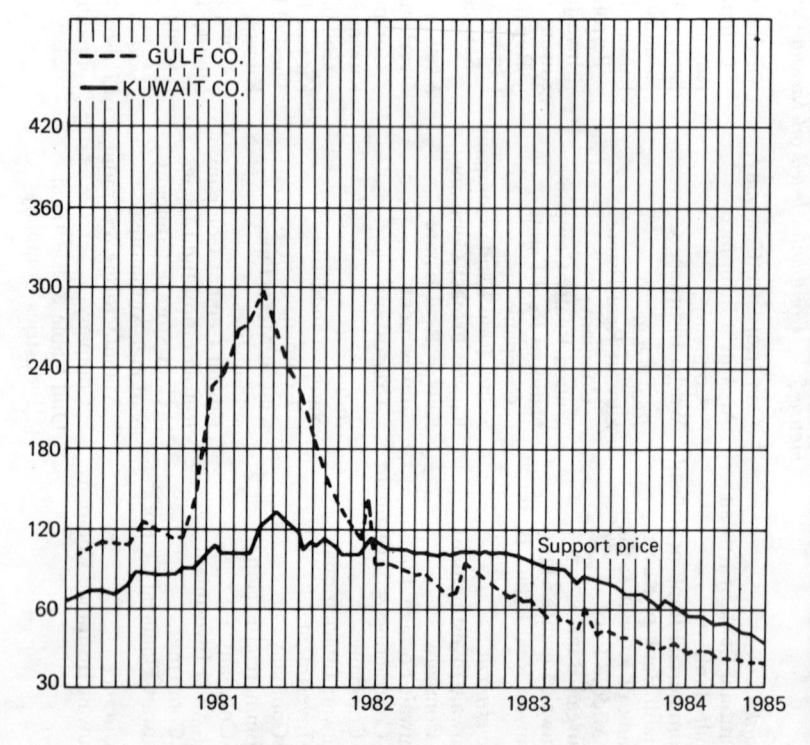

Figure 5.2 Kuwait Stock Exchange indices

Financial Development, Capital Markets: the Gulf

With the view of giving more depth to the stock market, and increase the number of investment tools available, Kuwait financial authorities approved in October 1985 the trading of bonds issued by Kuwaiti and non-Kuwaiti institutions on the country's stock exchange. Furthermore, both Kuwaiti and other nationals, whether residents of Kuwait or not, were allowed to trade in these bonds. The bonds, denominated in Kuwaiti dinars, could be acquired from either one of the three recognized brokers, the Kuwait Investment Company, the Kuwait International Investment Company and the Kuwait Foreign Trading, Contracting and Investment Company.

The government also introduced minimum requirements that have to be met by companies listed on the stock exchange. These included submission of balance sheets, and an indication of the basis on which receivables and other items were valued. The stock exchange committee also issued a set of rules governing share transactions. The regulations were designed to prevent a recurrence of the spate of 'speculation and fraudulence' which precipitated the Manakh crash and its legacy of $94 000 million in post-dated cheques. All brokers, for example, had to show a minimum capital of KD100 000 ($325 000) backed by bank guarantees of KD1 million $3.2 million). The 17 brokerage firms which were active on the old exchange have been merged into four companies and only those or their authorized representative were allowed on the trading floor.

Using purely financial criteria, Kuwaiti share prices were found in mid-1985 to be low in absolute terms however, still acceptable in relative terms. This comparison of the share's market value to its book value showed an increase ranging between 2 to 2.6 times on the average with respect to shares of Kuwaiti public companies over a two year period, while the rate stood at an average of 2 times in the case of international stocks. In other words, the 1985 prices of Kuwaiti share were not as low as often claimed, at least in relation to the shares' book value. Prices did tumble from the previous highs attained before the Manakh crisis buy were still at levels considered acceptable internationally.

A major factor that has restricted the effective functioning of the new exchange was the lack of buyers' interests. This problem has been aggravated by the fall in real estate values and rentals, which was likely to get worse as even more new property started coming on the market. It was estimated that in early 1986 there would be a minimum of three years' supply available even at the 1984 take-up rates.

In 1985, the Kuwaiti government owned one-third of the entire Kuwaiti stock market. Unless the government's holdings were sold back to the private sector, there could be an extreme shortage of tradeable stock. Other constraints hindering the growth of the stock market include a lack of understanding of accepted investment criteria, a scarcity of readily available investment analysis and advice, and the use of misleading appropriation statements in company reports.

Activities in the Kuwaiti Dinar Bond market has been proceeding very quietly in the last two years (see Figure 5.3). Accordingly to the National Bank of Kuwait Economic and Financial Bulletin of May, 1985, there has been a fundamental disequilibrium between investment demand and supply in the market. While demand for Kuwait paper was still high (as manifested in the enormous oversubscription to the 1984 Industrial Bank of Kuwait issue), the supply of new dinar bond issues has slowed to only 2 in 1984 (both issues on behalf of domestic issuer totalling KD24 million). This represented the lowest inflow of new inventory to this market since 1980, and constituted less than 16% of the investment assets created during 1978 which was the peak-year of activity in this market.

A secondary market in Kuwaiti dinar bonds has existed since the mid-70s, but has been mainly the domain of specialized financial institutions. The Arab company for Trading of Securities (ACTS) was the market maker in this respect. However the activities of this company declined considerably after the collapse of the Manakh stock market. More new issues were needed to stimulate liquidity in the Kuwaiti dinar bond market and reactivate the secondary market. Locally, there were only a few institutions whose credit standing would allow them to tap the market. However, these institutions alone cannot sustain a viable fixed income sector of the capital market.

The recent measure announced by the Kuwait Stock Exchange to permit the trading of bonds issued by Kuwaiti and non-Kuwaiti institutions on the Exchange is a welcome addition to the depth of the bond market and would greatly enhance, the market's liquidity.

Saudi Arabia

Development of a Saudi stock market proved to be quite a slow process, with monthly turnover in shares in 1985 estimate at no more than SR30 million ($8.3 million). The absence of a concerted ini-

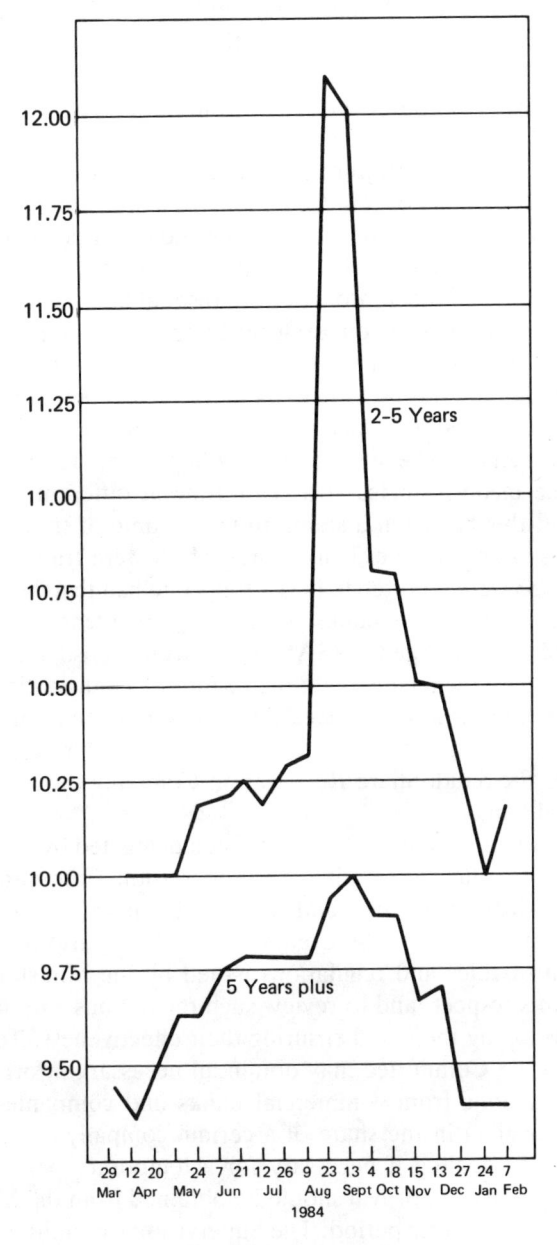

Figure 5.3 ACTS KD bond yield indices

tiative to establish a stock market was at least partly to blame. There was also considerable disquiet about the prolonged aftermath of the Souk al-Manakh crash in Kuwait. It seemed that the government wanted to ensure a gradual growth in trading so that speculation can be avoided.

In 1985, there were 38 joint stock Saudi companies having a total capital of SR14.7 billion ($4.03 billion), ten were financial companies, 13 industrial companies, 10 utilities and services companies and 5 agricultural companies. In September 1984 a new system was introduced. Private stock brokers were disqualified from trading and the business was passed on exclusively to the commercial banks. However, not all were reportedly happy with the new stock trading system in Saudi Arabia. Some bankers have complained of the cumbersome procedure which can take three to four weeks to conclude a transaction. The absence of a trading floor is reported to have led to price inconsistencies at a given time at different places. The result of all this has been a slump in the volume of trading and the price levels. For example, bank shares which were traded at around SR900 in 1983 were reported to have dropped to half that figure in 1985.

Until early 1985, the banks had been dependent on the Saudi Arabian Monetary Agency (SAMA) clearing house for recording changes in share ownership, with the result that confirmation of share sales was taking as long as check clearing – more than one week in some cases. It was hoped that matters would improve with the creation of the Saudi Share Registration Company owned by the 11 commercial banks.

Supervision of trading in shares has been delegated by a Ministerial Committee to officials forming the Supervision Committee drawn from the Ministry of Finance and National Economy, the Ministry of Commerce and SAMA. The Committee's job was also to insure the application of rules and regulations issued by the Ministerial Committee in this respect, and to review such regulations with the objective of developing them and ensuring their effectiveness. To conduct its business the Committee may obtain all necessary information on share transactions from commercial banks and companies. It may also block dealing in the share of a certain company or set a maximum limit for dealing if necessary for a temporary period not exceeding one week. Approval should be obtained from the Ministerial Committee for a longer period. The Supervision Committee may halt on prior approval of the Ministerial Committee all dealings in the market.

Dealing in deferred payment for share is forbidden in Saudi Arabia. Banks should not accept payment of the value of share purchased by deferred cheques, promissory notes or bills. The banks would be responsible for any violation in this respect.

Trading in shares should be confined to the shares of shareholding companies fully-owned by Saudi natural or legal persons, and to Saudi joint-stock companies with foreign participation in their capital provided that the ownership of share will not be transferred to foreigners.

To finalize the trading process the customer or his legal representative should fill a purchase or sale 'order form' indicating; name, identity card number and the maximum amount which he desires to pay in case of purchase or the minimum amount which he wished to receive in case of sale. The purchase and sale order provided for a clause in accordance with which the customer authorizes the bank to finalize the dealing operation as per the terms indicated in the form. The bank will charge a commission against finalizing the operation and registering the share certificates. The commission would be computed on the basis of a percentage of the market value of the shares to be determined by the Supervision Committee and at a maximum of no more than 1%.

To undertake the trading process, the brokers at the central dealing unit in the bank conduct a reconciliation process between sale and purchase orders coming from branch units and central units at other banks and relevant documents will be exchanged through a clearing room to be established at SAMA for this purpose. A company's shares may not be traded prior to the issue of a decision by the Minister of Trade announcing its establishment. However, provisional share certificates issued after the announcement of the formation of a company may be traded.

The record on flotation of shares in the Kingdom is somewhat mixed. Saudi Basic Industries Corporation (SABIC) was the first state concern to go public, with 20% of its stock, valued at SR2000 million ($555 million), coming to the market in January 1984. The issue – at SR1000 ($277) par value – was undersubscribed among GCC investors outside Saudi Arabia, but oversubscribed domestically. A second, 10% issue followed in April 1985, however, one month later, bid and offer prices for the SR1000 shares were down to SR550–70 ($152–8).

The public issue for National Industrialization Company (NIC) was not very successful, partly because the government announced it was not going to take a share of the equity, and partly because of the economic slowdown in the Kingdom. Around SR450 million ($123 million) was finally raised in the local market.

Besides SABIC and NIC, other flotations of stocks took place in the last few years. Among the issues that fared well were Saudi Livestock Company, the Tabuk and Qassim agricultural development companies, and the 1985 60% offering in the SR300 million ($83 million) capital of Saudi Pharmaceutical & Medical Appliances Company (Spimaco).

Of greater significance will be the flotation in 1986 of the Al Rajhi Company for Currency Exchange & Commerce. When it becomes Al Rajhi Banking Investment Corporation, 43% of its proposed SR750 million ($208 million) capital will go to the public, the original four shareholders in the company retaining 50%. Non-family founder shareholders are to be issued 5% and the remaining 2% will go to the staff.

Two other major corporations may come to the market by the end of 1986. Twenty-five percent of Petromin's capital in the lube oil, mining and refinery sectors will be issued, and it is expected to be at least two times oversubscribed. Petromin has already confirmed the selling-off of part of the lube oil operations, and if this proves to be successful other issues will follow. Parts of Saudia, the national airline, are also expected to be floated.

Given the right kind of incentives and regulations, Saudis, especially the smaller investors, have a number of good reasons other than a sense of national responsibility, for investing inside the Kingdom. They feel comfortable with their money invested in a familiar environment, there is no foreign exchange risk incurred and they often distrust the middlemen necessary for investment overseas. The message will eventually get through that it is unrealistic to expect guaranteed dividends in a normal market, and that the inflated prices quoted in the early 80s had no basis in relation to any company's financial status. When expectations are more in line with the real state of the economy, investors will be happy with the prevailing rates of return and would be willing to invest more locally.

Bahrain

Bahrain has been examining ways to establish a viable stock exchange since the early 80s. In 1985, the country had 21 joint-stock companies and several stock brokers, but no stock exchange. Dealings in domestically registered companies continued to be restrained throughout 1983–85 period. Of the 21 brokers issued licenses in 1983, only about six were active by late 1985. Even where there were requests for purchases of shares, those who held them were unwilling to sell. Their value had declined so sharply, they refused to trade until they can recoup at least some of the loss.

A committee representing the ministries of Commerce and Finance, the Bahrain Monetary Agency and the Chamber of Commerce & Industry, with assistance from the International Finance Corporation and looking into the prospects of establishing a stockmarket on the island recommended that a 'gradual approach' should be adopted. The committee called for the establishment of certain prerequisites including a securities information centre which would help informing dealers of trends in share prices and volume of trading.

The capital market law in Bahrain which was under review in 1985 by a team of legal experts called for an independent legal status to the proposed stock exchange. It aims at streamlining trading procedures and creating an environment in which share prices are influenced purely by market forces. It also calls for an expansion of the proposed stock exchange's activities to include trading in negotiable securities and bonds issued by the government as well as the private sector. Further, it lays down guidelines for the establishment of marketmakers and stockbroking firms. The stock exchange once established will be entrusted to an independent board of governors, who will finance their operations from fees levied on listed companies and brokers.

Despite the absence of a trading floor in Bahrain, approximately 191 shares of 21 locally incorporated joint stock companies with a total par value of BD133 million ($352 million) were being traded on the island in 1985. Also being traded were some six million shares (total par value BD525 million) of 13 companies with offshore Gulf ownership but based in Bahrain. Such companies are popularly known as 'Gulf companies'. Gulf companies have a huge capital base but small nominal face value of their share whereas the reverse is true for the Bahraini joint stock companies. The drop in prices of Gulf companies due to the Manakh crisis in Kuwait greatly affected the local Bahraini companies. Prices of Bahrain companies recorded a major drop since the hey days of 1982–83. In October 1985, the Bahrain companies price index was 50 compared to a base of 100 in May 1985.

United Arab Emirates

Establishment of a stock market in the UAE was still far off in 1985 despite moves to regulate and expand unofficial share dealing in the seven emirate federation. A 1983 draft stock market law was still on the shelf in late 1985. The slow implementation of a 1984 federal companies law and the lingering fear from the 1983 Al-Manakh stock market crisis in Kuwait continued to obstruct its revival.

However, cautious steps were taken recently to build a legal framework that could facilitate the eventual establishment of a stock market. A decree was issued in July 1985 listing the information a company must publish to issue shares. Twenty two banks were named as authorized brokers for new share issues. The National Bank of Abu Dhabi recently opened a share trading division that for the first time started to post prices twice weekly for a dozen publicly traded companies.

In 1985, the UAE had some 30 licensed brokers who dealt in 40 traded companies, 18 of them in Abu Dhabi. As many as 70 other brokers were informally involved in buying and selling of shares. The total share transaction in 1985 was estimated at $200 million dirhams ($54 million).

While share prices and transactions have declined over the 1983-85 period, the recent sale of shares in some government companies has attracted interest. In early 1985, the Abu Dhabi Government issued shares in the National Marine Dredging Company at 100 dirhams compared with a book value of 300 to 400 dirhams. The offer was 12 times oversubscribed and in late 1985, the share price moved up to 250 dirhams. The Government of Abu Dhabi is considering selling shares in other companies, particularly in the profitable oil services sector in the profitable oil services sector, in an effort to stimulate local investment.

Some investors have established a securities trading centre in the northern emirate of Umm Al Quwain without getting the final go-ahead from the relevant authorities and the Union of the UAE Chambers of Commerce. How quickly will the UAE establish a formal stock market may be as much a political as an economic decision. What is mostly needed as a prerequisite to such a development is a change in the disclosure requirements on company accounts and a bankruptcy law that would guarantee the rights of shareholders.

Other GCC Countries

No major progress in developing a stock exchange in Qatar and the Sultanate of Oman has been recorded recently, even though Oman had asked the International Financial Corporation to look into the matter and present its recommendation in this respect.

PROMOTION OF REGIONAL FINANCIAL INTEGRATION

Ideally, debt instruments introduced by one GCC member state should eventually be made available to other GCC citizens and institutions of other GCC countries. This would broaden the market for these instruments, mobilize regional financial resources, and circumvent the problem of limited domestic markets.

The promotion of regional financial integration requires constructive input from the GCC governments and financial institutions. The adjustments which the governments will have to make are concerned primarily with closer co-ordination of their exchange rates and monetary policies as well as harmonizing existing laws governing capital market transactions in their respective countries. Co-ordination of exchange rates among GCC countries would be a step forward towards achieving unification of these rates in the member states.

Discussion between the monetary authorities in the Gulf region have been held regularly with a view towards establishing a regional monetary zone, in which the various national currencies would fluctuate against each other within a strictly limited band. The adoption of a regional unit of account a 'Gulf dinar', for example, would be the next step, to be followed by the adoption of a single currency. However, this necessitates harmonization of domestic monetary policies, which has important implications on the control of credit levels of domestic interest rates and the role of banks. This is a very big step to take by the member countries, and if implemented could greatly promote monetary integration and economic unity in the GCC region and facilitate the gradual evolvement of a regional Gulf capital market.

There are three principal factors impeding progress towards incorporating a Gulf stock exchange. The first of these is the divergence of laws governing incorporation of joint stock companies with fully or partly non-national ownership. The second is the divergence of laws governing stock trading in the countries concerned. And the third factor is somewhat psychological in nature stemming from a fear that wealthy investors from other GCC countries would embark on a take-over spree of indigenous business if shares are issued for pan-Gulf subscription.

The GCC economic agreement on stock exchange activities has not yet been implemented, requiring each Gulf state to depend on its domestic capital market. This naturally restricts the scope of the markets and render them less liquid. One need not emphasize the importance of liberalizing the rules governing the existing and the proposed Gulf stock markets. As a first step GCC nationals should be allowed to get involved in cross border trading. The governments should also consider make use of the idle savings of non-GCC Arab workers living in the Gulf and induce them to become active participants in the region's capital markets. At a later stage, and as the Gulf capital markets come of age and exhibit stability and sophistication, a minority participation by investors from foreign countries should be considered.

The current regional GCC guidelines including freedom of exercising economic activities and the free movement of capital from one member state to another, together with the strong drive for regional co-operation and integration among the GCC countries, would make it possible for several capital markets in the Gulf to grow. Once stocks and bonds are marketed at the regional level, a secondary regional financial market would then develop. It would complement the primary capital markets in the various member states, and would allow them to benefit from the larger investment pool available in the region as a whole.[3]

Bahrain is well endowed to serve as a listing centre and as a secondary market for bonds and stocks issued for GCC nationals and to provide the financial advisory services and the international backstop needed in this respect. Bahrain market would complement the primary capital markets in the various member states and given its advanced financial infrastructure and its international network Bahrain would be able then to set the pace for financial development in the region as a whole.

At every step of its gradual growth, Bahrain market has to be efficient enough to offer competitive advantages to borrowers in the region, in terms of amounts, maturities, cost of funding and type of finance, as market would find it more advantageous to continue to deal with the established financial markets.

A regional governing body with representatives from all GCC countries would be formulated under the umbrella of GCC secretariat. It would be entrusted with the task of governing the regional secondary market in Bahrain and providing direction for its future growth. It will also make sure that Bahrain financial centre would in effect serve and complement the financial markets in the various GCC states and foster their activities.

Allowing nationals to own stocks in companies in the various Gulf countries and to acquire regional debt instrument, could help develop a sense of unity among Gulf citizens and a positive feeling that people are contributing to the well being of their region.

Notes

1. Saudi Arabian Monetary Agency, *Statistical Summary* (Riyadh, 1985).
2. The terms on which SAMA operated the facility were as follows:
   Amount of Facility: up to 75% of a bank's nominal holding of individual issue of BSDAs in multiples of SR1 million nominal. Transaction on any one day must not exceed 75% of a bank's total nominal subscription to any named single issue of BSDA (rounded up to the nearest million). The minimum amount for the repos will be SR3 million. In cases where the limit is under-utilized on any single BSDA held, the un-utilized portion will be eligible for future repos. The amount of Facility as detailed above will be available to be purchased and sold automatically once during their 91 day life of a certain issue. Banks will be required to specify on each occasion which holding they require to be utilized for the repos.
   Availability: Initial notification must be received by SAMA up to 12 noon on any day of the week except Friday.
   Term: The repurchase facility may be utilized for periods from overnight up to five days.
   Price: Prices (on a discount basis) will be based in light of the market conditions and will be at SAMA's absolute discretion.
3. Articles (8) and (22) of the United Economic Agreement of the GCC countries.

6 A New Era for Gulf Banking

INTRODUCTION

A combination of declining lending activities, rising number of non-performing loans, more competition and government regulation, squeezed margins and greater lending risks are pulling down earnings of Gulf banks. Meanwhile, international banking is becoming more competitive as financial institutions link up to provide round the clock service in the new globalized deregulated market. A new era for Gulf banking is dawning that requires long term structural adjustment to cope with the challenging economic and business environment.

During the 1974–83 boom, Gulf banks expanded rapidly and generated good profits, servicing economies growing at double digits growth rates. Governments were the main propellors of growth and banks thrived on huge public sector expenditures. However, in the first half of this decade, the GCC countries witnessed a dramatic transition from surpluses in the balance of payments and government budgets into corresponding deficits. Oil revenues are estimated to have dropped to less than 40% of the $150 billion recorded in 1980. It has become evident that the region is experiencing an extended period of consolidation and retrenchment. The GCC countries are preparing themselves to cope with lower oil revenues for sometime to come.

The ongoing period of retrenchment mirrors a new economic realism in the region. The fall in oil revenues coincided with the end of the first development cycle. Much of the necessary infrastructure has been completed and emphasis is now being shifted towards the industrial and services sectors and towards operating the economies more efficiently. The private sector is being induced to participate more actively in the overall development process.

Gulf central banks are also signalling the end of an era for free banking and lax financial reporting habits in the region. Regulators are determined to introduce reforms leading to better disclosure norms and to drive banks to reconsider their lending practices before the recent decline in the quality of loan portfolio becomes alarming. The increased supervisory role of the central banks are expected to be accompanied by new and more effective tools of monetary policy.

A New Era for Gulf Banking

The changing business opportunities in the Gulf and abroad are creating a more sophisticated financial services market to which banks in the region are expected to contribute. What is the outlook for Gulf banking? Can Gulf banks cope with the challenge? and What changes they need to implement in order to evolve into full service financial institutions?

CHANGING BANKING CONDITIONS IN THE GULF

The reduction in the pace of regional growth and development has led to an overall slackening of demand for finance. Guarantee business, contract financing and import financing, previously Gulf banks' core business, accounting for more than 70% of their loan commitments have fallen off sharply last year. A good portion of the loan demand for these sectors now takes the form of rollovers of existing credit. Banking environment in the region has become more testing and competition among banks all chasing fewer first-tier clients is leading to tighter profit margins.

Good commercial banking business is less easy to come by, running costs are being looked at more critically, and some loans which one to two years ago seemed sound enough now look more suspect. Depressed property and stock market have undermined even the best of the collaterals that banks hold.

Gulf Bankers, preoccupied mainly by asset growth in the 70s and early 80s, are now re-evaluating assets, insisting on quality, looking for opportunities abroad and specializing either in traditional trade financing, investment banking, financial serves or in portfolio management.

The economic slowdown in the region is bound to create cash flow problems especially among inefficient companies that have been mismanaged for sometime. Many Gulf companies expanded so rapidly in the boom period that they did not have time to build up an organizational structure to keep with the volume of work at hand. Provided they were technically competent, money kept flowing in and everyone made a profit. Cash and liability management did not seem important in the 70s and early 80s. Some companies took loans for construction purposes and 'downstreamed' them into property and financial transactions. Others tied up some of their own resources in investments at home and abroad which were not necessarily bad, but were too illiquid to be of use in a crisis.

While the underlying problems are the same, however, the symptoms have, under the influence of local conditions taken different forms in the various countries of the region. In Saudi Arabia, banks concerned in growth and market share competed with each other in the boom years to attract more borrowers. Many of these clients are now facing difficulties in making repayments, and the banks have no guarantee that the courts would rule in their favour if borrowers fail to repay their debt. In the absence of a modern banking law, courts resorting to Islamic Sharia will throw out cases where element of interest is involved.

Costly new technology and training have affected income while expanded branch network have enabled banks to increase customer deposits, and to build up their balance sheets. Nevertheless, Saudi banks were unwilling to commit further funds to a shrinking market threatened by more loan losses and new deposits are increasingly being channelled to assets abroad.

In Bahrain the offshore banks have been greatly affected by the overall recession in the gulf and the shift of the international market away from syndicated lending. Construction bonds and guarantees are drying up as infrastructural projects reach completion and new projects are either delayed, scaled down or shelved for lack of sufficient funds. Import finance has also declined. Total GCC imports from the main exporting countries, USA, Japan, UK and Germany, recorded major declines in 1983–85. Consumer demand decelerated as well, and business confidence has been adversely affected by Al-Manakh crisis in Kuwait and the Gulf war that has been raging for more than four years. The Iran–Iraq war has removed ample banking opportunities in both these two countries. At the same time official policy and the growing competence of the national banks have combined to exclude the OBUs from much of the available business.

The syndicated loan market, once Bahrain banks' bread and butter, has declined worldwide, and the deals that remain are becoming increasingly unattractive. Several banks are choosing not to increase their assets at dangerously low margins, and those institutions that have the technical expertise are moving onto a variety of other debt instruments.

On the liability side, the dependence of the Gulf offshore banks on interbank funding makes them vulnerable. International banks are wary of increasing their exposure to a region where the risk is perceived to be on the rise. The privately owned Arab OBU's have realized that without attaining a larger scale of business it would not be possible for them to support too costly an organization out of Bahrain. However, the gloomy regional prospects and the difficulty of achieving the required leverage ratio had convinced these banks to re-draw their strategies and concentrate more of their resources internationally.

In Kuwait the problems have been centred domestically on the collapse of Souk Al Manakh stock exchange. The decline in real estate and stock prices poses a threat to banks' collateral. However, the damage to the banks may not be very serious because of the huge hidden reserves built up over the years by the previously very profitable banking system.

The banks still have ample liquidity and a considerable cussion of capital to work with. It is evident that the big commercial banks and investment companies have as well, guaranteed government support through access to the Central Bank's discount window, swap and loan facilities. Their credit standing continue, therefore, to be good supported by the low sovereign risk of Kuwait.

There was a fundamental shift in Kuwait's banking system out of the non-interest bearing demand accounts into time deposits and foreign currency accounts. Current accounts steadily declined by 25% during 1984 as investors lost interest in speculative transactions either in stocks or real estate.

The major problem of UAE and Qatar is that they are over-banked. There are 102 banks and 284 branches for 1.3 million people in the UAE. While in Qatar, ten foreign banks and five local banks are chasing a small amount of business. The downturn in the local and regional economies has left its impact on banks operating in the two countries. Three banks in the UAE have run into difficulties in the last 18 months, and liquidity problems surfaced as well in Qatar. There will inevitably be more mergers in the future, and the bigger banks that are created would most probably reduce their exposure locally and internationalize more their operations.

THE INTERNATIONAL CHALLENGE

Gulf banks are making a big push towards internationalization. The narrow economic base at home, the decline in domestic lending opportunities, the legal uncertainties and low margins associated with commercial banking are forcing these banks to seek more business opportunities abroad.

Gulf banks find international expansion integral to their growth plans and an overseas presence improves the sources of assets to which they have direct access. Gulf banks do not have multinational corporations to follow into foreign markets, nevertheless, international expansion would help them cater better for their customers' international business needs. If they have representation in the major capital markets, Gulf institutions would be in a better position to provide a wider range of investment advisory and management services to their high net worth clients. Besides, relationships with major contractors working in the Gulf and major exporters to the region can be strengthened by a presence close to them.

Overseas presence will allow Gulf banks to become more directly involved in the trade patterns of their home countries. It could also help them develop new sources of money market deposits and new opportunities for lending to business outside their region. Their niche of having a presence in the main financial centres of the world is their ability to offer foreign companies the 'specialty' of knowing the Gulf region. International expansion is, therefore, pursued by the banks in the region as a means of achieving international eminence and facilitating international business and regional trade flows.

Most of the large Gulf banks already have a presence abroad. Some opened branches and representative offices in London, New York, Singapore and Hong Kong. Others are expanding internationally by acquiring well established institutions. ABC of Bahrain already has 70% stake in Madrid based Banco Attlantica and 75% share of Hong Kong's Sun Hungkai Bank. Bahrain Middle East Bank acquired interest in a joint venture bank in Switzerland and is planning to invest $35 million in a US bank.

In their international operations, Gulf banks are suffering from the decline of syndicated sovereign risk lending. The syndication market has shrunk in the last few years from around $96 billion in 1981 to around $42 billion in 1985. Table 6.1 traces the development of Arab bank's syndicated lending from 1977 to 1985, compared to the total size of the Eurocurrency credit market. During the 1981–85 period, Arab banks accounted for about 10% of the total Eurocredits. It is interesting to note that close to 45% of the Euroloans lead managed by Arab banks were for Arab borrowers.

International lending is becoming more difficult as the emphasis is

Table 6.1 Participation of Arab banks in syndicated loans

	Eurocurrency Credit ($bn)	Arab banks ($bn)	Arab banks (% of total)
1977	41.77	0.95	2.27
1978	70.18	2.32	3.31
1979	82.81	2.49	5.01
1980	77.39	3.58	4.69
1981	96.38	9.10	9.44
1982	82.51	9.80	11.50
1983	60.66	6.94	11.44
1984	59.47	6.33	10.64
1985	42.01	4.43	10.54

Source: OECD, June 1986.

shifting towards corporate rather than sovereign risk lending. Bonds and note issues, project finance and portfolio management require much more banking sophistication than simply participating in internationally arranged syndicated deals for sovereign borrowers.

The involvement of Gulf banks in international capital markets, mainly bonds, notes and CDs issues, has been quite modest up till now. Eurocredits which prior to 1982 used to outnumber Euro-bonds by a ratio of 2 : 1, hardly match them now. The Euro-bond market grew from $75 billion in 1981 to more than $214 billion in 1985, (Table 6.2). International bond issued have replaced syndicated lending as the dominant mode of international finance. The bond market is set for continued growth in the medium term, particularly the Eurocommercial paper sector which provides greater flexibility to the borrower.

Syndicated lending has been slowed by the tangle of developing country debt, but that's only one reason why bond activity is on the rise, what is more important is that banks are increasingly attracted to the high profitability and lower risk of acting as intermediaries rather than as basic sources of credit. Even some syndicated lending has been reconfigured so that it doesn't resemble loans. Intruments known as back-up and note-issuance facilities provide opportunities like those found in bond underwriting; they have no immediate impact on a bank's balance sheet. For a fee, a bank guarantees that a creditor will have access to funds, if needed. But since no lending occurs until the option is exercised, banks need not classify the

Table 6.2 Borrowing in international capital markets
($bn)

	1983	1984	1985	1986*
Floating-rate bonds	19.5	38.2	58.2	30.8
Fixed-rate bonds	547.6	73.3	109.3	191.1
Euronote facilities	9.5	28.8	46.8	23.0
Total	86.6	140.0	214.5	244.9
Syndicated loans	67.2	57.0	42.0	37.0

Source: OECD, June 1986.
* First half: annualized totals.

transaction as a loan. These credit developments meet the needs of a different clientele than was targeted by syndicated lending.

Gulf banks are finding it difficult to make an impact on this market. International banks and securities firms that excel at arranging bond issues often have long standing relationships with the borrowers. They also have the expertise needed to launch complex offers within hours of receiving permission, and have the necessary strong placing power to succeed. The expertise in the capital market will have to develop over time and Gulf banks may find it both profitable and strategically important to go more forcefully into the evolving securities market.

Dollar new issues have been the most important component of Gulf banks' Euro-bond activity. Within that sector, the main presence has been in floating rate notes (FRNs). Arab Banking Corporation, Saudi International Bank, Gulf International Bank and National Bank of Abu Dhabi were lead managers in many instances. Arab involvement in dollar straights has been confined largely to co-management and underwriting. Al-Mal was the only Arab house to lead-manage straight issues in the last three or four years.

A similar level of Gulf activity can be seen in dollar convertibles, with Kuwait International Investment Company (KIIC) lead-managing one issue. KIIC together with the other two Kuwaiti investment companies (Kuwaiti Investment Company and Kuwait Foreign Trading Contracting and Investment Company), Saudi Arabia's National Commercial Bank and Al-Mal account for the great majority of Arab involvement. Hikmat Nasheshibi *'Arab to Arab Eurobonds Can Work' Euromoney*, (London, May 1985)

Arab banks in general and Gulf banks in particular continue to show a preference for West European financing. Lending to clients in that region accounted for 41% of the total volume in 1983 and rose to 48% in 1984. There was also a 10% point jump in lending to the Asia-Pacific region constituting in 1984 around 27% of the total (see Table 6.3).

In 1984, North America became the third favorite place to lend accounting for almost 9% of all Arab financing as compared with 6.6% the previous year. Arab banks lending to Eastern Europe increased fourfold from 1983 to 1984, in both dollar and percentage terms. Middle East financing declined slightly in volume but maintained its fourth place. However, as percentage of total lending, the region accounted for only 6% of the total in 1984 down from 8% the year before.

Another area of international banking which is acquiring increasing importance is trade finance. A number of innovations have been introduced recently to this market, especially the 'a forfait' paper, barter trade, counter purchase and clearing or switch business. The availability of the financial futures markets will bring through an

Table 6.3 Breakdown of Arab banks' lending by region : 1984

	Total $ Volume (million)	Total No. of issues	Bonds $ Volume (million)	Bonds No. of issues	Loans $ Volume (million)	Loans No. of issues
Europe	18 222.8	107	6 841.2	59	11 381.6	48
Asia–Pacific	10 251.2	97	2 832.9	50	7 418.3	47
North America	3 325.0	18	1 875.0	13	1 450.0	5
Middle East	2 252.1	32	395.0	4	1 857.1	28
Eastern Europe	1 622.9	10	20.0	1	1 602.9	9
Africa	1 559.7	7	600.0	1	959.7	6
Supranationals	596.5	10	596.5	10	–	–
Latin America	75.0	1	–	–	75.0	1
Consortia	48.9	1	–	–	48.9	1

Source
Institutional Investor, (June 1985).

explosion of new ideas and instruments in this business. The Gulf banks have traditionally been strong in the trade field and in order for them to continue to benefit from this burgeoning fee generating business, they need to innovate and to continuously move up with the market.

Increasingly, more international competition is filtering into the domestic market of the Gulf and the governments of the region are finding it more difficult to protect their local institutions against the threat. In this era of electronic telecommunications, computerization and globalization of banking services foreign banks are able to penetrate the Gulf markets without necessarily having local offices. Gulf banks need to continuously improve their services and better manage their assets and liabilities in order to face the international challenge both domestically and abroad.

REGULATING THE BANKING SECTOR

Central banks and monetary authorities in the region are aware of the need to pursue more stringent monitoring practices on Gulf financial institutions. Up until recently there were no limits to the amounts that banks can lend to their own directors, nor did banks have to disclose their bad and doubtful loans. Disclosure requirements in general have been undemanding. Unspecified amounts can be placed in hidden reserves direct from income, making profits and loss accounts less meaningful. The end of the year figures did not provide detailed breakdowns of deposits by type, and of the maturity structure of banks' liabilities and assets.

Few unsound banking practices were not uncommon before. Many banks lent on the basis of the names of the borrowers, internal control was lacking and businessmen, particularly in UAE, set up banks to help them guarantee access to credit. Various financial institutions became involved in speculative activities at a time when monetary authorities exercised minimal control on these institutions. Many banks thought it was unnecessary to set aside sizeable provisions for non-performing loans and went on channelling their ample earnings to their shareholders in the form of dividends.

Tools of monetary policy are still lacking, changeable reserve ratios and open market operations have not been utilized, limiting as a result the ability of the monetary authorities to exercise direct control on domestic credit. The recent introduction of CDs by UAE central bank and the 90 days banking security deposit account introduced by SAMA are encouraging signs that more effective tools of monetary policy are gradually being introduced.

Central banks have recently started to move forcefully to bolster confidence in banking system. They have tightened their rules and have begun scrutinizing the banks' books and inquiring into the quality of the financial results presented. The Bahrain Monetary Agency has clamped down on banks lending to its own directors. Under a rule introduced recently, Bahrain banks can lend only a collective maximum of 30% of their capital and reserves to their directors or their companies and a maximum of 15% to any individual director. Credit is defined to include advances, guarantees, overdrafts, standby facilities, letters of credits, loans and any other related credit instruments.

In 1984 the UAE Central Bank issued a directive to local banks spelling out for the first time a compulsory procedure for categorizing bad or doubtful loans, whose incidence has increased with the slowdown of the national economy. As a result, UAE banks have now made larger provisions for such loans, which are estimated to comprise about 14% of all loans and advances.

A second measure of the UAE Central Bank was a circular issued in January 1985 which laid down a standard format for the presentation of annual balance sheets, requiring banks to explicitly reveal the existence of inner reserves and the state of liquidity. Together, the two measures helped to accelerate the merger process by revealing the actual position of each bank. Banks were also told to hold reserves within the country and were banned from announcing fictitious profits to attract investments.

In Kuwait, the Central Bank has been asking more information about how the banks were treating their loans and has made it known that loan provision policies should be tightened. The standing requirements are 100% provisions to be made for loans past due over one year, 45% for loans due over 270 days and 15% for loans past due up to 180 days. The Central Bank has been scrutinizing, as well, proposed dividends and share issues.

FUTURE OUTLOOK FOR GULF BANKING

There is nowadays ample ambiguity and confusion in the region as to where the market is heading in the second half of the 80s. With the lingering economic slowdown, good traditional banking business would be more difficult to come. The main subject of concern is the potential default of private borrowers and the difficulty of obtaining the repayment of loans. A group of customers in the region are beginning to shy away from their commitments to the banks, hiding behind religious objections to interest rates. Others have been genuinely hit by declining asset values and fell into the category of potential rescheduling.

The number of non-performing loans have been on the rise, and the depressed property and stock prices have undermined some of the best collateral that banks hold. The pile of good assets is, therefore, shrinking and banks who decide to mark time in the hope of better regional prospects, possibly in the 90s, are taking the risk of seeing themselves slowly dying on their feet.

The major financial institutions of the world are changing their character from asset based banks into financial trading firms, from being risk takers (extending commercial loans) to becoming brokers, fund managers, agents and advisors. The securitization of the banking industry coincided with the decline of sovereign lending due to the international debt problem, deregulation of the financial and banking industries, privatization and the rise of capitalism as well as the powerful technological developments in the communication that is gradually rendering the whole world into one huge global market.

The changing business opportunities in the Gulf and abroad are creating a more difficult and sophisticated financial market to which banks in the region are expected to adapt. Not only would the banks be operating in a less enticing economic environment and will be dealing with a clientele base facing liquidity problems, but also they would be subjected to more stringent supervision from the local monetary authorities. Gulf customers are becoming more sophisticated and are seeking new channels of savings and investments.

The outlook, however, is not entirely gloomy. In 1984, Gulf banks were among the least leveraged banks in the world. In Kuwait, for example, banks shareholders' equity (capital and reserves) was almost 18% of total credit facilities, compared with a norm among international banks of 3–7%. For Bahrain based Arab OBU's capital to total assets ratio averaged around 11% while that of the top ten banks in the UAE was around 10.6%. The ratio is equally high for domestic banks in the other GCC countries. The consolidated ratio of loans to deposits held by Saudi Arabia's eleven commercial banks was barely 55% in 1984. This undergearing renders Gulf banks solid financial institutions capable of withstanding any temporary set back in their local economies.

The long term prospects need not be discouraging provided that Gulf banks are capable and willing to adapt to the new business opportunities available in the region and abroad, and build the necessary management depth to meet the challenge ahead.

Banking Opportunities in the Region

GCC governments would like the commercial banks to expand their services to cover small businesses and extend longer term credit to the industrial sectors. Larger private sector participation and mobilization of private financial resources are major goals of the region's 1985–90 development plans.

There is no major source of finance available for small to medium size businesses in the region. These were previously ignored because of the lower volume of work and the perception of higher risk. The challenge for the banks is to determine which customers are creditworthy and have the ability to operate in the present environment. If the risk is properly assessed and collateralized, the new lending opportunities for Gulf banks would be quite rewarding. Banks should require stricter documentation from every customer. They may want to enforce putting up foreign assets as collateral. Clauses could be added to the loan agreement making it clearer that when signing the document the borrower is fully aware of the interest element involved and is willingly indulging in a non-Islamic banking practices. Those institutions which are able to manage risks most efficiently will be the market leaders in the time to come.

There are several companies in the region whose own credit risk was probably acceptable until they were forced into difficulties by the sudden withdrawal of credit lines from their traditional non-Gulf bankers. Perceiving less business opportunities in the Gulf, several international banks had decided to pull out or limit their overall exposure to the region. Additional opportunities are now available for Gulf banks who are more committed to their customers, many of whom are still basically solvent, even though some are facing liquidity problems. Only those financial institutions who know their customers well and who had positioned themselves for long term commitment in this part of the world can provide the needed support for Gulf businesses.

Ironically, the region's continuing economic retrenchment is likely to insure a wider role for Gulf banks in financing global trade with the region. Many foreign institutions are leaving the market for the locals who have a better grasp of the risks involved. The terms of executing the business are also changing. There is a shift from cash to credit and from sight to six months LCs. This opens new opportunities for Gulf Banks to cash in on their customer's new credit requirements. Gulf banks now face the challenge of responding to the needs of industry where growth prospects appear to be promising. However, the return schedules in these sectors are of a longer term nature. With the lack of medium and long term financing deposits or funds the banks may not be able to play a greater role in the mid-term and long term financing transactions. Mismatching assets and liabilities is a clear deviation from sound banking practices. Unless Gulf money and capital markets are developed to make it possible for banks to issue their own long and medium term debt instruments, Gulf commercial banks would not be in a position to channel funds to longer term investments. What would be very useful in this respect is a greater degree of direct funding support from Gulf government to their fledgeling financial institutions.

Gulf banks need position themselves to benefit from a noticeable trend in the region toward Islamic orientation and thinking. The banks should be able to provide Islamic banking services tailored to the needs of a large sector of Gulf customers. There is a large pool of 'interest free' funds that could be tapped and various forms of Islamic products that could be introduced. Customers who refuse to receive interest on savings accounts could be lured by offering them offsetting services such as no cost overdraft, or concessionary foreign exchange rates. It would not be too difficult for banks to 'Islamize' some parts of their lending; loans to contractors for equipment, for example, could be managed on a lease-back basis and Islamic consumer finance could be provided by purchasing consumer products, e.g. cars and selling them to customers on an installment payment plan. Profits to be made by a mark up on the price not by interest.

Furthermore, acting in conformity with Islamic principles, Islamic investment funds could be launched by the more sophisticated Gulf commercial banks. The small number of outlets is one of the most serious problems facing Islamic bankers. Several Gulf banks have already developed the expertise to invest in companies quoted on major stock markets, as well as in commodities and other non-interest bearing channels. There are, therefore, ample growth potentials in the field of Islamic banking for commercial banks in the region to explore.

The prominent Gulf banks are expected to take a leading role in developing financial and capital markets in the region. They need to introduce new financial instruments to the Gulf investors and eventually create secondary markets for these instruments. The experience of these banks in the world's major equity markets puts them in a unique position to become market makers in the emerging Gulf capital markets, provide advisory services in this respect and improve the quality of financial information and disclosure in the region.

The introduction to the region of new financial instruments dominated if needed in the local currencies, would make it possible for the private sector to raise its own medium term capital requirements at possibly cheaper rates. Euro-commercial paper, Certificate of Deposits (CDs), Floating Rate Notes (FRNs), Note Issuance Facility (NIF), Revolving Underwriting Facility (RUF), among other Euronote products are examples of such instruments.

For the borrower these facilities will open the market to longer maturities when bank lending tends to be short term. For the banks, Euronotes are better than lending because Banks are not putting up any money, it is no longer funding and adding to their asset base, but rather a commitment from the bank to ensure that the borrower will have access to funds when they are required. The bank, therefore, provides a service and gets a certain fee in return. The short term notes are normally placed among institutional investors in the region. Banks can also create secondary markets in trading paper, which increases their product lines and add new customers.

There are good opportunities for Gulf banks to contribute to the medium size companies in the region that are feeling the effect of the economic slowdown and require guidance to restructure their balance sheets and streamline their businesses. Banks can provide the needed advisory services in this respect and if the companies are basically solid they could arrange reschedule of payments and extend additional credit or other facilities. Clients will receive a more committed service from Gulf banks rather than international banks in this area. By acting as consultants and providing the needed advice to their customers, banks would be able to generate a lot of fee business in this field.

Banking is basically a secular activity and the Gulf is not a secular society. One of the reasons for the unattractiveness of the regional risk is the issue of legal framework. Local courts in Saudi Arabia and to lesser extent in the UAE are uncomfortable about enforcing non-Islamic law against defaulting borrowers in favour of banks.

When they do, their rules are not automatically feasible in political terms. Seizure of assets is difficult and time consuming, though new bankruptcy regulations issued by the Ministry of Commerce in Saudi Arabia should streamline the procedure somewhat. The Saudi Arabian Monetary Agency is also trying to establish some sort of mechanism for collecting debts. It has strengthened its arbitration board which has legal status to deal with disputes. These are encouraging measures but more need to be done to put in place a sound legal system governing the relationship between banks and borrowers in case of disputes.

Investment Banking

In addition to the search for new markets abroad and new business opportunities locally, Gulf banks like their counterparts worldwide will continue to gradually shift their emphasis away from commercial banking and into investment banking and financial services. In the new era of international finance, sophisticated savers will continue to withdraw deposits from banks to earn more by investing in securities, while corporate borrowers are letting their bank loans expire and tapping the capital market for cheaper funds.

Lending in the Euromarket, therefore, is moving gradually away from banks loans to bonds, and from sovereign risk lending towards corporate and project finance. The syndicated loan market has shrunk in the last few years from $91.3 billion in 1981 to $52.5 billion 1985 according to this year's OECD financial statistics. On the other hand the Eurobond market grew from $31 billion in 1981 to $135.4 billion in 1985 and the market is set for continued growth in the coming few years. Gulf banks can concentrate on Arab to Arab Eurobond activity, benefiting from the strong relationship that exists between Arab borrowers and the region's financial institutions. During 1980–84 for example, Arab banks accounted for 10% of the total Eurocredits. Close to 45% of the Euroloans lead managed by Arab banks were for Arab borrowers.

In an era of securitization, those commercial Gulf banks with sufficient trading expertise, and have the capacity to understand market risk besides the traditional credit risk, could not only generate large trading profits and off balance sheet fees, but also enjoy advantageous asset and liability management on a global scale. With enhanced trading capacity, Gulf banks will be in a better position to manage an increasing portion of the region's investment funds which had been primarily handled up till now by western financial institutions.

Gulf International Bank, for example, introduced lately the first uncommitted Eurocommercial paper issued by a Middle Eastern Bank. Such an innovative financial instrument provides Gulf's institutional investors an attractive investment opportunity characterized by high liquidity and good quality. GIB will use the proceeds to fund normal banking operation, thus diversifying its funding sources. This was the latest in a series of developments by GIB to offer alternative investment opportunities to the Gulf's individual and institutional investor and to help develop the region's capital and financial markets. Other banks and financial institutions in the region are floating various money market and investment funds to cater for the evolving needs of Gulf's savers and investors. Various Euronotes and underwriting facilities have also been issued and the trend is clearly towards greater utilization of financial instruments in the region.

Private Banking

As Gulf economies shift from infrastructure building economies to service economies, new generation of wealthy, and in many cases, young Arab investors are being created. Banks' focus on high net worth clients over the past ten years will broaden to encompass the less wealthy but well-to-do clients, and professionals who form the core of the new service-oriented economies. Consumers in the Gulf are now richer and on the average more sophisticated. The region's per capita income is among the highest in the world, and disposable incomes have increased significantly in the last 20 years. Fewer customers are leaving large sums of money on deposit without accepting interest, as they used to do before, and many are drawing down their savings accounts and venturing into higher yielding investment accounts.

The change of focus from commercial into personal banking or private banking, is a recent phenomenon worldwide. Even more recent is the focus on private banking in the Gulf, as demonstrated by the proliferation of ATMs in Kuwait, the introduction by Gulf International Bank of money market fund catering for the small investors and the intensified push into the market by the card and traveller check issuers.

The range of products that can be offered is extensive – money market funds, securities funds, investment trusts, commodity based funds and real estate funds are just examples. Clients both institutions and individuals are increasingly looking for the bank than can provide them with a comprehensive financial service. A bank that can fulfil their credit requirements, advise them on currency exposure and interest rate trends and provide them with channels to invest their savings.

CONCLUSION

The change in the banking industry and in the economies of the region represent a challenge rather than a threat to Gulf Banks. The outlook for Gulf banks in the coming five years is for the smaller institutions to specialize in a particular product, while the larger banks to develop into full service institutions capable of providing expertise in a wide range of specialized financial products backed by top class research and technology and executives who are capable of drawing strategic plans that would see their respective institutions into the 90s.

The 'full line' bank would provide products ranging from floating and fixed rate bonds to equities, from spot foreign exchange dealing to sophisticated arbitrage in the financial futures markets and from swaps to Euronote. Non-recourse project finance will be on the rise, and gradually more project co-financing with the World Bank and the various Arab Funds will be forthcoming. The region's international banks need to develop credible investment banking capabilities with emphasis on mergers and acquisitions, corporate advice, equity placement, portfolio management and stocks flotation. The ability to deal in the big financial markets will be crucial. This will help the banks boost their off-balance sheet income and reduce future debt-based risk.

Banks in the Gulf should aim at reducing their reliance on the interbank market and develop their own long term source of finance from the Eurobond market as well as by the direct acquisition of a retail deposit base either in the region or abroad. To beef up their Gulf currencies deposits, the blue chips banking institutions should work hard on attracting more government funds as well as private and pan Arab deposits. Professionalism, competitiveness, better management and continuous upgrading of banking services are prerequisites to such a development.

Mergers and closures may prove necessary, in fact it is already happening. Some local banks have merged or closed their doors in the UAE, others are considering merging in Bahrain while few are slimming their operations there. More international competition will continue to filter into the domestic markets and governments of the region are finding it more difficult to protect their local institutions against the threat. In this era of electronic telecommunications, computerization and globalization of banking services, foreign banks are able to penetrate the Gulf markets without necessarily having local offices. Gulf banks need to continuously improve their services, provide their clients with state-of-the-art financial instruments and build the necessary management depth in order to face the international challenge both domestically and abroad.

The longer term prospects need not, therefore, be discouraging provided that Gulf banks are capable and willing to adapt to the new business opportunities available in the region and abroad, and build the necessary management depth to meet the challenge ahead.

If Gulf banks want to survive, they should implement structural revisions, acquire recent development, computerize banking services and have a cadre of highly trained bankers capable of responding to the changing business environment. Whereas trade and contract financing require traditional banking expertise, the new areas of banking activities entail more specialized staff and new management structure that facilitates streamlining in the decision making process. The keener competition and the shift in market orientation towards merchant banking requires a faster response time. In financial services, sophisticated management and well trained human resources are perhaps even more important than the capital of the bank.

Banks are aware of the fact that the drive towards maturity cannot be realized without implementing revisions in their overall strategic outlook. For example, a shift in attitude from being asset managers to becoming liability managers, and from being commercial bankers working with credit risk only to becoming investment bankers capable of assessing market risks as well. In times of feeble economic conditions long term strategic planning would be quite useful to help banks succeed in this highly competitive environment. It could help them carve their niche in the domestic, regional and international markets.

7 The Declining Construction Sector

INTRODUCTION

With the completion of the major infrastructural projects, new construction activities in the GCC region recorded a sizeable decline in the last few years. After reaching a peak of $37.5 billion in 1982, the value of contracts awarded in the six Gulf countries dropped to an estimated $15.8 billion in 1985 and looks set to continue downwards.

Saudi Arabia, for example, is projecting an average decline of 2.8% per annum in the construction sector's GDP during the five years of the 1986–1990 development plan. While in Kuwait, where construction activities represent some 10% of non-oil GDP, the spending cuts decided by the government for the fiscal year 1986/87 will have a direct impact on overall construction expenditures. Similar declines in construction activities are expected in the other Gulf countries. Nevertheless, the contract market in the Gulf is still considered quite sizeable by international standards. The emphasis, however is changing from the high growth sectors of the 70s (roads, harbours, transport, electricity, schools, telecommunications and public facilities) to managing and maintaining the already built infrastructure, rural development and health and to support for industry, minerals and other natural resources.

The market shift from major primary construction projects to non-basic industries and operations and maintenance (O&M) is best exemplified in Saudi Arabia. The Kingdom's annual O&M market was estimated at SR25 billion ($6.7 billion), equivalent to more than 12% of total planned government spending in the 1985/86 budget. Little construction work is involved in an O&M contract and most spending goes on cleaning, operation, and replenishment or replacement of material and parts. As such, spare parts and labour account for most of the contract cost.

It is necessary for companies, whether local or international, to make sure they understand the changing character of the market they are dealing with. The construction market in the Gulf has progressed beyond the point of satisfying the most basic infrastructural needs. It is no longer a market where the contractor may be able to base his business entirely on projects conceived by others to which he responds. It has become necessary to research the market properly in order to uncover the most promising business prospects.

The Gulf region may well become a credit rather than a cash market. The increasing need to offer finance, engineering and project management in a single package will put pressure on the traditional consultant and contractor unless stronger links with the financial community can be forged. This is not just a matter of good relationships, but also of an ability to work together, possibly in joint ventures.

THE CHANGING CONTRACT MARKET

Total contract awards in the six GCC countries were estimated at about $15 755 million in 1985, a drop of 29% on the year before and less than half the amount awarded in 1980 (Table 7.1). Saudi Arabia was the largest market in the region throughout the 1980–85 period, capturing more than 70% of the amount of contracts awarded. Oman's share rose from 2.3% in 1980 to about 7% in 1985, while the UAE's share declined from 8.4% to 4.4% during the same period. Kuwait, Bahrain and Qatar accounted for 14.1%, 2.8% and 1% respectively of the GCC market for new awards in 1985. The decline in the value of annual contracts awarded in 1985 was the steepest in the UAE (–60%) followed by Qatar (–30.8%) and Saudi Arabia (–34.6%).

Even though expenditures on development projects have, on the average, been reduced in the various Gulf countries, the number of contracts in the last three years remained almost unchanged but much below the level of 1981. Except for Oman and Bahrain where the average amount per project had actually increased during the 1983–85 period, the amount recorded steep declines in the other Gulf countries. Whereas the amount per project was at an average of $56 million in 1982, it dropped to $29.6 million in 1985. Large scale projects of $100 million or more declined by around 30% in 1985 compared to 1984. This may be explained by the fact that governments' policy in the region of giving contract priority to domestic contractors has led to splitting up of contracts into smaller components.

In 1985, major declines of contract awards were recorded in three main sectors 'public facilities', 'housing' and 'health welfare', the

Table 7.1 Project contract awards in the GCC countries, 1980–85 (Million US$, %)

	1980 value	1980 share	1981 value	1981 share	1982 value	1982 share	1983 value	1983 share	1984 value	1984 share	1985 value	1985 share	1980/81	1981/82	1982/83	1983/84	1984/85
S. Arabia	24 716.1	75.5	21 846.9	73.1	27 540.9	73.5	13 998.9	64.7	17 041.1	76.6	11 148.2	70.8	−11.6	26.1	−49.2	21.7	−34.6
Kuwait	3 363.7	10.3	3 564.1	11.9	5 531.9	14.8	3 630.8	16.8	2 113.6	9.5	2 218.7	14.1	5.9	55.2	−34.4	−41.8	5.0
Bahrain	235.0	0.7	556.0	1.9	367.4	1.0	566.1	2.6	344.7	1.5	436.3	2.8	136.6	−33.9	54.1	−39.1	26.6
Qatar	925.4	2.8	537.5	1.8	929.1	2.5	91.3	0.4	218.2	1.0	150.9	1.0	−41.9	72.9	−90.2	139.0	−30.8
UAE	2 756.7	8.4	2 563.3	8.6	2 106.6	5.6	2 039.1	9.4	1 769.6	7.9	707.1	4.4	−7.1	−17.8	−3.8	−13.2	−60.0
Oman	725.4	2.3	819.0	2.7	991.5	2.6	1 319.1	6.1	757.9	3.5	1 094.2	6.9	12.9	21.1	33.0	−12.5	44.4
Total	32 722.3	100.0	29 886.8	100.0	37 467.4	100.0	21 645.3	100.0	22 245.1	100.0	15 755.4	100.0	−8.6	25.4	−42.2	2.7	−29.2

Sources: Tabulating various reports in MEED, 1980–86;
Other national and international sources, 1980–85.

latter consists largely of hospital construction. For each of the three sectors, the decline was by a billion dollars or more and the level of awards was at its lowest point since 1981. This reflects mainly the general levelling off of infrastructural construction activities and the re-ordering of priorities in favour of such sectors as 'defence', 'computer', 'water' and 'manufacturing'.

The decline in project scale was especially sizeable in Saudi Arabia due to the cutback in government expenditures on development projects in the last few years. Whereas in fiscal 1981/82, the government development expenditures were budgeted at SR206 billion (70% of the SR298 billion total budget for the year), in 1984/85 development expenditures were down to only 55% of that year's SR260 billion budget, or SR141 billion. The 1985/86 budget of SR200 billion had a smaller portion allocated to development projects estimated at around SR100 billion, half of what had been budgeted in 1981/82.

The 1986–90 development plan does not promise much improvement in the traditional contracting activities. The highway network in the Kingdom has been almost completed and the emphasis will be more on maintenance and efficiency utilization. The fourth plan calls for improvement in the quality of housing and the effective use of existing stock, as opposed to creating additional units.

A relatively favourable situation continues to exist in defence projects, petrochemicals power generation and desalination. Whereas contract amounts in the defence sector rose strongly in the last few years, activities in the other three sectors were less affected by the overall decline in development expeditions. In the petrochemical sector, several projects have been approved for construction in the coming few years. Also, plans are in progress to increase power generation in the Kingdom by 8 mkw by fiscal 1990/91.

In Kuwait, the slowdown in construction activity has also been quite evident. There is now a definite shift of emphasis from large scale projects to smaller housing projects and towards maintenance and improvement of existing facilities. The uncertainty that clouds the activities in this sector is mainly due to the excess supply conditions in the market, and the negative psychology overshadowing the overall economic activity in the country. Indicators such as imminent starts and construction permits continued to show sharp declines in 1985 (−31% and −35% respectively).

The largest drop in contract amounts in Kuwait was recorded in such sectors as 'harbours and shipping', 'power', 'desalination', 'housing' and 'hydrocarbons'. The sectors where construction activities continued to perform well in 1985 include public facilities, urban development, education and telecommunications.

A progressive retardation in construction has also been evident in the UAE. The value of contracts awarded dropped in 1985 to its lowest level in ten years. Since 1983, contracting companies operating in the country have cut their labour forces by up to 50%. The drop in contract activities was evident across sectors with sizeable declines recorded in 'manufacturing', 'water', 'harbours and shipping' and 'aviation'. The 70% decline in total contracts awarded in the last five years was the steepest in the region. It coincided with the completion of the major infrastructural projects in the country.

In 1982, Qatar was the fourth largest construction market in the region providing about $929 million worth of work. In 1985, contract amounts dropped to a trickle of $150 million. The decline in construction activities was evident in all the infrastructural sectors. The import of construction material in 1985 was down by 36% compared to the previous year. Cement imports registered the largest fall of 80% to 38 000 tons during 1984/85. Although the figure is slightly misleading, because it takes no account of an increase in local production, it is still a reasonable indicator of the decline in Qatar's construction activities.

The average contract value in Qatar has been of the order of $4 million. Only few major projects were under construction in 1985–86 and not many were being considered to be built over the coming few years. The contracts for the $575 million Wusail power generation and desalination plant project, the $43 million project for the construction of multiproduct pipeline to transport petroleum products for exports and local consumption and the $6 billion North Field gas project have not yet been awarded.

In Oman and Bahrain, the construction sectors have been less seriously affected. The two countries are not OPEC members and, therefore, were not seriously hindered by the declining oil revenues in 1984 and 1985 as was the case with the other GCC countries. As a matter of fact, the amount of contracts awarded recorded a noticeable increase in Oman and Bahrain during 1985. Oman still requires a broader infrastructural network, freeways, airports, harbours, schools, health centres, as well as extensive rural development construction projects. There should be, therefore, scope for additional construction activities in the Sultanate in the coming five years. However, this year's decline in oil prices has led Oman to reconsider its planned expenditures on infrastructure. Development related spending is projected to increase by only 2.6% in the Third Five-Year Plan (1986–90) relative to the level in the preceding plan, to about $6.4 billion.

The increase in the total amounts of contract awarded in Bahrain in 1985 was mainly due to a noticeable rise in the amount contracted to the 'defence' and 'aviation' sectors. The few mega-construction projects (e.g. Gulf University, the Tourist Centre in Zallak) are clearly not the sort of projects one should expect in the second half of the 80s. Indications are that in the future most projects lined up will be in the range of $10 to $25 million, which may not be of interest to the top international contractors. It is the second tier contractors that will find it profitable to tender for these projects. The government is putting more emphasis on housing and manufacturing, and the private sector is being called upon to participate more actively in future construction activities. The opening soon of the Bahrain-Saudia Arabia causeway may help in improving the general outlook of the construction sector.

THE CHANGING ROLE OF THE INTERNATIONAL CONTRACTORS

During the 70s and early 80s, the large international contractors dominated the construction market of the Middle Eastern countries. According to *Engineering News-Record*, the New York-based construction weekly, new contracts won by the top 250 international contractors in the Middle East (including the Arab countries of North Africa, Iran and Iraq) fell to $21.6 billion in 1985, down a marked 18.8% from the previous year, and drastically less than the $51.2 billion peak reached during 1982. This decline contrasts with worldwide foreign work won by the top firms, which increased by a marginal 1.4% to $81.6 billion last year, ending a three-year slide from a peak of $129.9 billion in 1981.

The most numerous firms in the Middle East during 1985 were 26 US firms working on $7.8 billion worth of contracts, or 36% of world-wide contracts in the Middle East. Following the US were 15 Korean firms, representing 15.6% of all contracts, or $3.4 billion in business. Fifteen Italian companies won 11% of world-wide business in the Mideast with $2.4 billion in contracts. Twenty-five Japanese firms followed with 8.8% of the total, or $1.9 billion. In fifth place among international contractors in the Mideast were six Turkish firms, who secured 4.5% of the market with $1 billion.

More specifically in the Gulf region, the declining fortunes of foreign firms are highlighted by the recent performance of South Korean contractors who captured a good portion of the market with their low pricing in the boom of the 70s. In 1985, South Korea's share of the market dropped to 7.4% with awards worth an estimated $840 million compared to awards worth $4.2 billion in 1982, accounting for 17.4% of the GCC market.

French, and West German contractors have suffered similarly. France saw the value of its new contracts in the GCC region decline from $4.9 billion in 1983 to $557 million in 1985, while Germany's share in the market dropped from 7.6% in 1983 to 2.3% in 1985.

The increase in defence contracts helped the United States to maintain its market share in 1985. The gulf region remained a productive market for American contractors accounting for 20% of their total foreign business. The United Kingdom was the primary beneficiary of the increase in defence spending. In 1985, UK contracts rose six times that of 1984 to $5.3 billion. Even though most of the contracts were generated in the defence sector, British contractors and consultants were able to secure several medium sized civil engineering projects.

Although Japan does not have an export-oriented defence industry, the country was able to increase its share in the GCC project market from 10.7% in 1984 to 16.9% in 1985. However, the decline in the performance of South Korean contractors who has had an advantage in construction related projects is not encouraging for Japanese firms seeking business in the region. Their comparative advantage would be to move up in the market and concentrate on consulting services, construction and management services including financing, and O&M projects.

Turkish firms entered the Gulf contracting market relatively late in the boom years, but managed initially to make headway, largely at the expense of the South Koreans. In 1985, however, they marked time, with new contracts a total of $736 million. At the peak of their gains in 1981, the Turks took $5535 million worth of new work. Their largest market in the region last year was Saudi Arabia, with new contracts totalling $387 million.

Many foreign firms have responded to the slump by cutting their labour forces and recalling expatriate staff, others have withdrawn from the region altogether. The pressure on foreign firms is all the greater given the emphasis that is spreading throughout the region to encourage local contractors. The trend has been most pronounced in Saudi Arabia, which early in spring 1983 introduced a regulation requiring foreign prime contractors to sublet locally at least 30% of all public sector awards. Furthermore, a royal decree has restricted the construction of roads, bridges, small and medium-size buildings as well as the execution of public contracts for catering, maintenance, operation, transportation and other similar activities to Saudi contractors only. All contractors must also use local firms for certain services considered vital to the Kingdom such as insurance and banking.

Kuwait has followed Saudi Arabia's example. A 30% rule was introduced in 1985, but individual government clients increasingly specify that up to 40% of contracts must be sublet locally. At the same time, much tighter restrictions have been imposed on imports of materials, and contractors have been instructed to buy locally wherever possible.

In the other Gulf countries, Qatar and the UAE have introduced grading of contractors. The aim is to spread available work around, opening up more opportunities for local firms. In the UAE, moves are afoot to introduce a ruling that gives preference to public works bidders prepared to buy materials from local suppliers for at least 10% of a contract's value.

FINANCING THE CONSTRUCTION SECTOR

A major problem facing local contractors in the region is lack of finance. With the decline in construction activities commercial banks have tightened up credit facilities to local contractors. Local firms and especially the smaller ones continue to find a gap between the credit they need and the sums available. Even Bahrain OBU's are unlikely to be able to bridge the gap. The tightening credit facilities may subject local firms to liquidity problems such that they cannot offer sufficient financial guarantees or even meet start-up costs on a contract. We will try to estimate here the expected unfulfilled financing needs of contractors for work to be carried out in Saudi Arabia and the other five GCC countries for the years 1985/86 till 1989/90. We will also point to the ample lending opportunities still available and to the changing face of contract financing in the region.

Saudi Arabia

According to 1985/86 government budget, total expenditures will be SR200 billion ($54.8 billion). Allocation for construction related activities take up a significant part of the budget. Total project related expenditures during the 1985/86 fiscal year estimated at around $20 billion or 36% of total allocation.

Given the decline in oil revenues, and the view that the Saudi authorities may not be willing to continue to draw on their foreign reserves at the same rate as before, the total budgeted government expenditures (and therefore the budgeted construction expenditures) are expected to decline by around 15% to accommodate the expected drop in oil revenues (from an estimated $47.6 billion in 1984 to around $38.08 billion in 1985) Construction expenditures are projected to decline further by around 10% per year in the next two years before stabilizing thereafter. The projected outlays on government construction projects in the five years period up till 1989/90 are as follows (in $ billion).

	1985/86	1986/87	1987/88	1988/89	1989/90
Estimated construction expenditures (government)	17.436	15.851	14.410	14.410	14.410

According to the latest reports available, total expenditures on private residential and non-residential construction were $6736 billion in 1982/83 and $6011 billion in 1981/82. The best estimates currently available indicate that private construction expenditure has been growing since 1982/83 at about 10% per year and is expected to stabilize in the next year or so. The projected outlays on private sector construction projects in the five years period under consideration would be $7.410 billion per year. The estimated total construction expenditures over the five years period would, therefore, be (in $ billion).

It is difficult to quantify precisely the size of banking business generated by such a volume of construction expenditures. A lot of contingent business would continue to be forthcoming, this includes advance payment guarantees of 10% of the value of the contract, 1%

	1985/86	1986/87	1987/88	1988/89	1989/90
Estimated total construction expenditures (private & government)	24.846	23.261	21.820	21.820	21.820

bid bonds and 5% performance bonds. Banks are normally called upon to provide bridge financing before government disbursements are received. The need for such credit facilities are expected to increase in the coming few years. The average period of 3 months bridge financing is expected to give way to periods of 6 or even 9 months, generating more financing opportunities for the banks.

In the past, about a quarter of total construction projects costs were spent on purchasing new construction equipment and machinery. This percentage is likely to decline because of the likelihood that contractors working in the region already have a reasonable amount of equipment in inventory. Besides, rentals of equipment rather than outright purchase may become more common. Consequently, about 20% of the total project cost would be a better estimate of the amount to be spent on purchasing equipment. Also, about half of the 10% advance payment received by contractors will be available for purchasing new equipment. This means demand for financing of construction equipment is estimated at around 15% of total construction expenditures (in $ billion).

	1985/86	1986/87	1987/88	1988/89	1989/90
Estimated demand for financing construction equipment (total)	3.727	3.489	3.273	3.273	3.273

Part of this total demand for financing will be fulfilled by loans provided by Saudi commercial banks. However, not all the financing requirements could be met locally as Saudi banks are expected to continue to follow sound banking procedures of risk diversification.

They have a need to diversify their loan assets into various national and international sectors. They will avoid getting over exposed to one sector of the economy especially when this sector has been witnessing consolidation of activities and will continue to set borrowing limits to their various clients in the contracting business.

In 1984/85 total commercial bank credit in the Kingdom grew by 7% to $16 887 billion from $15 785 billion in 1983/84. Loans and advances extended to the building and construction sector totalled $3621 billion compared to $3540 billion in the previous year, i.e. an increase of 2.2%. Saudi banks have been exercising more restraint when extending loans to contractors and were becoming more selective and prudent in their credit evaluation. With the present economic slowdown in the Kingdom, growth of commercial bank credit is expected to assume a consolidating trend with growth rates forecasted at 2% annually for the 5 year period under consideration. Also it is assumed that a declining percentage of loans and advances would go to the construction sector. This percentage dropped to 21% in the fiscal year 1984/85 from 23% in 1983/84, and would further decline to 18% in 1985/86 and 1986/87 and 15% thereafter.

	1985/86	1986/87	1987/88	1988/89	1989/90
Total Saudi bank loans (in $ billion)	17.224	17.569	17.920	18.279	18.645
Saudi Bank's loans to the construction sector (in $ billions)	3.100	3.160	2.688	2.742	2.797

The total unfulfilled financing needs of contractors working in the Kingdom would be as follows (in $ billion).

	1985/86	1986/87	1987/88	1988/89	1989/90
Residual financing needs of the construction sector (in $ billions)	0.627	0.329	0.585	0.531	0.476

Bahrain OBUs have been involved in the financing of the construction sector in Saudi Arabia. They are believed to have been generally more aggressive in seeking construction-related lending opportunities, while trade related banking has been the traditional strength of local Saudi banks. A breakdown of total loans of Bahrain OBUs to Saudi borrowers was not available by sector. It may be conjunctured that the construction sector received in 1983 around 17% of the total loans extended to corporates in the Kingdom or close to $515 million. The remaining balance was allocated to manufacturing, trade and other activities in the services and transportation sectors. This figure may have increased to $527 million in 1984/85 leaving an estimated financial gap of around $100 million. This gap is expected to have been closed by export credit from foreign governments and their specialized financial institutions providing back up support to contractors operating in the Kingdom.

Other GCC Countries

The budgetary allocation for development projects and construction-related activities in the other five GCC countries totalled around $6.2 billion in 1985/86 budgets; Kuwait with its allocation of about $3 billion is at the top, followed by UAE ($2 billion), Bahrain $500 million, Qatar ($400 million) and Oman ($300 million).

With the completion of the region's major infrastructural projects and with the present glut in the world oil market expected to prevail in the coming few years, construction outlays in the various GCC countries are projected to decline by around 5% in 1986/87 and the year to follow before stabilizing thereafter.

The following is a forecasted outlay of government construction expenditures in the five GCC countries: Kuwait, UAE, Bahrain, Qatar and Oman (in $ billion).

	1985/86	*1986/87*	*1987/88*	*1988/89*	*1989/90*
Estimated construction expenditures (government)	6200	5904	5624	5624	5624

Various estimates suggest that total expenditures on private residential and non-residential construction constituted, on the average around 30% of the corresponding governments' expenditures on construction activities in the five GCC countries. This percentage is expected to prevail in the foreseeable future and the projected total construction for these countries would, therefore, will be (in $ billion):

	1985/86	1986/87	1987/88	1988/89	1989/90
Estimated total construction expenditures for 5 GCC countries	8060	7675	7311	7311	7311

The important point to be made here is that there would continue to be ample lending opportunities for construction activities in the region. The risk, however, would be higher. Lending for construction activities in the coming few years would continue to shift from the foreign contractors who have proven track records and outside sources of cash to smaller and less capitalized Gulf companies or joint ventures involving local partners.

How will banks react to these changes? A bank is essentially looking at 3 factors when financing a contractor. First, the contractor's ability to perform on the project, second, if the cash flows on the project are realistic, and finally, the ability of the owner to pay. In the GCC countries, fortunately, there is little doubt on the governments' ability to pay. Several cases were reported accusing governments of delaying payments to contractors. However, government officials always justified the delayed payments on ground that the project has not been executed according to specification. In any case, revision of work as deemed appropriate had always led to payment being made.

For top tier international contractors, the ability to perform on a given project is of little concern, as they possess a high level of technical and managerial skills developed over many years and demonstrated on scores of complex projects. Furthermore, these contractors also possess adequate resources to absorb the effect of problems on a large project, including delays in payment. For such contractors therefore nothing much will have changed in their relationship with banks as they continue to be first class risks.

On the other hand, smaller contractors without the same resources and experience should be subjected to much closer scrutiny than before. Their ability to perform on projects cannot be taken for granted. They are also more vulnerable to payment delays which could convert a marginally profitable contract into a loss.

Not having recourse to the same kind of resources as larger contractors, smaller contractors may also find it difficult to continue to perform during prolonged periods of delay in progress payments. Thus, there is a greater likelihood of performance bonds being called. The perception hence is of heightened risk, which will translate into increased emphasis on financing of specific projects. Projects and cash flow should, therefore, be analysed to determine if the bid price makes sense and that cash flows are realistic. Banks should, therefore, insist on exercising more control of cash flows and an assignment of contract proceeds should almost be a prerequisite. These concerns may appear to be inflated to some local contractors, but they are clearly not unjustified. Once a bank extends financing on a project it becomes committed to its successful completion and is virtually a partner with the contractor.

CONCLUSION

The Gulf construction market will become stable within the next few years and only serious, efficient and well-managed companies will survive. Gulf contractors will have to meet the challenge and must invest heavily in improving their management techniques – the only ingredient of success in construction.

Non-specialized contractors with low technology to offer will be phased out completely from the market within the next few years. A contractor offering a high level of technology, with a strong financial backing will always find work.

In any case, the profit margins will never be the same again. Gone are those days when a contracting company with $10 million capital was charging over 20% profit on, say, a $200 million yearly turn-over – about 400% return on investment. Gone are those days when overheads were added as a percentage to each contract. Nowadays actual overhead costs are calculated individually and added to the contract price, while profit margins are becoming far more reasonable.

Even though the size of the construction market in the Gulf has declined, opportunities do still exist, albeit on a smaller scale and of a different nature than in the past. Private sector activities in construction will eventually pick up momentum as governments of the region continue to encourage private sector investment.

Managing existing physical assets which require rehabilitation, operation and continuous maintenance provides another business opportunity in the region. The original builders of a project or a plant will have a good starting position in negotiating subsequent management and rehabilitation contracts. There will be a need as well to help manage town and city services and for urban development in general. As some contractors are already finding, management rather than engineering is becoming the primary requirement. Foreign firms are called upon to provide managerial skills and broader technical capabilities, not only to operate industrial plants and city services but also to develop indigenous management capabilities by providing training for local cadre. The operation and management contracting, therefore, seems to be the follow up to the initial construction phase.

8 The Industrial Challenge in the GCC Region

INTRODUCTION

The industrial sectors of the various GCC countries are increasingly gaining prominence and gradually becoming viable and contributing more to the region's GDP. During the first half of the 80s the region witnessed a significant numerical growth in manufacturing enterprises. By 1985, according to the Gulf Organisation for Industrial Consulting, there were about 3600 licensed manufacturing enterprises operating in the region, with a total investment of $75 billion. The majority of these enterprises were engaged in import substitution products and depended mostly on imported skills for their operation. Nevertheless, the region remains characterized by excessive reliance on imports to meet consumption needs.

The contribution of the industrial sectors to GDP in the various GCC countries is still limited. The highest percentage is in Bahrain with around 12% of the country's gross domestic product being generated in the manufacturing and refining industries (Table 8.1). The industrial sector's output to total GDP in Kuwait, Qatar and UAE has been relatively stable in the last few years while that of Saudi Arabia increased from 5% in 1980 to around 8% in 1985. The lowest percentage of industrial sector output to GDP has been in Oman, close to 2.8% in 1984. However, Oman recorded the highest annual growth rate in industrial production for the period 1980–1985, of close to 50%.

Another indicator of the status of industry in the GCC region is the huge sums invested in this sector. In the first half of the 70s, the public sectors of the six Gulf states invested close to $560 million in manufacturing industry representing 4.8% of their total development expenditure during that period. In the second half of the decade, total investment in industry rose to $15 billion or close to 14% of their total investments, whereas in the 1980–85 period the figure rose to $40 billion representing 13% of total investments. This huge investment in industry and especially in petrochemicals, cement and chemical fertilizers raised the per capita contribution of industry to GDP from an average of $190 in 1970 to $839 in 1983/84.

Table 8.1 Contribution of manufacturing sectors to GDP in the GCC countries (percentage)

	1980	1982	1983	1984	1985
S. Arabia	5.0	4.3	5.8	7.5	8.3
Kuwait	5.9	6.6	6.4	6.3	6.6
UAE	3.8	8.2	8.7	8.7	9.0*
Oman	0.7	1.4	2.3	2.8	3.2
Bahrain	11.5	11.3	11.5	11.8	12.0*
Qatar	3.3	5.0	6.0	6.0	6.5*

Source: Various national and regional sources including *Unified Arab Economic Report*, 1985 edited by the Arab Monetary Fund.
* Estimates.

The challenge facing industrial development in the GCC countries is the ability to produce and sell competitively, despite the limited raw material base, high labour and management costs, a restricted home market, a gradual elimination of subsidies relating to electricity, water, land and industrial loans, and the limited protection offered by the tariff system which leads to the dumping of foreign products in the Gulf markets. Besides the GCC countries need to come up with a coherent industrial strategy for the region as a whole, that eliminates duplication and promotes complementarity of industrial ventures.

Gulf businessmen have been geared both psychologically and economically toward trade and services activities, where profits are easy and returns substantial and quick. This attitude has had a negative impact up till now on the expansion of the industrial sector. Private entrepreneurship has been to a larger extent, shying away from industrial activities, which involve more risks and long gestation periods for profitability.

With the special position of the resource ownership, coupled with the absence of entrepreneurial vigour of the private sector, GCC Governments have spearheaded the process of industrialization, hoping that through building a strong and viable industrial base and related infrastructure, the private sector would be motivated to take over the role.

Generally speaking, two independent patterns of industrial development are distinguishable. On the one hand, the private sector for the most part undertakes small-scale light industries oriented towards the internal consumer markets. On the other hand, the public sector undertakes large-scale, capital-intensive, export-oriented industrial schemes, mostly related to oil.

IS INDUSTRIALIZATION IN THE GCC REGION A RATIONAL POLICY?

The rationality of downstream oil investments in particular and industrialization in general in the GCC countries have been questioned. The argument often presented is that downstream industries do not reduce oil dependence since oil products and petrochemicals are part of the oil sector. Besides, the advantages accrued through lower prices of feedstocks, are eroded by the cost of transporting the products to the industrial countries and the higher maintenance cost. As for the non-oil industries, critics argue that due to the restricted home market base, limited raw material and high labour cost, it would be more advantageous for the GCC countries to continue importing their required capital and consumer goods at competitive prices from abroad instead of producing these products locally.

The economic theory of comparative advantage could be used to justify downstream oil investments in the GCC region. The real social value of the industrial projects should be considered to foster the commercial profitability argument and boost the overall viability of the project.

The Gulf region consists of capital and oil-rich countries with relatively small populations and limited agricultural potential. Hence, the theory of comparative advantage suggests that, in principle, capital intensive downstream investment would be an obvious choice for these countries. Apart from this general argument there is another, more specific one, which makes the Gulf countries' comparative advantage in developing downstream activities even more profound. Crude oil extraction is usually associated with natural gas (associated gas) which is produced in quite substantial quantities. It has been estimated that associated gas represents 10–12% of the energy content of the barrel of crude oil with which it is associated. Because associated gas has traditionally been flared as a waste product it can provide a very cheap feedstock to gas-related industries (petrochemicals, fertilizers, etc.) established close to oil extraction areas.

Even though, the theory of comparative advantage suggests that downstream investment is a sound policy for the Gulf countries, various feasibility studies carried out on refining and petrochemical industries in the region were critical of this policy. These studies concentrated on short-term profitability only, stressing the estimated losses of individual industries and measuring costs and benefits at market prices. However, market prices do not necessarily reflect the social marginal value of certain inputs and outputs to the oil producers.

The effective opportunity cost of capital to the Gulf countries need not necessarily be the current market interest rate. The alternative use of the surplus capital in the early 70s when the GCC countries decided to lock it into the construction of petrochemical complexes and other related industries would have been to invest it in foreign assets. But at that time, their experience of foreign investments was disappointing, having actually obtained negative real rates of return from their investment abroad. Furthermore, a policy of investing all their capital wealth in foreign assets would have been socially unacceptable as this would have implied the creation of a *rentier* society consisting of citizens living on assets held abroad and lacking opportunity to enjoy the benefits of productive employment. Such a situation would have led as well to fable social structure and with no clear commitment of citizens to their region.

Therefore, the opportunity cost of capital to the Gulf countries is less than the world market rate of return and, the 2-3% interest rate that the governments of these countries charge for their loans to finance their industrial sectors might actually represent the region's true opportunity cost of capital.

Another factor that would boost the profitability and viability of industrial investments in the region is the implementation of the GCC common economic agreement which went into effect in March 1983. It is designed to tear down economic barriers between the six member states and to encourage joint projects and investments by Gulf nationals. The ground for a common market in the region has, therefore, already been set eliminating as a result a major constraint for industrial development in the Gulf.

The other arguments that are normally presented to justify the industrial option in the region include the following:

1. to capture the value added from processing crude oil;
2. to provide opportunities for human resources development and the acquisition of useful skills;
3. to help in the transfer of technology to the region;
4. to contribute to the diversification of the sources of national income; and
5. to reduce the level of dependence on imports and achieve a higher degree of self-sufficiency in the field of production.

FACTORS HINDERING THE INDUSTRIALIZATION PROCESS

The factors limiting industrialization in the GCC region relate mostly to rigidities on the supply side. Despite the sizeable supply of the capital and foreign exchange, these countries are extremely deficient in the supply of labour at all levels. It is believed that it is not possible to enhance the capital absorptive capacity before transforming a considerable part of the financial resources into human and physical capital.

The small base of domestic manpower in the various GCC countries necessitates the use of expatriate labour who are normally more expensive to employ. Besides, the development of indigenous human resources is hindered by the clear bias that the nationals have for general education rather than technical training. This entails as well a preference to work in the government, trade and services sectors rather than the productive sectors of the economy. The unskilled national labourer tends to look down on blue collar jobs. He would choose to be self-employed and work as a guard or a taxi driver rather than seek employment in a factory or in a construction site.

It is important to realize that the highly concentrated development phenomenon in the GCC countries and the comparable resource base of these countries are leading to the creation of similar industrial bases. This would definitely reduce the scope for regional trade, and may increase considerably the danger of ruinous competition in the export markets, whether within the region or outside it. In addition, most of the basic industries created in the oil countries, especially in petrochemicals, fertilizers and iron and steel, tend to operate much below design capacity. This does not only increase the unit cost of production, but also threaten to wipe out most of the cost advantage arising from the domestic abundance of energy and raw materials.

The high cost of imported intermediate material, and equipment as well as the dependence on expensive expatriate labour, increase still further the average cost of production and render locally-produced commodities less competitive. In addition, there are operational and organizational constraints that adversely affect the cost of production such as the ineffectiveness of existing marketing systems, rigidly centralized management structures, and the shortage of a sound information base.

Another obstacle facing industrialization in the region is the low price of competitive imports and the dumping policies followed by certain countries exporting to the region. Several exporters have adopted cut-price policies to preserve their markets in the Gulf countries, even if their profit margins would be drastically reduced.

Another hindrance to industrialization in the Gulf countries is the small size of the domestic markets. Attempts have already started to formulate a regional approach to industrialization, and create inter-industry and inter-country linkages. This does not only help to expand the size of the domestic market, but also to create foreword and backward linkages so that investment in one industry may make investments in others more profitable.

It is becoming increasingly evident that the next phase of industrialization will require, in addition to the regional dimension, an international dimension. Future industries are likely to depend more on export markets and need, therefore, to face the challenge of international competition.

What can be discerned from the foregoing is that the emerging patterns of industrialization are carrying with them certain challenges that need to be faced with careful national planning and regional co-operative outlook.

PROSPECTS FOR NEW INDUSTRIES

There is still ample scope for the development of new industrial ventures in the GCC region that enjoy a comparative advantage at the present time or in the foreseeable future. In more than 100 studies carried out in the last two years, one has come across very few sectors where local industrial output was capable of supplying the bulk of the market. Tentatively the following areas can be identified:

1. *The industries that depend on the by-product of the refining industry.* The local oil refining capacity has considerably increased to meet local consumption and export requirements. The numerous by-products of the refining industry can be collected in appropriate quantities to support significant industries in the field of petrochemicals and in the field of chemical industry in general.
2. *The downstream industries in the petroleum and petrochemical sectors.* These include petrochemical intermediates, plastics intermediates, solvent fertilizers, tyres, rubber products, paints, nylon and polyester fibres, detergents, animal feeds and other miscellaneous products (see figures 8.1–8.3 for petroleum derivatives

```
┌─────────────────────────────────────────────┐
│              PETROCHEMICAL                  │
├──────────────────────┬──────────────────────┤
│ PRIMARY INDUSTRIES   │ SECONDARY PRODUCTS   │
│                      │ INDUSTRIAL USES      │
└──────────────────────┴──────────────────────┘
```

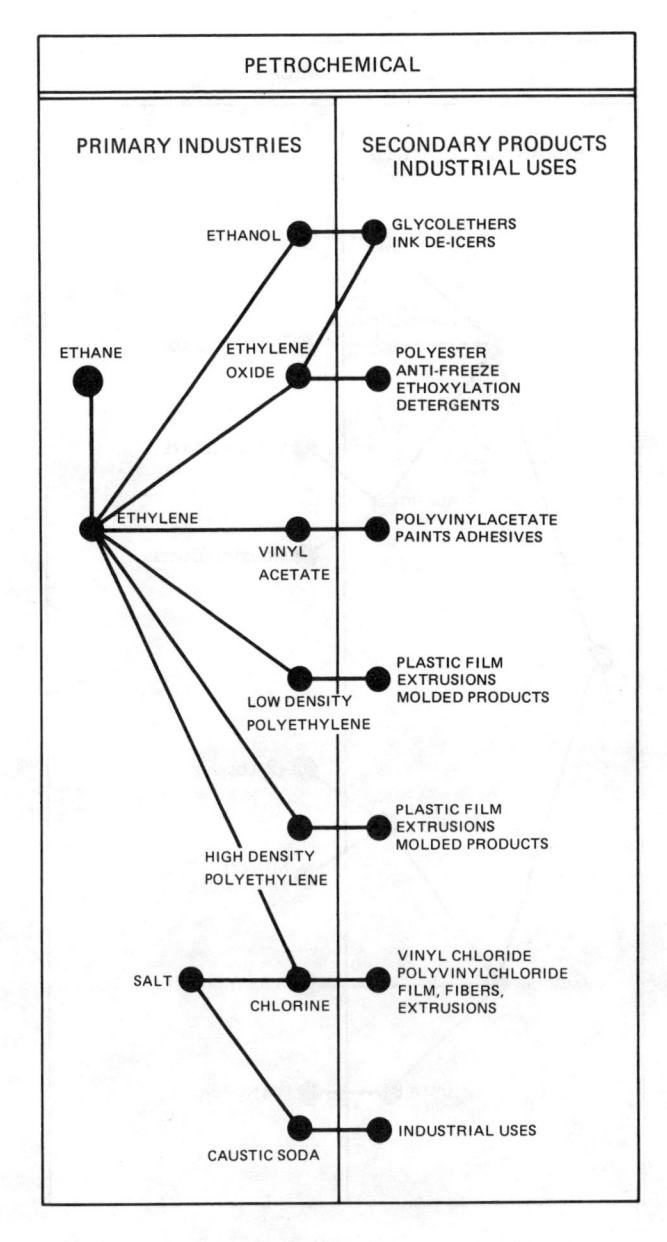

- ETHANOL — GLYCOLETHERS, INK DE-ICERS
- ETHANE
- ETHYLENE OXIDE — POLYESTER, ANTI-FREEZE, ETHOXYLATION, DETERGENTS
- ETHYLENE
- VINYL ACETATE — POLYVINYLACETATE, PAINTS ADHESIVES
- LOW DENSITY POLYETHYLENE — PLASTIC FILM EXTRUSIONS, MOLDED PRODUCTS
- HIGH DENSITY POLYETHYLENE — PLASTIC FILM EXTRUSIONS, MOLDED PRODUCTS
- SALT
- CHLORINE — VINYL CHLORIDE, POLYVINYLCHLORIDE, FILM, FIBERS, EXTRUSIONS
- CAUSTIC SODA — INDUSTRIAL USES

Figure 8.1

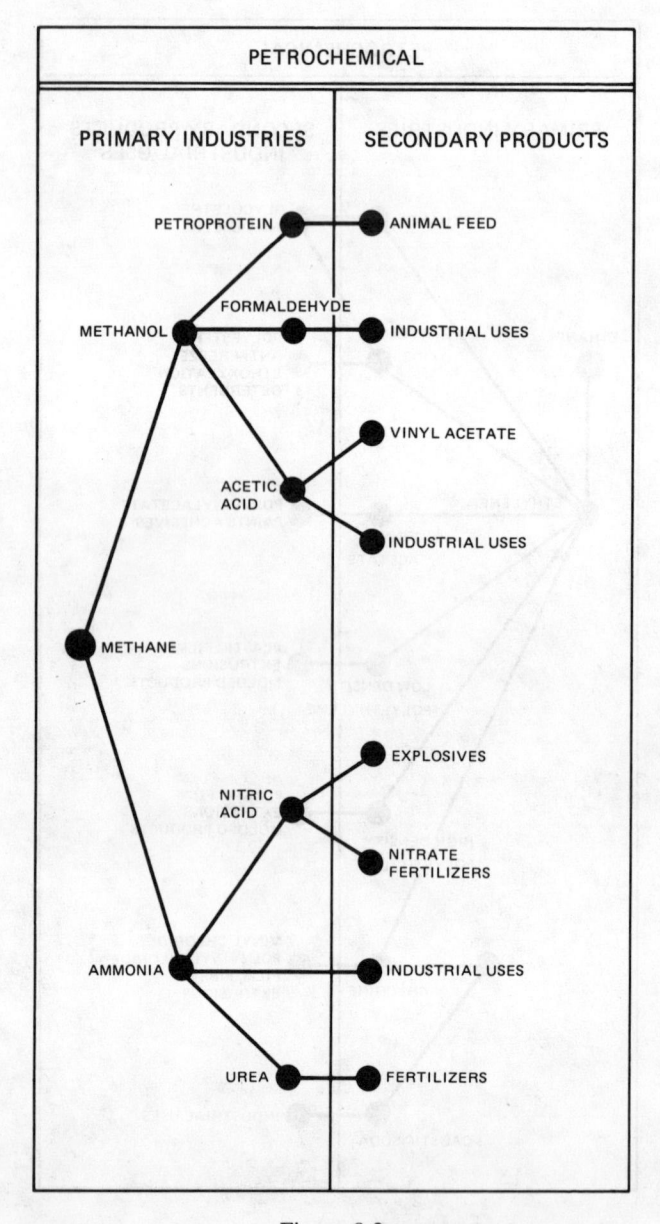

Figure 8.2

Industrial Challenge in the GCC Region

PETROLEUM DERIVATIVES

PRIMARY INDUSTRIES | SECONDARY PRODUCTS

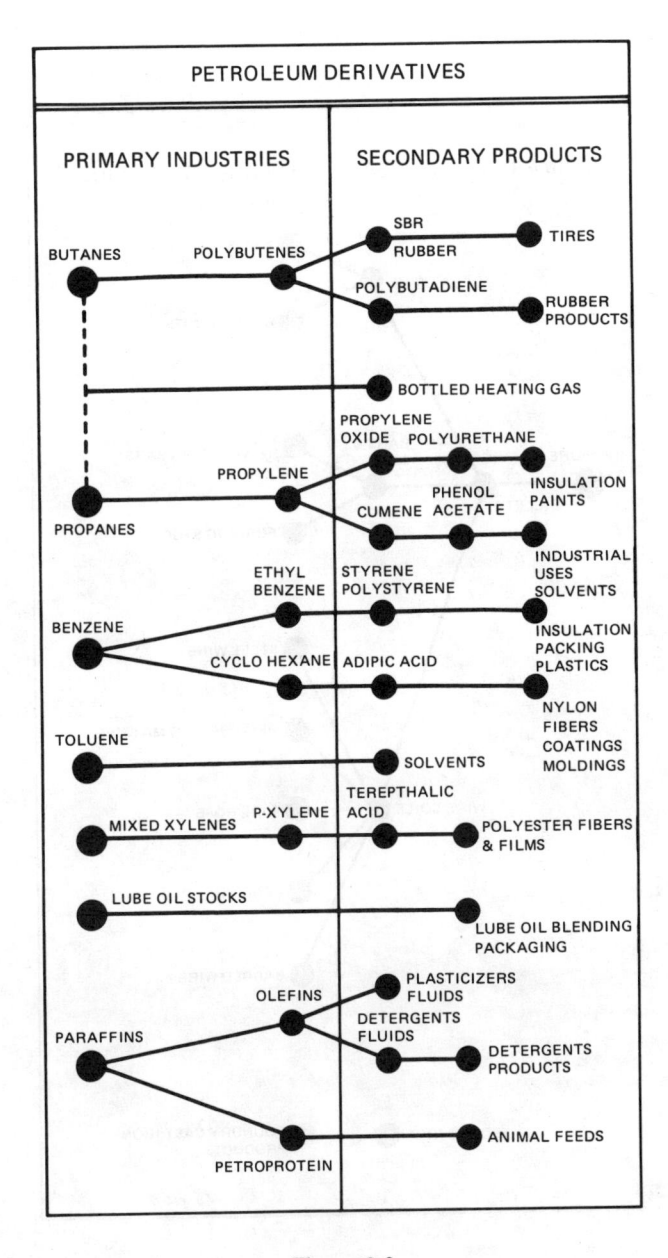

- BUTANES → POLYBUTENES → SBR RUBBER → TIRES
- POLYBUTADIENE → RUBBER PRODUCTS
- BOTTLED HEATING GAS
- PROPANES → PROPYLENE → PROPYLENE OXIDE → POLYURETHANE
  - CUMENE → PHENOL ACETATE → INSULATION PAINTS
- BENZENE → ETHYL BENZENE → STYRENE POLYSTYRENE → INDUSTRIAL USES SOLVENTS
  - CYCLO HEXANE → ADIPIC ACID → INSULATION PACKING PLASTICS
  - → NYLON FIBERS COATINGS MOLDINGS
- TOLUENE → SOLVENTS
- MIXED XYLENES → P-XYLENE → TEREPTHALIC ACID → POLYESTER FIBERS & FILMS
- LUBE OIL STOCKS → LUBE OIL BLENDING PACKAGING
- PARAFFINS → OLEFINS → PLASTICIZERS FLUIDS
  - DETERGENTS FLUIDS → DETERGENTS PRODUCTS
- PETROPROTEIN → ANIMAL FEEDS

Figure 8.3

130   *The Gulf Economies in Transition*

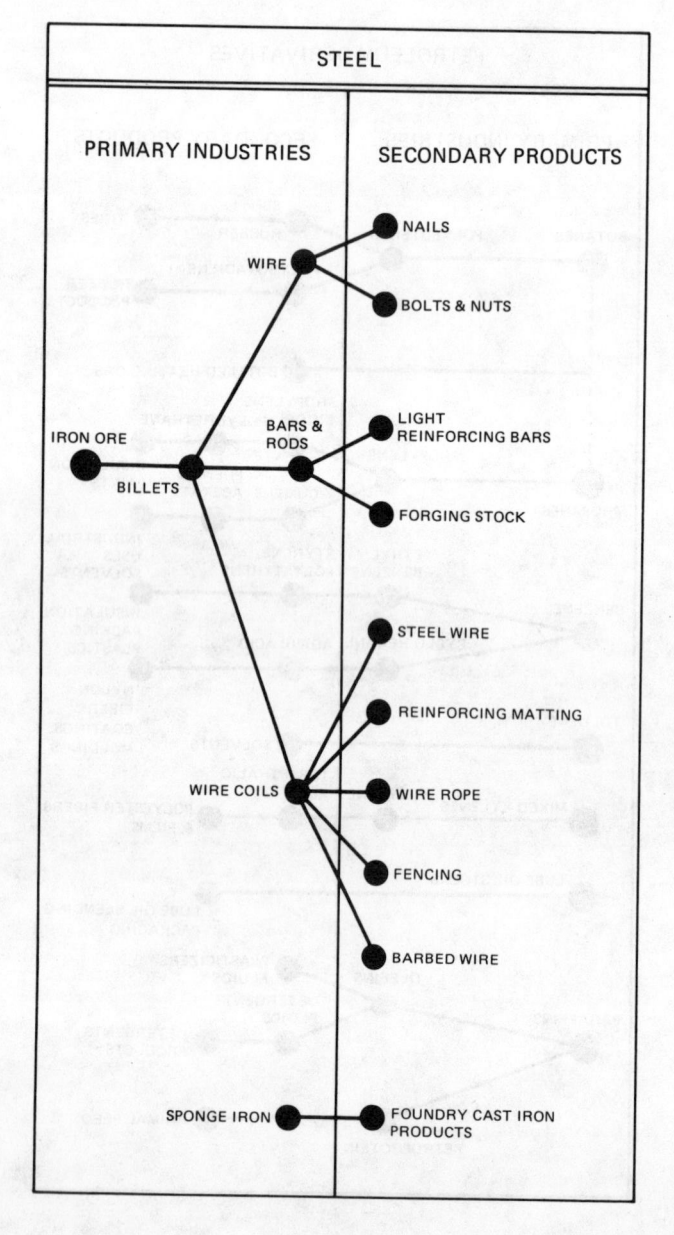

```
┌─────────────────────────────────────────┐
│                 STEEL                   │
├──────────────────────┬──────────────────┤
│  PRIMARY INDUSTRIES  │ SECONDARY PRODUCTS│
│                                         │
│                        ● NAILS          │
│              ● WIRE                     │
│             /    \                      │
│            /       ● BOLTS & NUTS       │
│           /                             │
│          /           ● LIGHT            │
│         /    ● BARS &  REINFORCING BARS │
│  ● IRON ORE — ● BILLETS / RODS          │
│                      \                  │
│                       ● FORGING STOCK   │
│                                         │
│                                         │
│                        ● STEEL WIRE     │
│                                         │
│                        ● REINFORCING    │
│                          MATTING        │
│          ● WIRE COILS — ● WIRE ROPE     │
│                                         │
│                        ● FENCING        │
│                                         │
│                        ● BARBED WIRE    │
│                                         │
│                                         │
│   ● SPONGE IRON — ● FOUNDRY CAST IRON   │
│                     PRODUCTS            │
└─────────────────────────────────────────┘
```

Figure 8.4

and petrochemical-related secondary industries). These industries can draw on relatively cheap basic products as well as cheap intermediate and finished products, including those processable on an export basis. They also enjoy a major comparative advantage available in the region, namely, the abundant and low cost source of energy, such as gas and hydrocarbon fuels in general.

3. *The industries based on mineral resources which exist in economic quantities in Saudi Arabia, Oman and UAE.* These include iron ore, potash, copper, phosphate, gold, limestone, etc. These industries are characterized as being capital and energy intensive. Developing such mineral-based primary industries normally creates external economies and forward linkages that would render investments in derived secondary product industries more profitable (see Figure 8.4 for steel-related secondary industries).

4. *There are also good potentials to develop industries in the consumer products field.* The easiest way to seek opportunities here is to look at the leading brands in the market and then see if these can be produced locally. Only two such examples of extremely promising and successful ventures will be mentioned here. One is the new plant in Saudi Arabia to produce Pampers nappies, which will certainly be a success, and the other is the joint venture between Basmah and Nestlé for the production of dairy products. Once the established brands start being manufactured locally it will immediately enjoy a secure market. The manufacture of these products locally would also create demand for a whole range of other related products and materials.

5. *Other prospects include the synthetic and assembling industries.* These are those that depend on the preceding industries, or are characterized with the presence of large markets for their products in the Gulf area in particular and in the Arab region in general. Examples of these industries include: the ones for manufacturing and for assembling of certain types of automobiles, and industrial requirements that serve other sectors such as the oil industry, agriculture, light industries, manufacture of household durable commodities, metal constructions and medical products.

6. *The industries that serve the construction process of infrastructure in the GCC region and in the Arab world in general.* The Arab region is still in need of large efforts to achieve appropriate standards of local and regional infrastructure, such as the projects of desalination, transportation, and communications. Among these infrastructure projects are also included the power projects,

electric interconnection projects, educational projects, and information communication and linkage projects. We can identify numerous industries that can help achieve this important construction process with local capabilities.
7. *The industries that serve the national and regional defence and security sectors.* Requirements in these two sectors are large and regenerating. We can identify dozens of industrial projects that serve this sector and hence minimize dependence on other countries for obtaining all the manufactured requirements.
8. *The industries that serve the oil industry.* This is absolutely the largest industry in the region and its needs and requirements are numerous during the different stages of oil production (exploration, extraction, transportation and refining). Since its beginning, this industry has been contributing to the development of a large associated business sector, and many industrial projects could emerge to serve this industry.
9. *The virtual absence of engineering industries is a major weakness of the region's industrial strategies.* The development of selective high technological and engineering industries would make it possible for countries of the region to attain a certain degree of technological independence and would help in the transfer and assimilation of technology.

An exhibit of investment opportunities for small and medium industrial enterprises with significant raw material base in the GCC region is provided by the Gulf Organization for Industrial Consulting and is given here in Figure 8.5.

OPPORTUNITIES FOR PROFITABLE JOINT VENTURES

The Gulf is still a tax-free region and has not yet experienced the bureaucratic bottlenecks that have hampered investments in other developing countries. It provides a tension-free industrial atmosphere, solid government support and ample financial backing which should attract many foreign investors to seek partnership with national industrialists.

The environment in the Gulf for joint ventures today is different from the 70s. Then you could see 35% return on assets. Now it is all more sophisticated. Development is related to the country's absorptive capacity and profit levels are therefore more normal.

Industrial Challenge in the GCC Region

The changing economic situation is pointing the way to the decrease of the importance of Gulf countries as markets for simple exports of goods and services. Instead, the significance of the role of the joint venture between the foreign supplier of such goods and services and the local partner will be on the rise. We have seen the significant growth of this pattern over the last two to three years. Ultimately this could turn out to be the only way in which the foreign suppliers can maintain or possibly even expand their share of these important markets.

It is therefore of paramount importance for companies involved in export trade to the Gulf region to recognize this fact in time and act accordingly. Foreign partners require specialist advice on the developments that are taking place in the local and regional markets. The use of the correct sequence of actions to be taken by an international company is very important and the correct timing is critical in minimizing the time and cost of the venture. The overseas partners, for example, should make it a point to have the joint venture agreement written in Arabic and to see that it observes the region's rules and regulations.

Joint ventures have become a major business development tool in the GCC region, where government policies have, in many cases, given very broad encouragement for overseas partners to participate (see Figure 8.6). The package of incentives differs from one country to another, however, the one provided by Saudi Arabia is quite representative in this respect. It includes the following:

1 50% of the invested capital is provided by the Saudi Industrial Development Fund at very low rates;
2 fully-serviced sites are provided in the industrial cities for an annual rental of just 20 centimes a square metre;
3 raw materials are exempted from customs duties;
4 preferences are granted to locally-manufactured products for government contracts;
5 financial grants and free training facilities are provided to train Saudi staff;
6 there are no restrictions on the repatriation of profits or foreign currency transactions; and
7 ten-year tax holiday is given to industrial projects, and there are no personal income taxes on expatriate staff.

It is important to note that there is no standard co-operation

Figure 8.5 *Investment outlets for small and medium industrial enterprises with significant local raw material base (Market potential valid between 1985 & 1990)*

Production category	Summary description	Minimum efficient production	Manpower category*	Investment cost category**
1. Infant Foods	Plain and flavoured cereal milk-based infant foods.	5,000 tpa	1	2
2. Medical Textiles	Bleached cotton gauze bandages, adhesive bandages, plasters and bandages impregnated with plaster of Paris.	500 tpa	2	1
3. Travel Goods	Soft and hard luggage using thermo-formed ABS sheets of superior quality.	Soft 50,000 sets/yr Hard 100,000 "	2	2
4. Edible Oils	Refined non-saturated vegetable oils in plastic containers.	50,000 tpa	1	2
5. Garment Making	Production of children outwear and play suits etc.	1,000,000 units/yr	2	2
6. Tubular structures and Scaffoldings	Cross beams, spacer bars, bracers, jacks, fixed cap head pans, road frames and refined spacers.	1,000 tpa	2	2
7. Animal Feed	Prepared from locally grown grains and by-products and fortified for specific use.	1,000 tpa	1	2
8. Gypsum Boards	For dry walls residential and commercial construction.	150,000 M²/yr	2	2
9. Toys and Baby Cots/	Leisure and educational toys based on PVC & ABS, rocking chairs, swings and baby carriages and cots etc.	500 tpa	2	2
10. Green Houses	Manufacture of metallic and plastic components for assembling greenhouses for private and commercial use.	100,000 M²/yr	2	2

11. Tea and Coffee Bag Plant	Packaged tea/coffee bags.	1,000,000 bags/yr	2	1
12. Alkyd Resins	Important constituent for the paint industry, for which raw materials (such as glycol) would become locally available. Presently alkyd resins are imported.	1,000 tpa	1	1
13. Mineral Turpentine	Paint thinning solvent produced by oil refineries out of the kerosene cut.	1,000 KL	2	1
14. Unsaturated Polyster Resins	Comprising industrial and household articles GRP pipes, fishing boats, roof structures and furniture items etc.	1,500 tpa	2	1
15. Specialty Chemicals/Paint Raw Materials. Comprising the following product-lines:				
i) Precipitated Calcium Carbonate	i) Important raw material in processing of plastics, toiletries, printing ink, and oil drilling etc.	1,500 tpa	2	1
ii) Calcium chloride	ii) Used as drying agent in food processing besides concrete conditioning and brine refrigerant.	1,000 tpa	2	1
iii) Carboxy methyl cellulose (CMC)	iii) Several applications in detergents, textiles, cosmetics, toiletries, etc.	1,000 tpa	2	1
iv) Salt fine technical grades (NaCl)	iv) Human consumption and fish preservation, ice making, etc.	500 tpa	2	1
v) Pregelatinized starch	v) Used in various industries such as paper, adhesives, paints	1,000 tpa	2	1
16. Animal House Products	Recovery of by-products; animal fat, bone meal and hides may be recovered from the slaughtered animals.	250–500 sheep/goat heads per day	2	1

continued on page 136

Figure 8.5 continued

Production category	Summary description	Minimum efficient production	Manpower category*	Investment cost category**
17. Manufacture of Wet Blue Leather	First step in the production of light blue leather from dried hides and skins.	8,000–10,000 Nos. of hides, 40–50,000 Nos. of skins.	2	1
18. Plastic Containers	Made out of LDPE for use in packing of vegetable oils and paints in two sizes: 3 kg & 1 kg.	1,500,000 ppa	2	1
19. Pesticide Formulations	In the form of emulsofiable concentrates, wetable powders that are used in agricultural farms.	350 tpa	1	1
20. Herbicides	Tailored and blended for specific agricultural uses based on locally available Butadiene & Meleic Anhydride	500 tpa	1	1
21. Milk Cans	Transport aluminium milk cans of 25 and 40 litres.	100,000 pieces/yr	1	1
22. Gas cylinders	Aluminium gas cylinders of capacities between 15 and 50 litres.	500,000 pieces/yr	2	2
23. Cream Syphons	1 litre soda water syphons and 0.5 litre cream syphons for cream/fruit cream and use the syphons containing CO_2 & N_2O. The bottles and heads are made from aluminium and plastics.	500,000 pieces/yr	1	1
24. Radiators and Heat Exchangers	Production of small ribbed (fined surface) heat exchangers and radiators from extruded aluminium shapes and strips.	200,000 M^2	1	2

25. Lamp posts	Stepped diameter (3–9m) roadside aluminium lamp-posts (with/without arm) for public lighting, traffic lights, and other purposes.	100,000 ppa	1	1
26. Rain Gutters	Rain gutters and their accessories such as shapes, fall tubes and clamps.	1,000,000 ppa	2	1
27. Ladders and furniture skeletons	Fitter's shop to manufacture aluminium ladders, scaffolds and furniture skeletons.	2,000 tpa	2	1
28. Facades and Portal Frames	Fitter's shop to manufacture inner room-forming elements, facades, portal frames and pavilions.	500,000 M^2/yr	2	1
29. Containers and Tanks	Of diameters ranging from 1.4 to 2.6 m and of volumes ranging from 3 to 41 M^3 for food and chemical industry.	55,000 M^3/yr	2	1
30. TV Aerials	Based on aluminium, manufacture of over-head, outdoor, TV aerials and antennas.	550,000 ppa	2	1
31. Office/Students' Stationery	Exercise/copy/drawing books, pencils (all types), sharpeners, erazors, arithmetic/geometry box sets.		2	2

NOTES: M^3 = cubic metre
M^2 = square metre
tpa = tonne per annum
ppa = pieces per annum

Investment Category consisting of machine costs only.
Cat. 1 = up to $1 million
Cat. 2 = between 1–3 million

Manpower Category (production level only)
Cat. 1 = up to 10 Nos.
Cat. 2 = between 10–30 Nos.

Source
Mohyuddin Badr, Gulf Organization for Industrial Consulting, Doha, Qatar, 1985.

	Licences issued to date	United Kingdom	Benelux	France	Germany	Ireland	Italy	Austria	Switzerland	Scandinavia	Other European	USA/North American	China	Korea	Japan	Taiwan	Other S.E. Asian	Arab States	India and Pakistan	Not elsewhere specified	Total of foreign firms in sector	Approximate % of firms with foreign investment (rounded)
Foodstuffs, drinks and tobacco	540	4	1	3	4	3	3	1	–	9	–	3	–	1	–	–	–	21	–	1	54	10%
Ready made clothes and textiles	83	1	–	–	–	2	–	2	–	–	–	1	–	–	–	–	–	9	–	1	16	19%
Manufacture of leather products	33	1	–	–	–	–	–	–	–	–	–	–	–	–	–	–	–	1	1	1	4	12%
Manufacture of wood products	114	1	1	1	–	–	–	–	–	–	–	–	–	3	1	–	–	10	–	–	17	15%
Manufacture of paper products, printing and publishing	152	1	–	–	1	–	–	–	1	–	1	–	–	–	–	–	1	20	–	–	25	16%
Chemical industry including petro-chem, coal, rubber and plastics	395	5	3	1	5	–	2	–	15	9	–	24	–	1	2	–	1	21	4	3	96	24%
Manufacture of china, pottery, glass, etc.	21	–	–	–	–	–	–	–	–	–	–	1	–	–	–	–	–	2	–	–	3	14%
Manufacture of building materials	662	6	5	5	12	–	7	2	6	10	2	8	–	1	3	1	2	34	2	11	112	17%
Metal industry	571	10	1	1	10	–	5	1	6	5	–	11	–	1	3	–	3	52	4	7	112	21%
Manufacture of other products	221	5	1	5	1	–	2	–	3	–	–	14	–	–	–	1	–	30	5	2	69	31%
Shipbuilding and repairs, automotive and automotive parts, railways, bicycles	79	1	–	2	1	–	–	–	1	–	–	1	–	–	1	–	–	7	–	1	15	19%
Storage	58	–	–	–	–	–	–	–	–	–	–	–	–	–	–	–	–	–	–	–	–	–

Percentage of licensed companies with foreign participation – 18%.

Figure 8.6 Foreign participation in joint ventures in Saudi Arabia by nationality and industrial sector, 1985

Source
(John Walmsley, *Arab Industry Review* Bahrain, Falcon Publishing, 1985).

formula to apply when going into the joint venture business in the region. There is also no substitute for detailed research effort to explore the feasibility of the proposed venture. Potential foreign partners should evaluate the long-term working environment in which they are going to operate, the business and social laws that they are going to work with, as well as, the customer profile and the payment practices that are normally followed.

An example of the various steps to be taken by an overseas partner to develop a typical manufacturing project in the Gulf is given here:

1. Market Assessment – allowing for regional competition and trading.
2. Decision on timing the venture – this depends also on the existence of competitive projects and may require quick action on:

    (a) selection of local partner;
    (b) application for operating licence;
    (c) application for funds/subsidized loans;

Such action usually requires the preparation of a competent feasibility study.

3. Agreement with local partner on:
    (a) methods of funding for equipment, supplies and services;
    (b) sources of supply of equipment and services (the local partner may have his own interests in trading, construction or transport);
    (c) degree of technical support required from foreign partner e.g. technical sales, servicing facilities, etc;
    (d) technical input from the foreign partner;
    (e) staffing of the venture (technical and management).

4. Application for land for the project – this may require comprehensive technical information on the project e.g. plant and site layouts, details of plant, equipment and services, etc.
5. Preparation of realistic capital cost estimates for the project although the need for this is obvious, it is surprising how often the estimates are inadequate as they do not include realistic provisions for the cost of infrastructure and services, nor are correctly based on local unit costs for materials and services.
6. Provision of adequate technical and project management and site

supervision for the project. This is most important right from the inception of the project and will minimize any over-run on time and money, which again can be considerable.
7. Arrangements for the development of local skills for plant operation and management.

A similar guideline can also be prepared for the development of a joint venture for the provision of services.

If reference is made to joint ventures in Saudi Arabia for example, Exhibit 6 shows the overall complexity of joint venture arrangements. In the first instance, the variety of partners will immediately be apparent. Apart from a few essentially large high technology ventures, most of the activity is in the low or medium technology areas.

MAIN INDUSTRIES IN THE REGION[1]

This section presents a brief view of the major industries in the region – petrochemicals, cement, iron and steel, fertilizers, aluminum and light industries. The advantages, and limitations of these industries are discussed and some light is shed on their present status and future growth prospects.

Petrochemicals[1]

During the last ten years Saudi Arabia in particular and the GCC countries in general invested billions of dollars to develop a viable petrochemical industry in the region. Downstream petrochemical industries are given special emphasis in the current development plans. For example, SABIC of Saudi Arabia plans to invest more than $4.43 billion during the current development plan (1985–90) in plastics, fertilizers and other downstream industries. The main spending sectors in the development plan is given in Table 8.1.

Success of the Petrochemical industry is, therefore, considered to be of strategic interest to the Gulf countries. Given the region's apparent resource advantage, their efficient low cost production plants and a hoped breakthrough in marketing petrochemical products, the industry is looked upon as being the cornerstone of GCC industrial development.

Three petrochemical products dominated the Gulf production

Table 8.1 Saudi Arabia: main spending sectors in the fourth five-year plan (1985–90) (SR million)

Sector	Allocation	%
Natural resources	55 037	100
Water	31 789	58
Energy	18 821	34
Mining	4 427	8
Productive sector	87 054	100
Electricity	41 932	48
Royal Commission for Jubail & Yanbu	30 000	35
Agriculture	10 810	12
Industry	4 241	5
Service sector	64 821	100
Commercial services	825	1
Banking and finance	60 100	93
Meteorology and environment protection	2 831	4
Standards and specifications	507	1
Information and statistical data	558	1
Social and cultural development	108 637	100
Health	62 239	57
Judicial and religious sectors	18 501	17
Cultural information and youth welfare	13 617	13
Social services	14 280	13
Human resources	133 173	100
General education	85 232	62
Higher education	40 291	30
Technical education and vocational training	6 586	5
Institute of Public Administration	1 053	1
Workforce development	1 195	1
Science and technology	1 816	1
Physical infrastructure	150 760	100
Transport	54 851	36
Postal services and telecommunications	28 581	19
Municipal and public works	63 500	42
Housing	3 828	3

Source
Planning Ministry (Riyadh, 1985).

scene in 1985: enthylene, methanol and ammonia (see Table 8.2). These products were likely to account for almost 75–80% of the total basic products to be produced in the region by the close of the century. Raw material and energy cost comprise a large fraction of

Table 8.2 Capacities of basic petrochemicals in the Gulf Region [a]
(000 tons per year)

Country/product	Bahrain	Kuwait	Saudi Arabia	Qatar	UAE
A. Olefin					
Ethylene	–	350	1606	280	–
Propylene	–	–	–	5	–
Butadiene	–	–	124	–	–
Butene-1	–	–	80	–	–
Acetylene	–	–	40[b]	–	–
B. Aromatica					
Tolouene	–	–	–	–	–
Benzene	–	284	–	–	–
Oxylene	–	60	–	–	–
Pxylene	–	90	–	–	–
Benzine only	–	–	–	–	300
C. Alcohol					
Methanol	300	–	1250	–	1325
Ethanol	–	–	281	–	–
Oxo-alcohol	–	–	–	–	–

Notes
[a] Actual and planned projects.
[b] Cu. ft per day.

Source
Gulf Organization for Industrial Consulting, Doha, Qatar.

production costs of these basic products. Going further downstream, a somewhat limited range of intermediate products has been developed. The production of final products was, however, limited to polyester fibres and thermoplastics. Several other downstream industries were being developed, these included rubber products, tires, insulation paints, solvents, plastic, nylon, polyester products, detergents, animal feeds and fertilizers among others.

It is unfortunate that the output from the Gulf's petrochemical plants is arriving on the market when demand has started to slacken, and while there is still substantial over-capacity in the established petrochemical industry, particularly in Western Europe.

In the last five years, Europeans, Japanese, and American producers of petrochemicals have sought to combat world overproduction with rationalization measures. Western Europe has reduced its annual ethylene capacity by 3.5 million tons since 1980. A

Industrial Challenge in the GCC Region

2 million-ton-capacity of polyvinyl chloride, the substance from which plastics and fibres are made, has been shut down. The capacity of Western Europe to produce polyolefins, likewise, has been cut by 2 million tons and its polyolefins by 1 million tons. The US, which produced 18.3 million tons of ethylene in 1981, has cut back its production by 1.4 million tons to 16.9 million tons a year.

A recent report from the Organization for Economic Co-operation and Development (OECD) was critical of the attempt made so far by West European companies to restructure their industry, saying that by 1990, OECD member countries need to implement additional costs in their production capacity of up to 15%.

There is little doubt that on a flexible cost basis, Gulf petrochemicals – based on gas which, priced at 50 cents per million BTU, is half the US price, up to one-eighth the European relative price and one-tenth that of Japan – are very competitive on a world market. However, high construction costs, plus shipping costs to markets of the developed countries raise the price of individual petrochemicals to near parity with certain efficient European and US producers.

Furthermore, if the price of oil continues to fall, the declining cost of feedstock would give an additional boost to the competitiveness of the European products. The general view is, though, that at oil prices of around $25 per barrel, Gulf petrochemicals would continue to be competitive worldwide.

The impact of new petrochemical products from the Gulf on the world markets has been over dramatized. Several European countries are calling for tariff shelters. They are arguing that petrochemical exports from the Gulf are the result of subsidized capital and feedstock prices. Price competition is being interpreted as 'dumping' and the EC commission was asked to set quotas and impose tariffs on petrochemicals imported from the Middle East.

The Gulf producers are very keen not to engage in dumping their products at artificially low prices. But instead, to enter the world market in an orderly and controlled manner. Besides, the GCC countries are not likely to produce a sizeable portion of any single petrochemical product to make a significant impact at the global level. Even when all the Gulf petrochemical products come on stream, by late 1986 early 1987, the region will produce no more than 6% of the world's petrochemicals. This would not represent more than one year of projected global industry growth.

The Gulf countries, quite naturally, are opposed to exorbitant tariff barriers as a means of neutralising their present comparative advantage. The average duty on goods imported into the region, including petrochemical products, is no more than 4%. If the European Community chooses not to reciprocate in its trade relations with the GCC countries, the Community may turn out to be the net loser. The European Economic Community (EEC) has a large trade surplus with the Gulf countries, which in the case of chemicals, such as detergents and other households goods, is weighted around ten to one. Close to $356 billion worth of goods are exported annually from the EEC to Saudi Arabia and the other GCC countries. No European country would want to jeopardize that, so even if there were pressure from the petrochemical industry to protect its markets with tariffs, it is not the European commission best interest to take very much action in this respect.

In Early August 1985, the EEC imposed at 13.4% custom duties on polyethylene from Saudi Arabia claiming that Saudi exports of this product exceeded 15% of annual EEC consumption in the first half of 1985. Saudi Arabia insisted that the data was grossly exaggerated and threatened to increase custom duties on certain European products from 4% to 20% if the EEC failed to rescind the tariff. The other GCC countries may follow suit as well.

In the longer term, the Third World markets, especially the Arab countries and those of South East Asia offer the greatest growth prospects for petrochemical products. In the meantime, it is to the developed countries' advantage to weed out their portfolios of basic and intermediate grade products and move up market to concentrate on producing advanced new products.

Saudi Arabia
Saudi Arabia has three major ethylene crackers, with a total capacity of 1.6 million tons a year, all entered commissioning phase in late 1984, six months ahead of schedule. These companies are Arabian Petrochemical Co. (Petrochemya) is fully owned by Sabic, since Dow Chemical pulled out of the project in 1981. Saudi Yanbu Petrochemical Co. (Sadaf) is a joint venture with Mobil and is located in Yanbu. Saudi Petrochemical Company (Sadaf) is a joint venture with Shell and, like Petrokemya, is located at Jubail.

The Yanpet cracker which supplies feedstock to downstream units producing 290 000 tons a linear low density polyethylene or high density polyethylene, started up in February 1985. The ethylene glycol unit (220 000 tons) came on stream a month later. In 1984, nine projects came on stream, enabling SABIC to put 950 000 tons of

Industrial Challenge in the GCC Region

methanol on the international market. Methanol sales amounted to $42.9 million compared to $19.5 million in 1983, polyethylene, $27.8 million, and urea $44.9 million.

In the initial stages marketing of most of the product from the Yanpet plants will be handled by Mobil. The Petrokemya plant supplies ethylene to the Al Jubail Petrochemical (Kemya) joint venture between Sabic and Exxon. This project has the capacity to produce 260 000 tons of linear low density polyethylene.

The Petrokemya cracker also supplies ethylene to the Eastern Petrochemical Company (Sharq) a joint venture between Sabic and a Japanese consortium led by Mitsubishi. This complex moved into production ahead of schedule in the first quarter of 1985. Sharq has a capacity to produce 130 000 tons of LDPE and 300 000 tons of glycol. Some ethylene from Petrokemya is also to be supplied to the Sabic/Lucky Goldstar VCM/PVC plant, due for completion in 1986. This will produce 300 000 tons VCM and 200 000 tons PVC.

It is likely that the next round of chemical investment in the kingdom will be dominated by the private sector. Sabic proposes to sell 75% of its shares to private citizens, with the first 20% having been offered in 1984.

The National Industrialization (NIC) which was successfully floated in November 1984, has proposals for several joint investments. Its major project concerns a $300 million synthetic rubber plant to be built at Yanbu under a joint venture with France's Michelin.

NIC also has plans for polyester fibre plant based on ethylene glycol feedstock from the Sharq project at Jubail. ICI already has plans for production of polyester terephthalate (PET) bottle resin. Production of detergents in another prospect, if the local market justifies a $100 million investment, bearing in mind that Iraq is building a 50 000 ton LAB plant. Other private-sector ventures includes proposed pharmaceuticals production, involving Saudi Pharmaceuticals (SPC) in which NIC has a share. Hoechst has been linked with a drugs investment in Saudi Arabia. *Upjohn* of the US was considering a polyurethanes investment in the Kingdom as well.

An interesting private sector proposal, revealed in March 1985, was that by the Saudi firm, IDI Ltd, to construct a 50 000 ton titanioum dioxide pigment plant at Jubail. This unit, which would use chloride route technology, may be built by Lurgi of West Germany and would supply local and exports markets. More investment announcements from the private sector are anticipated during the course of 1985 and 1986 and it has been suggested that proposals for downstream petrochemicals investment in the Kingdom might total $4 billion.

Kuwait

Kuwait's plans for a 350 000 ton ethylene glycol, benzene, styrene, orthoxylene and paraxylene, seem to have been delayed. A primary reason is a shortage of ettane feedstock due to depressed crude oil production. However, the Kuwait Petrochemical Corporation has become particularly concerned with the investment in overseas companies. For example, it has taken a 25% interest in Hoechst of West Germany, and KPC also owns Santa Fe International of the US, parent company of engineers CF Braun.

However, Kuwait is pressing ahead with plans for certain downstream petrochemicals plants. Towards the end of 1984 processes were selected for two of three planned products and a construction contract was awarded to CF Braun. Kuwait Petroleum Products Company plans to build a 20 000 ton phthalic anhydride plant, based on technology supplied by Lurgi of West Germany. The same company also plans to make 20 000 tons of expandable polystyrene and 12 000 tons of high impact polystyrene.

Petrochemical Industries Company, a subsidiary of KPC, is to build a 62 000 ton polypropylene plant, based on technology supplied by Himont/Mitsui. All three units are to be based at Shuaiba and will have common utilities. Raw materials for the plants (some 35 000 tons of styrene monomer and 10 000 tons of orthoxylene) will be purchased on the international market. Although there has been no official request for Saudi Arabia, there is considered to be sufficient styrene available at the Sadaf plant to supply polystyrene units in Kuwait. As Sabic's intentions for polystyrene are not clear, it seems that it may phase its own entry into the PS market to make room for the Kuwait plant. The KPC plants are valued at $60 million and are due to be completed by 1987.

Qatar

Although Qatar has moved successfully into petrochemical production, being the first Gulf state to actually bring plants on stream, there has been some trouble with gas supplies and development of downstream units has been hindered. The Qatar Petrochemical Company (Qapco) 280 000 ton ethylene and 140 000 ton linear low density polyethylene plants, jointly owned by Qatar General Petroleum Corporation and DdF Chimie of France, went on stream in

1981. Cutbacks in Qatar's oil production has caused ethylene output to be somewhat erratic, because of limitations of gas supply, plans for a 70 000 ton high density polyethylene unit have been delayed indefinitely.

Bahrain

Bahrain's petrochemicals investment has revolved around gas-based ammonia and methanol plants. The country has pressed ahead with construction of a complex at Sitra to produce 330 000 tons ammonia and 330 000 tons methanol. It is owned by Bahrain, Kuwait and Saudi Arabia and operated by the tripartite Gulf Petrochemical Industries Company. The complex, which is already in operation was built by Italy's Snamprogetti. It has been decided to let Sabic handle marketing of methanol from the plant worldwide.

UAE

Several West European companies, e.g. ICI and France's CdF Chimie, have considered investing in gas-based projects in Sharjah. Early in 1984 there were reports that ICI was planning a world-scale methanol plant, but the company has since decided not to go ahead with such a project. France's CdF Chimie, however, is pressing ahead with an ammonia/urea plant.

Cement

The cement producers in the Gulf countries are facing a series of difficult decisions. New plants may have to be shelved – and output from existing ones co-ordinated – if a glut in supply is to be avoided. Drastic measures are needed because ambitious demand projections have been undermined by the cutbacks in development programmes brought about by the declining oil revenues.

The problem is that the high growth in the demand for cement over the past 10 years was exceptional and cannot continue at the same level. In fact demand in 1986 is expected to show a significant drop over the 1984 and the 1985 levels.

The problem has been exacerbated by recession on the world market. Asian and European products – notably Japan, South Korea, Spain and Greece – are dumping their surpluses in the Gulf at prices local companies cannot afford to match. At the same time, their domestic markets are protected by tariff barriers which are lacking in the GCC countries. The position is most acute in the UAE – the only Gulf country to produce a cement surplus.

Demand for cement in the Gulf countries is continuing to rise: a recent study estimates it will reach 32.7 million tons a year by 1988 – double the 1981 figure. However, the resulting annual 6% increase represents a considerable slowdown from the average 28.5% a year rise recorded between 1974–81.

While in 1981, 35% of cement used in the region was imported, in 1988, not more than 8% of the total is projected to be imported. The latest report of the Gulf's 29 cement factories reveals a total output of 23.6 million tons in 1985 and projected to reach 30 million tons in 1988. Saudi Arabia makes the lion's share with 36%, then comes Iraq with 33%, UAE with 20%, Kuwait 6%, Qatar 3% and Bahrain 2%.

Measures designed to reduce imports and strengthen regional co-ordination in marketing of GCC cement products are already in the pipeline. In October 1984, the Gulf Organization for Industrial Consulting (GOIC) initiated a study on ways to protect local industries against foreign dumping; it also examined the possibility of distributing surpluses among member countries of the Gulf Co-operation Council that do not produce enough cement to meet their needs. The GOIC study recommends the introduction of a common policy whereby surplus cement produced in the UAE is given preference by other GCC states over imports from outside suppliers. It also argues that surpluses could be provided as aid-in-kind to developing countries.

Another element of the GOIC strategy calls on the UAE authorities – and other governments – to stop issuing licenses for new works, and instead concentrate on co-ordinating clinkers supply and grinding capacity. Most UAE plants were operating in 1985 at just 35.40% of grinding capacity, while construction of a 500 000-ton-a-year unit for the Umm al Qaiwan Cement Company is proceeding apace.

The cement surplus of the UAE is expected to reach 4 million tons a year by 1988, assuming plants being built are completed on time, and produce at 100% of design capacity. The agreement to fix a minimum price among local producers had eased the cash flow problems of these producers and prevented some from going under in 1984. No improvement is expected in 1986, when most producers are projected either barely to break even, or to make a loss.

UAE companies also supply Qatar whose import needs totalled 38 000 tons in 1984 – sharply down from the previous year's 189 970 tons. Much of the demand came in the first half of the year; the Qatar National Cement Company was able to meet most of the second-half requirements. According to GOIC, Qatar should produce a 160 000 ton surplus in 1988, after the completion of various expansion schemes.

Unlike Qatar, which applies a general GCC free-trade ruling to cement, Oman has been given permission to protect its fledgling industry with a 20% import tariff. UAE exporters can match Omani prices even with duty and transport costs included, but they may eventually be squeezed out of the market by a planned 50% increase in the capacity of the larger of the country's two plants. However, GOIC estimates Oman will still experience a local supply deficit of about 600 000 tons in 1988.

Saudi Arabia is the Gulf region's long-term hope in terms both of construction and cement demand, although the downturn in new project in the Kingdom is expected to accelerate in 1985. Total demand in the kingdom fell by about 10%, to 20 million tons in 1984, and is expected to shrink further to about 16 million tons, in 1985 while 1989 demand is estimated at 18 million tons. An increase in local production to 11 million tons in 1985 – up from the previous year's 9 million tons – will further reduce opportunities for foreign suppliers. Saudi production capacity is projected to reach 15 million tons a year in 1986/87 on completion of works planned or at the construction stage.

The kingdom's largest cement importer, Arabian Bulk Trade, expects to see a slump of more than 25% – to 2.8 million tons – in 1985, compared with the previous fiscal year. GOIC says the kingdom will still require imports totalling 5 million tons in 1988, and suggests it should forge ahead with studies for new plants, and optimise production at existing works. It also recommends the construction of clinker kilns with a total output of 1 million tons a year.

GOIC is less sanguine about other Gulf markets, and recommends the shelving of Kuwait Cement Company's expansion plans – despite an estimated yearly shortfall of 950 000 tons by 1988. The organization also recommends that Bahrain should clamp down on new works licensing because an expected supply deficit of 147 000 tons in 1988 does not justify the installation of new plant.

Like many international contractors, UAE cement exporters are looking for salvation to an early end to the war between Iraq and Iran, and a surge in cement demand to supply reconstruction work in both countries. However, Iraq produced about 10 million tons of cement in 1984 and has already stopped importing. By the end of 1986, it will have total capacity of about 22 million tons a year. In turn, Iraqi producers may be forced to export to the already saturated Gulf markets.

A case can, therefore, be made for rationalization and co-ordination of production among the Gulf states, support of national and Gulf industries and the combat of imported cement from countries flooding the Gulf market. Some effective government measures are already in existence such as the obligation on contracts with government work to buy from national industry. Others such as a tariff surcharge may need further examination.

Iron and Steel

Iron and steel industry in the Gulf countries is a relatively new comer which virtually did not exist prior to the early 70s. However, the remarkable economic growth in the region over the past two decades has been accompanied by an expression in the construction sector and a growing demand for steel products.

Forecasts for the 90s estimate that steel consumption in the GCC countries will reach 15 million tons in 1990, and more than 18 million tons in 1995, compared to 11 million tons in 1985 and one million in the early 70s. This represents only 7.5% annual growth rates compared to the 27% annual growth rates registered in the 70s.

On the other hand, the projected production forecast will continue to lag behind consumption. Existing production capacity now stands at 2 million tons per year. At best and if all projects in the conceptual stage materialize, the local production of steel will not exceed 4.4 million tons per year. With the normal lead time required for implementation of steel plants, this production will not be available before 1991. It is evident, therefore, that the expected shortfall of steel produced in the Gulf states would amount to 11.4 million tons in 1990 and 16.7 million tons per year in 1995.

The Gulf area is characterized by supply insufficiency in all product categories. Despite the fact that three fully integrated steel plants and three rolling mills are involved in the production of long products, they do not meet the current demand for such products. According to the Gulf Organization for Industrial Consulting (GOIC) the supply gap by 1990 will be: Long Products, 2 500 000; Flat Products, 6 200 000; Pipe (Welded), 600 000; Seamless, 900 000; Cast Pipe, 600 000.

The Saudi Arabian Petroleum and Mineral Organization (Petromin) introduced the first generation of steel plants in the Gulf by establishing a steel rolling plant in Jeddah in 1966 with an annual capacity of 45 000 tons. The plant's capacity was increased to 140 000 tons in 1981. Another SABIC owned iron and steel plant, Hadeed in Jubail has a production capacity of 850 000 tons annually.

Three other steel rolling plants followed – in Dubai and Abu Dhabi (each 25 000 tons capacity) and Ras Al Khaimah (10 000 tons) – but each has closed down after a comparatively short period of time. In 1975, Dubai established the first iron-casting plant with a capacity of 30 000 tons a year, the first of a chain of similar plants in the region, and Qatar began steel production in 1978. However, the largest steel complex in the Gulf region is located in Saudi Arabia's industrial area of Jubail and has a capacity of 800 000 tons a year.

To meet the demand of the construction sector, the Gulf countries, established three plants for the production of construction bars with a total capacity of 1.6 million tons a year. Growing demand for iron construction bars was reflected in a dramatic increase of local output from 130 000 tons in 1972 to 622 000 tons in 1982.

There are several steel projects under study in Oman, Bahrain, UAE and Kuwait, all aimed at increasing steel output to meet a rapid growth in demand which is expected to continue up till the turn of the century.

Given the ability of the Gulf countries to introduce new technologies, the availability of capital and raw materials and the existence of energy – for running steel mills, especially gas where total reserves are estimated at more than 10 trillion cubic metres, it becomes evident that the region, has a comparative advantage for iron and steel industries. Equally important, the industry has the highest combined backward and forward linkage effects, i.e. steel plants would eventually trigger upstream and downstream industries. All this, coupled with the obvious shortfall in steel supply render the future prospects of iron and steel industry in the region quite promising.

Fertilizers

In their drive for industrialization, the Gulf countries have given priority to the fertilizer industry, taking advantage of the abundance of natural gas which is a basic intermediate for the production of nitrogenous fertilizers.

The relative importance of nitrogenous fertilizers in total world consumption of fertilizers has been on the rise. It went up from 30% in 1950 to more than 50% in 1984. The potentials for this industry is, therefore, promising, and the GCC countries are planning to capitalize on the comparative advantage they have and draw on their resource endowment to assume a key position in the world market for nitrogen.

Kuwait was the first in the region to establish in 1966 an export oriented fertilizer plant, producing urea and ammonium sulphate. Petrochemical Industries Company has the largest nitrogenous complex in the region, with three ammonia plants and three urea plants having combined daily capacities of 2000 tons and 2500 tons, respectively. A fourth ammonia plant with a capacity of 1000 tons per day started operations in late 1984, and its output will be used by a new 1000 tonnes per day di-ammonium phosphate (DAP) project planned by the Arab Company for Compound Fertilizers.

In Saudi Arabia the Al-Jubail Fertilizer Co. (Samad) a joint venture between Saudi Basic Industries Corporation (Sabic) and Taiwan Fertilizer Co. began production at its 500 000 tons per year capacity plant at Jubail in March 1983 producing urea from a methane feedstock. Working at full capacity, the plant is producing 1000 tons a day of ammonia from which 1600 tons per day of urea is formed.

Established in 1964, the Saudi Arabian Fertilizers Company (Safco) has been producing urea since 1970 with annual production topping 300 000 tons since 1981. In 1984 production output was 350 650 tons, more than 106% of the plant's design capacity. The previous best production output was 346 000 tons in 1982.

The Qatar Fertiliser company (QAFCO) plant first went into production in 1974 with a design capacity of 900 tons per day of ammonia and 1000 tons per day of urea. A second ammonia and second urea process line, exactly doubling the overall plant capacity, were commissioned in early 1979 and are expected to become operational soon.

Ammonia production in 1984 was 631 760 tons, a 7.8% increase over the 1983 figure. Urea production reached 734 020 tons in 1984, a 7.1% increase compared with 1983.

The UAE has one major gas-based fertilizer project, the Ruwais Fertilizer Industries Company (FERTL), which is two-thirds owned by the Abu Dhabi National Oil Co. and one-third by Compagnie Francaise des Petroies. It has a capacity to produce 272 000 tons of ammonia and 228 000 tons of urea. It is envisaged that all output will be exported, and Mitsubishi agreed to market 4500 tons of urea in 1984, with the intention of increasing the annual quantity to 100 000 tons by 1988.

In Bahrain, the complex of the Gulf Petrochemical Industries (a joint venture between Bahrain National Oil Company, Kuwait Petrochemical Industries and SABIC) started operation in 1985. It consists of two separate process plants, one for producing 1000 tons per day of ammonia and the other 1000 tons of methanol. Output of this complex is destined for export markets.

Aluminium

The world aluminium industry is passing through a period of fundamental transition. Growth in demand for aluminium products has been slowing down and a free market pricing system has emerged. A number of key outlets which have been responsible for the sharp growth in aluminium's popularity, have now 'matured'. The pattern of world production, has been changing, with new projects concentrated in areas where cheaper energy resources are available.

The Arab World's most important aluminium smelters are located in Bahrain, where Aluminium Bahrain (Alba) produced its first ingots in 1971, and in the United Arab Emirates where Dubai Aluminium's (Dubai) $1.4 billion smelter came on stream in October 1979. Both operations are based on the abundant local availability of cheap energy – natural gas to fuel the gas fired turbines, which provide a constant flow of electricity. This first vital prerequisite was supplemented by a second – the availability of local capital. Together, these two advantages have been more than sufficient to offset the cost of importing key raw materials – bauxite from Brazil and Australia, petroleum coke from the United States and aluminium fluoride and cryolite from Italy.

In 1984 Alba overall output reached 177 285 tons and most of it was exported. About one-quarter of the exports go to the Arab countries, and two-thirds of it to the Far East. As downstream Arab aluminium industries continue to develop, however, they are expected to take up close to 40% of Alba's production. Aluminium provides perfect sealing against sand and rain and fits exactly the building requirements of the region. The GCC countries are unique in that 50% of all exterior windows and doors are aluminium, because the harsh environment precludes the use of wood.

Several downstream aluminium based industries were set up in Bahrain starting with Bahrain Atomizers in 1972 that utilizes around 3850 tons of liquid metal from Alba. The next company to come on stream was Balexco in 1977, which in 1984 purchased 6748 tons of billet from Alba. Another company Midal Sables was established in 1979 whose current capacity stands at around 20 000 tons.

The latest and most important downstream development in Bahrain is a new Gulf Aluminium Rolling Mill (Garmco) with an annual rated capacity of 40 000 tons designed to be on stream in 1986. The mill is being constructed by Japan's Kobe Steel under the terms of a $100 million turnkey contract and it is jointly owned by the six Gulf countries. Saudi Arabia is likely to uptake a large portion of Gramco's eventual annual output of rolled aluminium sheet and coil and also offers the greatest potential for further downstream usage of aluminium product in general.

While the GRAMCO Project nears completion the company has also been handed the opportunity of setting-up a proposed aluminium foil factory. The proposed cost of the factory is $35–40 million and the initially proposed output is around 6000 tons of foil annually.

Despite the growth in Bahrain's downstream potential coupled with that of neighbouring countries, aluminium products continue to pour into the region – a measure of the level of the demand to be satisfied. Such has been the influx of imported aluminium that a technical committee of the Gulf Co-Operation Council has recently imposed a 20% duty on imported aluminium for two years. This will operate alongside protective measures already implemented by the region's producing states.

Dubai Aluminium (Dubal) $1.4 billion smelter came on stream in 1979 with a name plate capacity of 135 000 tons a year from three potlines. Actual production in 1985 jumped considerably beyond capacity to 150 000 tons a year. As with Alba, Dubal is entirely dependant on imported raw material. In the long term, the two companies may co-operate under the auspices of GCC to jointly purchase the required raw material and share marketing and technical expertise.

Light and Intermediate Industries

Major industrial projects have already been established in the region and there are encouraging signs of a trickle down effect that secondary industries will soon take off as well. For several years in the 70s, allocation went principally to construction materials sector, in which cement, pre-cast concrete and brick-making plants were established to meet the apparently insatiable needs developed during the construction boom. With this sector now saturated, activities are being shifted towards the production of consumer goods, chemicals and plastics, pharmaceutical products, vehicles, engineering equipment, machinery and appliances and in general import substituting industries.

Government planners in the region will continue to encourage the emergence of more of the diversified industrial groups that have appeared over the past five years. Organizations like Zamil and Jaffali in Saudi Arabia and Alghanim in Kuwait are beginning to give Gulf industries a more substantial posture. These groups are integrated vertically into heavy industries, and horizontally into a wide range of services.

While the growth of such conglomerates is inevitably slow, there has been a mushrooming of single manufacturing industries all over the Gulf. Bahrain, for example, issued more than 200 industrial licences over the 1981–85 period. In 1979, the government set up the Bahrain Light Industries Co. as a holding company to promote and develop private industry in the Island. Nearly 80 small scale industries have been licensed in Qatar since the beginning to 1981. In the UAE there was a total of 800 small to medium size manufacturing companies, in 1985 employing close to 10% of the country's total workforce.

In Saudi Arabia, the Saudi Industrial Development Fund had up until 1985 provided finance for more than 1000 projects at a total cost of over $10 billion. In 1984 and 1985, the Kingdom approved more than 300 industrial projects covering a whole range of industries – engineering, chemicals, food industries, building materials, pharmaceuticals, oil field equipment among others. The number of factories that were in production in the Kingdom in 1985 was around 2700 and covering 15% of local demand. By 1990 Saudi Arabia is aiming at producing 30% of its industrial needs locally.

The Saudi Government had identified some 25 secondary industries and around 80 light industries opened for investments utilizing the Kingdom's hydrocarbon and mineral resources. Businessmen who would invest in these industries will be granted attractive investment facilities by the various financial institutions in the Kingdom including 10 year tax holiday, low and favourable utility rates and exemptions from customs and import duties of raw materials. In addition to these incentives, the investors would also be given government priority in the provision of feedstocks and priority to sell their products to the government or to domestic market.

A remarkable surge in demand for local products has been recently noted in the region. The various GCC countries were obliging contractors to buy local products and to give a minimum of 30% of their awarded contracts to national subcontractors. Besides, maintenance and operation jobs have been gradually restricted to local companies. The GCC countries would be spending around $100 billion during the period 1985–90 for operating and maintaining the establishments built over the last decade. Services which are supplementary to the industrial activity and are deemed essential for the transfer of technology will, therefore, witness a major boom in the coming years.

The GCC countries have also been paying increasing attention to food industries so that development at home might cut back swelling food imports. The emphasis was to develop such sectors as grain, milk products, vegetable oil, soft drinks, dates, etc. Kuwait and Bahrain have already made strides in dairy industries. In Saudi Arabia the National Industrialization Co. (NIC) has set up a separate Saudi Company for food products with a capital of $27 million. NIC was looking for investment in the Kingdom's industry of the order of $1.6 billion over the next 5 years.

The market for plastics and paints in the Gulf has great potentials. It is hoped that the petrochemical complexes being set up in the region would generate downstream industries that could provide the necessary raw material for the paints and plastic industries.

Other light industries that have good potential in the region with significant local raw material base include fibreglass, wires and cables, synthetic rubber, paper, cartoon detergents, luggage, toys, animal feed, garments, plastic containers, milk cans, TV aerials, stationery, herbicides and pesticides among others.

Inspite of the fact that machinery and appliances were the largest single heading in private sector imports constituting close to 18% on the average of total GCC imports in 1984, development of the intermediate industrial processes and equipment has lagged behind the growth of both the major public sector base industries and the small scale finished goods production.

If Gulf industrial entrepreneurs were to go for manufacture of machinery and industrial equipment and spares, the markets for such would have to lie in servicing the base industries – the oil sectors and the chemical, cement, aluminium, power and desalination plants. While identification of components and spares for these industries is not easy, one ingredient in the equation is likely to be economies of scale. Power, desalination and oil are the most mature sectors, the base chemical industries and export refineries are only now coming on stream. Co-ordinated industrial spares manufacture for the GCC area would complement current GCC discussions on industrial standardization and centralized warehousing.

POLICY GUIDELINES TO BOOST GCC INDUSTRIALIZATION

Deficiencies of the sector may, as well, be traced back to the lack of an overall industrialization strategy, to the bureaucracy and administrative routine, to the instability of the industrial labour force (almost exclusively expatriate), to the unbalanced consumer consciousness, to the inadequacy of incentives at both production and export levels and to the insufficient protection *vis-à-vis* competition from abroad. To counteract these difficiencies and activitate the industrial sector, the following policy guidelines are deemed instrumental:

1. Setting up a comprehensive strategic outlook for industrial development at both the national and regional level. This encompasses fundamental decisions such as import-substitution or export oriented strategies.
2. Priority should be given to those new projects ensuring complementarity (through either backward or foreward linkages) with the existing capacity.
3. Implementing a sliding scale protection-tariff formula directly proportional to the ratio of value added to total value.
4. Besides, infant industries would benefit from higher (than provided for in the previous point) tariff rates for a period of five years.
5. Governments' tenders are to be drawn out in such a way as to favour locally processed products.
6. Part of the governments' foreign aid might be provided in kind. It will then consist of domestic industrial products.
7. Trading companies would be encouraged to take in charge part of the marketing responsibilities, so far assumed by the industrial units.
8. Adjustment of the educational curriculum to provide more opportunities for technical training.
9. Introduction of unified GCC policies, subsidies and tariff rates.
10. Industries which are not viable economically and which should not have been established in the first place could as well be liquidated.
11. Enhance consumer consciousness towards locally produced commodities.
12. Cut down on bureaucracy and administrative routine that normally delay the takeoff of new ventures.

Notes

1. This section draws selectively on various studies prepared by the Gulf Organization for Industrial Consulting (GOIC) in Doha, Qatar. For other references see also Lyn Tattum, 'Petrochemicals: Are the Europeans Over-reaching to Arab Market Penetration'; Elias Ghantus 'Fertilizers: Self Sufficiency an Attainable Target' and Allan Spence 'Aluminum: Climb Out of Recession Needs Boost of New Product Market'. All appear in the *Arab Industry Review, 1985* (Bahrain, Falcon Publishing WLL).

9 Gulf Currencies, Foreign Investments and External Balances

GULF CURRENCIES AND THE US DOLLAR

In the light of recent volatility of international currencies exchange rates, questions are often asked of the relationship between Gulf currencies and the US$. What governs this relationship and how would the region's currencies react to a declining dollar?

In the 50s and 60s the newly created Gulf currencies were expressed in terms of gold. At that time most of them were still strongly linked to sterling, except the Saudi riyal which was fixed in 1960 at SR4.50 for each US$.

After the sterling was devalued in 1967 and the dollar price of gold was changed in 1971 and 1973, the daily value of Gulf currencies started to be expressed in dollars although still technically linked to the gold par value. IMF regulations required dollar exchange rates to be held within 2¼% on either side of the dollar gold parity.

As the dollar value continued to fall in the international markets during the first half of the 70s, the Gulf states were attracted to the IMF's Special Drawing Right (SDR) as a substitute for the dollar. Politically, it seemed better to have a currency pegged to the SDR rather than the dollar especially when the dollar came consistently under pressure during the 70s. Saudi Arabia shifted to the SDR in 1975, while Bahrain, UAE and Qatar announced the change in 1978. Oman continues to have its currency pegged to the dollar, while Kuwait decided to link the KD to a 'basket' of currencies of its own choice.

Prior to July 1974, the SDR was valued at par with the US dollar, i.e. US$ = SDR1. Since July 1974 the value of the SDR has been determined daily by the IMF on the basis of a basket of currencies with each currency assigned a weight in the determination of that value. The weights reflect the importance of these currencies in international trade and finance. The 1985 SDR valuation basket constituted the following: US$ – 42% weight, West German mark 19%, Japanese yen, French franc and UK sterling – 13% each.

The Saudi riyal parity value was set in 1975 at SR4.28 per SDR, with a margin of 7.25% on either side of this parity value. This means that the riyal can surge or fall against the SDR within a 14.5% margin. The Saudi authorities retained, therefore, the flexibility to control and direct the value of the Saudi riyal in a way that suits the financial priorities of the country. The Saudi Arabian Monetary Agency (SAMA) did from time to time change the exchange rate of the riyal against the dollar presumably to reflect movements of the riyal *vis-à-vis* the SDR.

Exchange rate figures for the first half of the 1980s show a stronger relationship between the Saudi riyal and the dollar than between the riyal and the SDR. While the riyal depreciated from SR3.326 to the dollar in 1980 to SR3.65 to the dollar in 1985 (an overall decline of 8.9% over a 5 year period) the riyal appreciated by 8% in value *vis-à-vis* the SDR, from SR4.329 to SDR to SR4.007 (Tables 9.1 and 9.2). The corresponding increase in the value of the dollar to the SDR was around 28%.

This suggests that SAMA has been placing more weight on the dollar than the SDR when determining the exchange rate of the riyal, and the dollar continued to be the main intervention currency. During 1984–85, the riyal was devalued several times *vis-à-vis* the dollar but the drop has been small. The devaluation of the riyal from SR3.65 to the dollar to SR3.75, in June 1986 a drop of 2.7% (following a 1% decline in June 1985), has been the largest decline recorded in the 1980s and it was implemented when the dollar was not flying high in the exchange markets. However, it did come at a time when the Kingdom's oil revenues were running low (daily production of 2.5 mb/d compared to projected projection level of 4 mb/d). The devaluation of the riyal may have been an attempt by the Saudi authorities to boost the riyal value of the Kingdom's declining dollar oil revenues. In a way, therefore, it may be considered as a controlled adjustment to a current account imbalance.

If the Kingdom's foreign oil revenues continue to be depressed and the dollar preserves its strong position in the foreign currency market then the riyal may witness other devaluations. However, there have been times in the past when the riyal exchange rate was deliberately moved against the direction generally expected in the market, presumably to introduce an element of uncertainty in order to prevent over speculation in the currency.

For Bahrain, UAE and Qatar the move from the dollar to the SDR was in fact less significant than it appeared to be. The SDR parity

Gulf Currencies, Foreign Investments . . . 161

Table 9.1 Gulf currencies per US$
(average period rates)

	Qatar QR/$	Bahrain BHD/$	Saudi Arabia SR/$	Oman OR/$	UAE DH/$	Kuwait KD/$
1978	3.8767	0.3875	3.3996	0.3454	3.8712	0.2750
1979	3.7727	0.3816	3.3608	0.3454	3.8157	0.2762
1980	3.6568	0.3770	3.3267	0.3454	3.7074	0.2703
1981	3.6399	0.3760	3.3826	0.3451	3.6710	0.2787
1982	3.6399	0.3760	3.4274	0.3454	3.6710	0.2879
1983	3.6399	0.3760	3.4547	0.3454	3.6710	0.2915
1984	3.6399	0.3760	3.5238	0.3454	3.6710	0.2960
1985	3.6399	0.3760	3.6221	0.3454	3.6710	0.2901

Source
IMF International Financial Statistics, Jan. 1986.

Table 9.2 Saudi riyal per dollar and per SDR and dollar per SDR
(average period rates)

	SR/$	$/SDR	SR/SDR
1978	3.3996	1.25200	4.2563
1979	3.3608	1.29200	4.3422
1980	3.3267	1.30153	4.3298
1981	3.3825	1.17916	3.9885
1982	3.4274	1.10401	3.7839
1983	3.4547	1.06900	3.6931
1984	3.5238	1.02501	3.6119
1985	3.6221	1.01534	3.6777
Jan. 86	3.6502	1.09786	4.0074
Feb. 86	3.6514	1.123941	4.1040
Mar. 86	3.6517	1.149757	4.1986

chosen was the pre-1973 SDR which was very close to the dollar parity and the dollar continued to be the intervention currency. Since 1979 the three countries have been adopting a virtually fixed dollar rate. In order to make possible fixed exchange parity, and to guarantee full convertibility of the Gulf currencies, ample foreign reserves need to be maintained. The monetary authorities, therefore, are keeping close control on money supply in their respective countries. If commercial banks need more liquidity, they can buy local currencies from the central banks in return say for dollars and sell them forward through well established swap operations. This process preserves the ratio of local currencies to foreign reserves and guarantees full convertibility.

The Kuwaiti authorities devised their own basket of currencies (linked to a weighted average of currencies of their major trading partners). The value of this basket is calculated every day and the Central Bank produces a daily fixing price of the Kuwaiti dinar. Drawing on historic data of the KD *vis-à-vis* the dollar and the other currencies, one can make inferences of the various weights used in the basket of currencies. The dollar weight appears to be in the range of 70%, the Japanese yen 12%, German mark 8%, UK sterling 5% and other currencies 5%. These weights may change over time reflecting the actual dominance of the international currencies in Kuwait's foreign trade.

Data shows that between 1980 and August 1985, the dinar retreated by 13.5% *vis-à-vis* the dollar but gained 27% against the sterling and 5.6% and 15.5% against the yen and the mark respectively.

In April 1984, a temporary two-tier exchange rate system was introduced, with a view to stem the accelerated pace of capital outflow from the country. While market forces remained at free-play to determine the financial rate, documented commercial transactions were provided at a 'subsidized' declared rate. By mid-1984, the Central Bank deeming circumstances suitable, decided to bring the financial rate to parity with the commercial rate. The country thus reverted, *de facto*, to the unified exchange rate system.

The main difficulty in establishing market exchange rates for Gulf currencies is that most of the region's exports are oil related and prices are denominated in dollars irrespective of the cost of production. Foreign investment income is also mostly dollar denominated. A stable exchange rate system is believed to achieve a better purchasing power for revenues from exports and would dampen inflationary expectations. Adopting a floating exchange rate would make it difficult for the GCC governments to forecast their budgets in the local currencies, and it would as well introduce an exchange risk element to capital flows and trade transactions. The impact on the value of existing foreign assets owned both by the private and public sectors of a local currency revaluation and devaluation is considered to be psychologically damaging and could hinder perfect capital mobility.

The exchange rates of the Gulf currencies do not necessarily reflect strength and weakness of Gulf economies nor do their exchange value adjust regularly to trade and current account imbalances. The exchange markets are basically a channel through which governments convert oil revenues to finance their local currency expenditures, and the private sector draws on these markets to meet its international requirements. Exchange rates are in effect a technical device than a truly market determined relationship, and they are expected to continue to be so as long as oil revenues remain the main source of the region's foreign income.

On the other hand, following a fixed exchange rate policy between the US$ and the various Gulf currencies could lead to the loss of foreign reserves by the monetary authorities and place upward pressure on domestic interest rates. With limited exchange risk involved, interest differential between dollar deposits and deposits in local currencies is a clear invitation for speculation and capital outflow. If domestic interest rates were allowed to match the rates on the dollar then the local economies would, *de facto*, be subjected to contractionary monetary policy when the opposite is actually needed.

The Gulf economies are highly exchange orientated with a predominantly external sector which constitutes around 80% of the Gross Domestic Product of these countries. In comparison, the external sector in the US, the UK, Japan and India accounts for 15%, 47%, 25% and 12% of their respective GDPs. These comparative ratios show the extent of vulnerability of Gulf economies to exchange rate fluctuations.

This worked in favour of the Gulf countries during the period 1981–84 and throughout most of 1985 when the dollar was appreciating in value on the world exchange markets. With approximately three-quarters of the region's imports being paid for by currencies that were depreciating *vis-à-vis* the US dollar, the benefits in terms of lower unit cost of imports, and therefore, lower inflation were considerable. During 1984, most GCC countries recorded declines in consumer prices ranging from −5% for the UAE to −0.4% for Saudi Arabia. The rate of increase in prices in Oman declined from about 15% in 1983 to 6.5% in 1984.

How would the Gulf currencies be affected if the dollar continues its gradual slide on the international exchange markets? The GCC countries stand to lose on two fronts, their oil revenues would decline by the same percentage as the drop in the dollar and their income from foreign investment, the bulk of which is dominated in dollars, would also be affected. However, the reduced purchasing power of the GCC currencies would be made for, at least partially, through buying American goods at a lower dollar rate, and in the longer term through the increase in world oil consumption, especially outside the US. The cheaper dollar oil prices measured in yens, marks, pounds and francs would eventually bring forth a higher level of oil consumption.

It is logical to argue that if each dollar buys less marks and yens then the region cannot afford to import as many German and Japanese products as before, and the depreciation of the Gulf currencies against the mark and the yen is the best way of insuring that imports are redirected away from the expensive countries. This would be similar to what had happened in the 1980–85 period when the dollar was on the rise. In 1984, the drop in the region's imports from the US exceeded the corresponding drop in imports from Japan (for the six GCC countries the drop in imports from the US was 37% compared to a drop of 18% in imports from Japan).

However, if the dollar records an abrupt drop in its value, the Gulf currencies need not necessarily follow suit. Instead, the monetary authorities could revert back to the SDR to which most of the GCC currencies are officially pegged and where they enjoy a trading margin of 14.5% around the official SDR parity. This could help smooth out the effect of the major drop in the international value of the dollar on the economies of the region.

GULF FOREIGN INVESTMENTS

According to the Bank of England and US Treasury figures, governments of OPEC countries have managed to accumulate net foreign assets of roughly $345 billion over the 1973–84 period with the GCC countries accounting for 70% of the total. By the end of 1985, Government placed overseas investments of the six Gulf countries are estimated to have dropped to $205 billion. Saudi Arabia is believed to have $90 billion, Kuwait $80 billion, UAE $20 billion and a total of $15 billion for Qatar, Oman and Bahrain (Table 9.3).

An estimated 28% of the assets ($58 billion) were held in the form of bank deposits in twenty or so industrialized countries. Nearly 70% of these deposits ($40 billion) were in dollars while rather more than 25% were denominated in DM, sterling, yen and Swiss and French francs. It is these bank deposits that take the immediate impact of

Table 9.3 Gulf foreign investments: 1985
($ billion)

	Amount[a]	Percentage	Amount invested in the US
Bank deposit	58	28	6.8
Government securities	55	27	32.5
Foreign exchange reserves	12	6	–
Equity & direct investment	49	24	14.9
Loans to LDC's	31	15	–
Others	–	–	7.7
Total	205	100	61.9

Note
[a] Estimates based on Bank of England quarterly Bulletin, March 1985 and US Treasury Dept, International Captial reports, July 1985.

fluctuations in current account balances. In the last three years, it is estimated that there were net withdrawals of these deposits amounting to around $34 billion.

Government securities in the USA, UK and Germany had always been attractive investment channels to the Gulf countries. By the end of 1985 an estimated $55 billion was invested in this category, around 60% of that ($33 billion) was in US Treasury bonds and notes.

The third category is the deployment of funds in foreign exchange reserves – gold, SDRs, reserves with the IMF and bonds of the World Bank. These reserves differed widely from country to country and the total figures were heavily influenced by Saudi Arabia's loans to the IMF. The aggregate in this category is believed to be around $12 billion or 6% of the total.

Following all these liquid assets comes direct loans, equity holdings (corporate bonds and stocks), property and other investments in the industrialized countries. These constituted around 24% of total foreign investment or $49 billion in 1985. Finally, outstanding loans to the less developed countries by the end of last year were around $31 billion or 15% of the Gulf's total foreign assets.

The investment position of the Gulf countries' public sectors in the US was estimated at around $62 billion by the end of 1985, more than half of it in US government securities. The figure for mid-1985 was $65 billion down from $67 billion at the end of 1984. Actual totals are believed to be considerably higher. The US government is unable to track all stock purchases of less than 5% of a company's equity, nor can it identify the Middle Eastern element in investment portfolio which comes through third countries such as Switzerland or the UK.

Total investment in the US on the part of the Gulf countries is estimated to have slumped by around 8.5% in 1985 following a drop of 10% the year before. The disinvestment trend that started in 1983, reflects lower oil revenues and the need of countries like Saudi Arabia to finance current account deficits.

Disinvestment from the US in the last three years would have been much higher had the Gulf countries run down their dollar and non-dollar based investments at the same rate. It is believed that, for purely investment reasons, countries of the region had liquidated a higher proportion of their non-dollar dominated securities, because of the lower yield of these assets compared to the dollar assets.

The latest freeze of the Libyan assets in the US may accelerate a trend already apparent in Arab Investment strategy, to shift more business to non-US banks and to diversify into German, Swiss and Japanese equities and bonds. Any time the US acts to freeze assets in response to political circumstances, it raises a little alarm bell. It becomes another factor influencing foreign investment decisions in the US.

A sudden massive divestiture out of the dollar is not expected as it would place additional pressure on the American currency which is the mainstay of Gulf countries' monetary reserves. The European capital markets are not large enough to absorb all the funds available and the Japanese market is still seen as restrictive. It is more likely that Gulf investors, both private and public, would shift some dollar holdings out of the US markets into Eurodollar bank deposits and Eurodollar bonds. Some transfers to stocks and bonds are expected as these are more difficult to be frozen than bank deposits.

GCC EXTERNAL BALANCES

The current accounts of the 6 Gulf countries witnessed a dramatic shift from a surplus of well over $70 billion in 1980 to a much smaller surplus of around $13 billion in 1982 to an estimated deficit of around 4.3 billion in 1985. Another deficit is projected for 1986 based on the sizeable drop in the region's oil revenues. Only Saudi Arabia recorded a deficit in 1985, the other four Gulf countries continued to show a surplus (Table 9.4).

Table 9.4 Current account balances of the GCC Countries
($ billion)

	1980	1981	1982	1983	1984	1985	1986[a]
Saudi Arabia	41.40	38.36	−1.04	−16.06	−19.04	−17.50	−20.00
Kuwait	16.16	14.68	5.01	5.12	5.57	4.40	2.76
UAE	10.17	9.21	7.00	5.62	7.13	7.08	3.81
Qatar	2.65	2.38	1.13	0.31	1.20	1.00	−0.19
Oman	1.10	1.36	0.55	0.36	0.11	0.11	−0.06
Bahrain	0.38	0.55	0.64	0.12	0.61	−0.61	−0.05
Total	71.86	66.54	13.29	−4.54	−5.14	−4.30	−13.64

Note
[a] Projected.

Sources:
National and international sources.

The main reason behind the deterioration of the current account balances was the huge drop in the region's oil exports. Oil revenues continue to be the major source of income for the various GCC countries constituting in 1984 up to 95% of total exports for Saudi Arabia, 90% for Kuwait and Qatar, 87% for UAE and 65% for Bahrain. GCC current account balances would continue to hinge, therefore, on future developments in the world oil market.

The large deficit in the services account for Saudi Arabia, Oman, Qatar and Bahrain, even after taking into consideration investment income, remains a noteworthy feature. In fact the run down of net cash holding to finance the deficit in the last two years has sharply reduced net interest receipts. Adjusting imbalances in GCC current accounts, and halting the drawdown on foreign reserves is actually becoming a major policy goal in the region.

Impact of Lower Oil Prices

Falling oil prices have both direct and indirect effects upon the countries of the region. The most direct effect is the loss of export oil revenues which are normally translated into declining government expenditures, retarding as a result overall economic growth. The loss in oil revenues can be estimated assuming a certain average price and production levels for the various GCC countries. Table 9.5 gives the estimated crude oil production and export earning for the six Gulf

Table 9.5 Impact of lower oil prices on Gulf countries' oil revenues

	1984 Production (mb/d)	1984 Earnings ($ million)	1985[a] Production (mb/d)	1985[a] Earnings[d] ($ million)	1986[b] Production (mb/d)	1986[b] Earnings[e] ($ million)
S. Arabia	4.10	36 186	3.25[c]	27 367	4.35	19 069
Kuwait	1.16	12 345	1.06	10 994	1.32	7 127
UAE	1.10	11 707	1.05	10 890	1.30	7 022
Qatar	0.38	4 225	0.30	3 130	0.30	1 628
Oman	0.42	3 829	0.50	4 440	0.55	2 540
Bahrain	0.04	1 008	0.04	958	0.04	527

Sources: Compiled from National and International sources including International Energy Agency, Paris, Apr. 1986. IMF, *International Financial Statistics*, Apr. 1985; GCC, *Central Banks and Monetary Agencies Annual Reports* (various issues: 1983–85).
[a] Estimates.
[b] Projections.
[c] Based on average production of 3.7 mb/d in first quarter, 2.7 mb/d in the second quarter, 2.4 mb/d in the third quarter and 4.2 mb/d in the fourth quarter.
[d] Average price per barrel of Gulf crude oil estimated at $27 compared to an average price of $28.3 in 1984.
[e] Projections based on an average price per barrel of Gulf crude oil of $14 in 1986.

countries, assuming an average price per barrel of Gulf crude oil for 1986 of around $14. The indirect effects include a lower income generated from the region's sizeable foreign assets due to lower international interest rates and generally higher domestic inflation brought forth by rising non-dollar import prices.

The indirect effects are more difficult to quantify. Lower interest rates and declining dollar exchange rates are not, of course, a guaranteed accompaniment to lower oil prices. But by helping to dampen inflationary expectations, lower oil prices were instrumental in lowering bond yields. Short term rates are less directly influenced by inflationary expectations as these depend more on changes in monetary policies. Lower oil prices are also reducing the import bill of the major oil importing countries, boosting their external balance of payment position and strengthening the exchange rates of their respective currencies. The impact is more favourable for the non-oil producing countries such as Japan and Germany and less so for the US which is both a major oil producing and oil importing country. This explains, at least partially, the drop in the value of the US dollar *vis-à-vis* the other major world currencies.

An average drop in interest rates of around 20%, coupled with about 18% decline in dollar exchange rate *vis-à-vis* the other major currencies, are likely to reduce the region's income from foreign investment by up to 25%. Of course, the impact differs from one country to another depending on the composition of the portfolio of foreign assets held by the various Gulf countries.

Another indirect effect of declining oil prices is possibly higher inflationary pressures in the region. Even though, on the domestic scene, the depressionary internal factors are still holding. However, the inflationary impact of higher import prices (other than US products) due to a declining dollar are already being felt in the region. Inflationary pressures will be more visible if governments of the region continue to administer devaluation of the Gulf currencies in an effort to boost local currency value of their declining oil revenues.

SAUDI ARABIA

Saudi Arabia is seen succeeding in pushing production to its OPEC quota of 4.35 mb/d. The postulated 48% drop in oil prices in 1986 (from $27 to $14) will be partially offset by the expected 34% increase in output. The country's oil revenues would accordingly be reduced to

$19 billion in 1986 down from $36 billion in 1984. The declining oil revenues may imply further austerity budgets with no major new projects to be undertaken. The budgets for 1986–87, and 1987–88 are expected to be balanced, reflecting the Kingdom's policy of holding the drawdown of its foreign assets and trying instead to fine-tune expenditures to match projected revenues.

The decline in oil revenues would generate another current account deficit in Saudi Arabia's balance of payment in 1986. The projected 30% drop in oil revenues will be partially offset by an increase in petrochemicals and other exports. Total merchandise exports are forecasted to be in the range of $20 billion compared with about $28 billion in the year before. Merchandise imports may be slashed to about $15 billion in 1986 (down from an estimated $20 billion in 1985) giving a favourable trade balance of around $5 billion.

In the services and transfers account, a fall in the number of foreign workers in the Kingdom means a fall in remittances from $5.28 billion in 1984 to an estimated $4.5 billion in 1985 and $4 billion in 1986. On the other hand, the decline in interest rate and the running down of foreign assets implies a drop in investment and other income from $17.6 billion in 1984 to $14 billion in 1985 and possibly $11 billion in 1986. As to the import of services which includes training contracts, freight and insurance, civilian and defence related maintenance among others, the drop is expected to be from $45.5 billion in 1984 to an estimated $40 billion in 1985 and $36 billion in 1986. A current account deficit of $20 billion is therefore projected for 1986 (Table 9.6).

KUWAIT

The Gross Domestic Product of Kuwait is estimated to have contracted by 9.6% during 1985, resulting from a 12% decline in oil sector's production with a 6% decline in non-oil GDP. This follows a 4.5% growth in current GDP in 1984.

Kuwait's 1986/87 budget has been cut in line with projected oil revenues. Total expenditures dropped by 11.3% from the previous fiscal year. Kuwait is expected to maintain the much larger share in the oil market acquired during the first half of 1986. A 25% increase in production is forecasted this year to 1.32 mb/d. This would limit the impact of lower prices on the country's export revenues. For the first time in Kuwait's modern history the country is projecting a real

Table 9.6 Saudi Arabia: current account balance: actual and projections ($ billion)

	1980	1981	1982	1983	1984	1985[a]	1986[a]
Exports	100.72	111.12	73.11	45.68	37.44	28.32	19.73
Imports	-28.24	-33.96	-34.45	-33.22	-28.55	-20.00	-15.00
Trade balance	72.48	77.16	38.66	12.46	8.89	8.32	4.73
Services and transfers	-31.08	-38.80	-39.70	-28.75	-27.93	-25.82	-25.00
(a) Receipts	11.26	16.24	18.96	21.30	17.57	14.18	11.00
(i) Investment income[b]	7.44	10.96	12.00	10.00	13.36	10.00	9.00
(ii) Other income	3.82	5.28	6.96	11.30	4.21	4.18	3.00
(b) Payments	-42.34	-55.04	-58.66	-50.05	-45.50	-40.00	-36.00
(i) Private transfers	-4.06	-4.10	-5.21	-5.23	-5.28	-4.50	-4.00
(ii) Oil sector investment income	-6.92	-9.50	-3.58	-3.29	-3.60	-3.00	-2.00
(iii) Others[c]	-31.36	-41.44	-49.87	-41.53	-36.62	-32.50	-30.00
Current account[d]	-41.40	38.36	-1.04	-16.29	-19.04	-17.50	-20.27
Cumulative surplus[e]	114.31	152.67	151.63	135.34	116.30	98.80	78.53

Notes
[a] Projected.
[b] Investment income includes foreign earnings accruing for both private and public sectors.
[c] Other payments includes freight and insurance and other private and government services.
[d] Current account = trade balance + services and transfers.
[e] Since 1974.

Sources: IMF, *International Financial Statistics* (Sept. 1985), and SAMA publications.

deficit in its 1986/87 budget. However, Kuwait's substantial foreign reserves, around $80 billion, will make it much easier to absorb the deficit compared to the other oil exporting countries.

Kuwait's balance of payment position remains healthy despite falling oil revenues. The outlook for 1986 is less favourable. The decline in merchandise exports and the expected drop in income from investment abroad due to lower interest rates will be partially offset by decreasing remittances of foreign workers in the country. This should result in current account surplus of $2.76 billion in 1986 compared with $4.4 billion in 1985 (Table 9.7). Kuwait's liquid reserves are enough to cover imports for more than a year. The problem facing the country is how best to adjust internally, as its external position remains healthy.

UNITED ARAB EMIRATES

The fall in real gross domestic product (by 3–4% in 1985) is expected to continue in 1986 for the fifth consecutive year. The value of 1985 oil exports, amounting to around $10 890 million (down from $11 707 million in the year before), are forecasted to drop by around 36% in 1986 to $7092 million. UAE is trying to compensate for the drop in oil prices by boosting its production. A 24% increase in 1986 daily oil production is expected to dampen the impact of lower oil prices on the country's export revenues.

Central bank figures indicate that the actual budget deficit for 1985 was more than twice the planned deficit and close to 38% higher than the 1984 deficit of $245 million. The government's continued inability to control expenditures is likely to lead to greater restrictions in the 1986 and 1987 budgets. Official statements have suggested that expenditures will be cut by 15%. However, the projected 36% drop in oil revenues and the cost over run from 1985 may lead to larger cuts in expenditures.

Total exports are forecasted to drop to $9408 million in 1986 down from $14 700 million in 1985. Imports will also be curtailed due to the decline in the US dollar and the slowdown in domestic economic activities. The value of imports fell in 1985 to $6398 million and are projected to drop further to $4800 million in 1986 generating a trade surplus of $4608 million. Other current account items, services, private and public transfers which recorded $1220 million deficit in 1985 are forecasted to shrink to a deficit of $800 million. This leaves a

Table 9.7 Kuwait: current account balance: actual and projections ($ billion)

	1980	1981	1982	1983	1984	1985	1986[a]
Exports[b]	20.60	15.96	10.72	11.27	11.63	10.57	6.85
Imports	-6.75	-6.74	-7.80	-6.98	-7.14	-7.00	-4.85
Trade balance	13.85	9.22	2.92	4.29	4.49	3.57	2.00
Services and transfers	2.31	5.46	2.18	0.90	1.09	0.82	0.76
(a) Receipts	6.71	9.80	7.29	6.14	6.44	6.00	5.90
(i) Investment income	5.49	8.41	6.35	5.31	5.57	5.25	5.15
(ii) Other income	1.22	1.39	0.94	0.83	0.87	0.75	0.75
(b) Payments	-4.40	-4.34	-5.11	-5.24	-5.35	-5.18	-5.14
(i) Private transfers	-0.69	-0.69	-0.87	-0.91	-0.90	-0.88	-0.80
(ii) Others	-3.71	-3.65	-4.24	-4.33	-4.45	-4.30	-4.34
Current account	16.16	14.68	5.10	5.19	5.58	4.39	2.76
Cumulative surplus[c]	71.60	86.28	91.38	96.57	101.75	106.14	108.90

Notes
[a] Projected.
[b] Exports include both oil and non-oil merchandise exports.
[c] Since 1975.

Source
Economic and Financial Bulletin, no. 8, National Bank of Kuwait, May 1985.

current account surplus of $3808 million in 1986 down from $7080 million the year before (Table 9.8).

QATAR

Qatar did not increase its oil production to try to compensate for the substantial drop in prices. Consequently, oil revenues are forecasted to decline by around 48% from 1985's estimated $3130 million. Production in 1986 is expected to average 300 000 b/d, close to the levels of 1985.

With the drop in oil revenues, total exports are forecasted to fall to $1808 million from the 1985 level of $3478 million. Imports have been declining in the last few years, they are projected to drop still further by around 25% in 1986. Spending on new projects has been frozen and overall economic activities have been on a declining trend. 1986 imports could drop to $800 million giving a trade surplus of $1008 million. The estimated $1200 million deficit in the income and transfers balance would exceed the trade surplus this year and generate a deficit in the current account of around $192 000 dollars (Table 9.9).

Qatar has not yet announced its 1986/87 budget. The indications are that public expenditures will be lower than the estimated $2700 million spent in the previous fiscal year. With the drop in oil revenues, a larger deficit budget should be expected. This would further accentuate the depressionary trends in the country and lead to another drop in GDP.

OMAN

Oil represents 90% of Oman's exports and close to 80% of the government's revenues. The country was able to increase its production capacity from 416 000 b/d in 1984 to 500 000 b/d in 1985, with average daily production expected to reach 550 000 barrels in 1986. However, the fall in oil prices will reduce Oman's earnings from oil exports from $4440 million in 1985 to an estimated $2540 million in 1986. This is expected to cause a sharp contraction in the Omani economy after years of sizeable growth.

Even if imports were slashed by around 30%, a much smaller trade surplus of $344 million will be recorded (compared to a provisional $1546 in 1985). The deficit in the services and transfers balance is

Table 9.8 United Arab Emirates: current account balance – actual and projections ($ billion)

	1980	1981	1982	1983	1984	1985[a]	1986[a]
Exports	22.18	21.79	18.22	15.38	15.84	14.70	9.41
Imports	-8.72	-9.80	-9.26	-8.27	-7.35	-6.40	-4.80
Trade balance	13.46	11.99	8.96	7.11	8.49	8.30	4.61
Services and transfers balances	-3.29	-2.78	-1.96	-1.49	-1.36	-1.22	-0.80
Current account	10.17	9.21	7.00	5.62	7.13	7.08	3.81

Note
[a] Projected.

Source
Central Bank Bulletin, 1985.

Table 9.9 Qatar: current account balance – actual and projections ($ billion)

	1980	1981	1982	1983	1984	1985	1986[a]
Exports	5.71	5.84	4.51	3.30	3.85	3.48	1.81
Imports	-1.45	-1.52	-1.95	-1.56	-1.30	-1.00	-0.80
Trade balance	4.26	4.32	2.56	1.74	2.55	2.48	1.01
Services and transfers balances	-1.61	-1.94	-1.43	-1.43	-1.35	-1.48	–
Current account	2.65	2.38	1.13	0.31	1.20	1.00	0.19

Note
[a] Projected.

Source
Qatar Monetary Agency.

forecasted to decline to $1134 million from $1300 million in 1985 due mainly to the expected drop in workers remittances and the reduction in services expenditures. A current account deficit of $60 million is accordingly forecasted for 1986 compared to a provisional surplus of $113 million in 1985 (Table 9.10).

Oman's 1986 budget was formulated based on an oil price of $22 a barrel. The drop in oil prices to less than $15 a barrel implies a much larger budget deficit for fiscal 1986/87 than the originally estimated $585 million. The budgeted public expenditures of $5414 million may be slashed to reflect measures introduced by the government to restructure the economy.

BAHRAIN

Bahrain which has one of the region's most diversified economies, has also been affected by the decline in oil prices. Real GDP growth is estimated to have been in the range of 1% in 1985 down from 3% and 4% in the two previous years respectively. Oil still accounts for about 60% of government revenues, and Bahrain's economy is strongly linked to the economies of the other Gulf countries. The current slowdown in the economies of the region has left its impact on Bahrain with banking, trade, real estate and construction feeling the pinch most.

Bahrain has been producing oil at close to its full capacity of 43 000 b/d in 1985 and is striving to maintain that level this year. However, with the drop in oil prices, oil revenues for 1986 are expected to decline to around $500 million, down from $958 million last year. Budgeted expenditures are expected to be slashed and the economy will record negative growth for the first time in ten years.

Bahrain recorded its first current account deficit in 1984 of around $10.6 million. The deficit was turned into $610 million surplus in 1985, however, the decline in oil revenues in 1986 would bring forth a projected current account deficit of $50 million.

THE POLICY RESPONSE

With the exception of Saudi Arabia, all the other GCC countries are either enjoying a surplus in their trade and current account balances or are projected to record small deficits that are not at all alarming.

Table 9.10 Oman: current account balance – actual projections ($ billion)

	1980	1981	1982	1983	1984	1985	1986[a]
Exports	3.75	4.70	4.42	4.26	4.42	4.97	3.42
Imports	-1.86	-2.40	-2.58	-2.36	-2.64	-3.36	-2.35
Trade balance	1.89	2.30	1.84	1.89	1.78	1.61	1.07
Services and transfers	-0.79	-0.94	-1.29	-1.41	-1.63	-1.50	-1.13
(a) Receipts	0.24	0.33	0.43	0.46	0.42	0.40	0.40
(b) Payments	-1.03	-1.27	-1.72	-1.87	-2.05	-1.90	-1.53
Current account	1.10	1.36	0.55	0.48	0.15	0.11	-0.06

Note
[a] Projected.
Source
IMF, *International Financial Statistics* (Sept, 1985).

Table 9.11 Bahrain: current account balance – actual and projections ($ billion)

	1980	1981	1982	1983	1984	1985	1986[a]
Exports	3.54	4.18	3.69	3.12	3.12	2.80	1.46
Imports	-3.02	-3.56	-3.04	-2.87	-3.51	-3.12	-2.18
Trade balance	0.52	0.62	0.65	0.25	-0.39	-0.32	-0.72
Services and transfers	-0.14	-0.07	-0.01	-0.01	0.28	0.93	0.67
(a) Receipts	0.71	0.96	1.13	0.84	1.03	1.58	1.22
(b) Payments	-0.85	-1.03	-1.12	-0.85	-0.75	-0.65	-0.55
Current account	0.38	0.55	0.64	0.24	-0.11	0.61	-0.05

Note
[a] Projected.

Source
IMF, *International Financial Statistics* (Sept, 1985).

The swing of the Kingdom into current account deficit since 1982 led to a rundown of bank deposits which are the most liquid of the country's foreign assets. By 1984, government securities, the next most liquid category of foreign investments also began to be liquidated.

It is estimated that Saudi Arabia's official sector had in 1985 access to around $90 billion of invested assets that were either liquid or could become liquid within two to three years. These assets were sufficient to cover current account deficits of $20 billion annually for more than four years. However, Saudi policy makers were clearly not willing to watch their reserves dwindle away so quickly, not only because of the income foregone generated by these invested assets, but also because they were keenly aware of the uncertainties of the oil market and the disruptions this may have on their future development plans.

Historically, Saudi Arabia had born most of the responsibility to support the benchmark price of OPEC. In 1982–85, the Kingdom slashed its oil production, reduced domestic expenditures and drew down on its foreign reserves. Many businesses in the country were affected, salaries and benefits were trimmed, and the economic slowdown filtered to all sectors of the economy. Saudi Arabia's political and economic weight in the world has been undermined to some extent by its decline as a major oil producer.

Because of its low oil production level the Kingdom has not been able to produce enough natural gas to supply its massive new petrochemical complexes, nor has it been able to meet its foreign contractual commitments. It is absurd to see Saudi Arabia importing gas while it has huge resources domestically.

It was not therefore, in the Kingdom's best interest to continue to play the role of a swing producer and end up subsidizing everyone else in order to promote a stable oil market. If other OPEC members were not willing to put OPEC's common good ahead of their own economic needs. Saudi Arabia cannot be blamed for choosing to follow a similar course of action.

The price shock of 1986 offers both risks and opportunities that Gulf countries need to cope with. The strategy of reducing oil prices to capture a "fair share" of the world oil market would imply lower oil revenues for a few years to come. Nevertheless, the new strategy may have a far reaching positive impact on the economies of the region in the long term. It could eventually restore the high share of world oil provided by the Gulf countries and could also lay the ground for a gradual and orderly rise in oil prices. Meanwhile, Gulf countries' huge official foreign reserves (estimated at around $205 billion) should protect them from serious liquidity problems in the short term.

10 Other Economic Sectors

This chapter presents a brief review of the other economic sectors in the region, namely agriculture and services sectors. The latter does not include banking and financial sectors as these have already been discussed in Chapters 5 and 6, while trading activities were picked up in Chapter 9. The presentation under other services will, therefore, be confined to insurance, aviation, hotels and shipping.

AGRICULTURE: CULTIVATING A NEW IMAGE

The GCC countries have mounted an aggressive campaign to improve their agricultural sector, which so far has played a limited role in the region's economy. The contribution of this sector to gross domestic product is still very low ranging from 4% in Oman to 2.5% in Saudi Arabia and to less than 0.04% in Qatar. The reason for such a marginal role include deficiencies in the soil, scarcity of irrigation water, climatic conditions of the desert including low annual rainfall and the limited supply of manpower trained in agriculture. Despite these limitations, efforts are now being intensified to improve agricultural performance and cultivate a new image for the agricultural sectors.

Agricultural self sufficiency is continuously being called for at all levels in the various GCC countries. A recent study by the Federation of Gulf Chamber of Commerce, Industry and Agriculture warns of a serious shortage of food in the Gulf region if no immediate measures are taken to achieve self sufficiency. The study recommends reclamation of additional land, encouragement and incentives to the private sector, increased use of advanced scientific methods to deal with the region's harsh climate, and establishment of local fertilizer and insecticide industries. The study expects that by the end of the century, the countries of the region would have achieved as a group self sufficiency in wheat, maize, poultry and other various agricultural and dairy products.

Agricultural area in the Gulf states totals 6.16 million hectares, of which only 2.8 million hectares are being cultivated. Rainfed agriculture is possible only where the average annual rainfall is at least 200 mm, a condition met nowhere in the GCC countries except for 3% of

Saudi Arabia and 12% for Oman. Furthermore, the geographical structure means that rainfed agriculture can only be carried out in a small proportion of the area meeting the 200 mm criterion.

The countries of the region have therefore turned into irrigation using mostly ground water. Acquifers have been tapped at ever increasing depth and it is estimated that by the turn of the century non-renewable water resources will in some regions of Saudi Arabia and Bahrain be fully exhausted if the current extraction rates are maintained.

Agriculture did not feature strongly in Gulf investment plans of the 70s. Between 1975 and 1980 only 9% of total investment went to agriculture. However, agricultural investment jumped to 13% of total development expenditure in the 1980–85 period. More than $2.5 billion was spent in the region to provide incentives to farmers and agricultural companies which included leasing land, financial assistance, to boy agricultural equipment and fertilizers and, loans for modernizing agricultural methods and techniques.

Of the six GCC states, the UAE, Oman and Saudi Arabia are believed to have the most promising future in agriculture. The agricultural sector in Qatar is rather dormant and its contribution to the total output is expected to continue to be minimal. Kuwait on the other hand, has mounted an aggressive campaign to improve its agricultural sector. Kuwait's total cultivable area is estimated at 2800 hectares, most of it used for vegetables (tomatoes, cucumbers, melons and radishes). Orchards and timber took out another 1000. In 1983, there were more than 1500 agricultural holdings including 313 specializing in vegetables, 86 in poultry and 40 in dairy products. Kuwait produces almost 50% of its fresh vegetable needs, and more than 35% of its eggs. The fishing industry provides 99% of local consumption with about 20% exported to neighbouring countries.

The main source of irrigation in Kuwait is the underground water which has a salinity range between 0.3% and 1.1%. Experiments are underway to use recycled sewage water for irrigation. Farming remains by and large an expensive industry in the country. To encourage agriculture the government gives attractive incentives including subsidies for digging wells, building greenhouses, and it heavily subsidizes seeds, equipment and fertilizers. The Agricultural Credit Bank normally gives additional loans on a low interest between 2% and 3%, with repayment three years after the farm becomes operational.

In Bahrain, the agricultural sector is witnessing a revival despite the island's dwindling water resources. More than $100 million has been alloted to agricultural schemes during the first half of the 80s. One of success has been egg production, which has reached self sufficiency. The government is also aiming to help the island's small band of dairy farmers.

In another move to increase Bahrain's agricultural productivity, a large date-processing factory was built near Mina Salman to process up to 1500 tons of dates annually. About 12 000 tons of dates a year are harvested from local farms with a good part of it is exported.

Prospects of agricultural development are more promising in Saudi Arabia, UAE and Oman. Here is a brief review of the agricultural sectors in the three countries.

Saudi Arabia

The Kingdom is the shining star of Gulf agriculture. The Saudi government is strongly committed to developing this sector, and has invested heavily in it. The third five year plan (1980–85) allocated around $21 billion to the sector. Close to $42 billion was extended in medium term loans to farmers, helping food production achieve an annual growth rate of 65%, and generating a higher standard of living for nearly half the Kingdom's population currently employed in the agricultural sector. The size of cultivated land grew by over 1300% from 150 000 hectares in 1980 to over 2.3 million hectares in 1985. The growth rate attained in the agricultural sector exceeded the target of the third five year plan. In 1984, food exports amounted to 36% of all non-oil exports, some 22% went to the other Gulf states.

The 1985–90 plan provides for continuing large scale investments in the agricultural sector. More than 5000 hectares are to be irrigated, a further 8000 hectares will be transformed into pasture, and annual output from the Kingdom's flour mills is projected to reach 979 000 tons, up from the present 750 000 tons.

However, loans from the Saudi Arabian Agricultural Bank (SAAB) will be cut to $2900 million in 1985–90, compared to $16 900 million in the third plan period. Table 10.1 gives the number of loans and the amounts allocated to projects financed by SAAB in 1982-1984.

Wheat production had increased from 3000 tons to over 1.3 million tons during the 1980–85 period, and the Kingdom has become one of the few grain exporting countries in the Middle East. Dairy production which in 1976, met only five percent of local demand, covered all domestic needs in 1985. The same was true with veg-

Table 10.1   *Projects financed by Saudi Arabian agricultural bank (SR million)*

	1982/83 No. of loans	1982/83 Amount	1984/85 No. of loans	1984/85 Amount
Broiler chickens	59	263.3	45	150.5
Layers	33	142.9	25	58.9
Dairy production	4	57.5	3	19.6
Greenhouses	38	212.3	29	193.0
Animal Feed	59	391.9	45	206.0
Livestock raising	67	233.9	42	150.0
Others[a]	3	4.2	4	21.6
Total	263	1,306.0	193	809.2

Notes
[a] Bee-keeping and fruit seedling nurseries.
Exchange rates: 1982: $1 = SR 3 4274; 1983: = SR 3 4547; 1984: $1 = SR 3 5219

Source
SAAB annual report, 1984.

etable, and fruit production. Saudi Arabia now exports eggs to Kuwait and UAE.

The Saudi farmers, who in the early 70s, used to achieve self sufficiency only in dates and some livestock, have been quite successful in converting deserts into green fields and achieving average yields of wheat comparable to those in the EEC and the US. The Saudi farmers had clearly benefited from the generosity of the government. The farmer is usually given the land he wants to farm by the government. He then receives a cash subsidy of between 20–50% of the cost of all machinery (except irrigation equipment). Over and above, the farmers can raise an interest free loan repayable over a 10 year period from the Saudi Arabian Agricultural Bank.

The farmers have benefited even more from the subsidized price of wheat. Until the price was cut in November 1984, to $555 a ton the government granted farmers close to $1000 for each ton they harvested, more than five times as much as it costs to import a ton of wheat (up to $200 cif). Buying all the wheat produced cost the Saudi government $1 billion more in 1984. Table 10.2 gives various levels of wheat production and consumption in the Kingdom.

The reduction in the wheat subsidy has encouraged the Saudi

Table 10.2 Wheat Production and consumption (tons)

Year	Local production[a]	Imports	Consumption	% of consumption produced locally
1978/79	17 505	828 336	845 841	2.1
1979/80	32 882	544 312	877 194	5.7
1980/81	85 435	673 652	759 087	11.3
1981/82	239 690	716 364	956 054	25.1
1982/83	674 631	283 000	957 631	70.5
1983/84	1,300 000	30 000	1,330 000	99.8

Note
[a] Deliveries to Grain Silos & Flour Mills Organization (GSFMO).

Source
GSFMO.

farmers to switch to the production of other grains. Barley production for animal feed has been on the rise recently allowing Saudi Arabia to build up its livestock herds and reduce its dependence on imports of frozen meat.

Saudi planners anticipate that annual milk production will rise to 500 000 tons by 1986 with Saudi firms becoming fresh milk exporters, especially to the neighbouring Gulf countries. The Kingdom is also hoping to become self sufficient in poultry within 10 years. The government sees poultry products as a Key dietary element and is working hard to encourage development of the industry.

Saudi Arabia is already exporting one of its traditional crops – dates. By 1985, the Kingdom was producing close to 400 000 tons of dates annually. The ministry of agriculture continues to offer a $15 subsidy for every date palm planted and further incentives for every kilogram of dates harvested. There are currently some 11 million date palms in the country.

Another area of food production that has been strongly encouraged by the government is that of fishing. In 1985, Saudi Fisheries, a company established in 1961, caught 5000 tons of fish and shrimp. The fish catch met over 90% of the local demand and a good portion of it was exported to the US and Japan.

Remarkable as the story of Saudi farming may be, it still has major limitations. The most important of which is the long term cost of the Kingdom on the drain on its underground water reserves. Even though there is apparently no major sign of water depletion yet, there are worries that the kingdom's resources may eventually fall, causing wells to start running dry.

Another worrying feature is that farming has not succeeded in halting the drift of small farmers to the cities. This is because the attractions of education, industry and city life have proved too strong and their agricultural holdings are not sufficient in size to encourage large scale mechanization. As a result, the traditional work force in the agricultural areas is declining.

Modern Saudi agriculture is more a matter of urban based business than farming in the traditional sense. Many of the newly established country farms are run by foreigners. Management is most often provided by Europeans or Americans while the workforce is comprised mostly of Yemenis, Pakistanis, Indians or Filipinos.

There is no doubt, however, that the agricultural programme in the Kingdom will continue, although the priorities will change. Subsidies will gradually decline and higher technology and efficiency especially in utilizing water resources will become the key elements. Training of Saudis also ranks high on the government's priorities so that Saudi management will start to take over and provide continuation to the Kingdom's agricultural sector.

United Arab Emirates

The agricultural sector in the UAE, generously funded by the government over the last ten years, has reached a stage where over 40% of the country's annual food consumption is produced locally. The country is also a surplus producer in some food items, such as vegetables where seasonal surpluses in the past few years were recorded and date production has been at record levels as well.

Farming in the UAE is concentrated in Al Ain and Ras-al-Khaima in the north. The greatest success here have been in winter vegetables rather than in wheat crops. Major crops production, livestock and forestry projects were started up in the early 70s, a period which has seen a huge population explosion in the Emirates.

The area of land cultivated in the UAE has increased five fold since 1972 and agricultural contribution to GNP has been on the rise in the last few years. Local catch of fish, estimated at 70 000 tons a year, meets 91% of the demand while vegetable crops estimated at 300 000 tons a year supply more than 50% of the local consumption. In milk and dairy products, eggs, mutton, chicken and fodder, the local

Table 10.3 Development aspects of agriculture in UAE

	Unit	1977	1984	Development %
Total number of farms	farm	7 759	12 917	166
Total cultivated area	hectare	15 339	29 500	192
Total plant production	ton	102 000	588 000	576
Total area with vegetables	hectare	1 600	10 290	643
Total production of vegetables	ton	40 300	300 000	744

output ranges between 8% and 33% of the country's requirements.

Government inputs that have helped boost agricultural production include subsidies, developed land, fertilizer, manpower costs and continuous advice through government appointed experts. The effort is backed by a chain of research stations working to insure the adoption of the most proper farming practices and techniques.

All these inputs provided generously over the years were aimed at securing food supplies from within the country and giving the nomadic people a settled way of life. More than 15 000 nomads responded to the invitation. Half of them have made farming their mainstay, while the other half, continued to pursue agriculture as an additonal source of income.

Several farmers are resorting to the use of covered plastic houses which provide the possibility of growing more than one crop in a season, higher yield and the conservation of water resources. In 1982 the number of protected agricultural houses was 480, by the end of 1984 the number had risen to 1500.

In 1985, there were 25 vegetable crops grown in the country. Of these, 8 crops represented 80% of the total vegetable production. These are tomato, cauliflower, cabbage, eggplant, cucumber, watermelon, sweet melon and squash. While the growing of these crops has been determined by their suitability to local climatic conditions, and their ready marketability, the government have been working hard to induce farmers to cultivate other crops such as potato, onions and other beans. The development aspects of the agricultural sector in the Emirates is given in Table 10.3.

The latest move towards achieving the goal of self sufficiency was demonstrated by the establishment in 1985 of an Agriculture Credit Fund. The Fund's aim is to assist and fund all agricultural and fishery activities, including light food industries and livestock farms. It offers loans to individuals, companies, co-operative societies and other organizations engaged in farming and fishing. The fund also provides subsidy in cash for the purchase of equipment such as pumps and boat engines. The fund assists investors as well with studies and researches in raising production and in improving and marketing efficiency.

The loans will be extended in accordance with the categories in which the projects are classified. For instance, agricultural projects for developing or expanding wells and water resources would qualify for 75% of the project cost while projects involving livestocks and poultry farms will get 80%, fishery projects 90%, and a light food industry 60% of the project cost.

There will be short term loans for obtaining the annual requirements for cultivating or marketing seasonal crops, and for meeting the needs of poultry and livestock farms and fishing operations. These would be payable within 18 months.

Medium term loans, repayable within five years, are given for buying equipment, including tractors, heavy machinery, motor boats, incubators, green houses, etc, and canal works and irrigation network reconstruction.

Long term loans, with a ten year repayment period, are given for setting up farms, fishery and livestock projects and for part financing a light food industry projects.

The most severe constraint to the expansion of agricultural activity in the UAE is the availability of water. Irrigation in the country depended mostly on pumping out underground water. While in the most places the underground level had dropped, in few areas the wells have dried out completely. In the coastal regions where agricultural areas are near the sea, pumping has resulted in a marked deterioration in the quality of water.

Several steps were taken to alleviate this problem. The government has been consistently trying to educate the farming community in the efficient use of water resources. Several dams were constructed to collect rain water and thus recharge the underground reserves. Five dams with a total capacity of 15 million cubic metres a year have been completed and nine others are planned. Modern irrigation techniques are also being introduced aimed at cutting down labour by 50% and conserve up to 60% in the utilization of water.

Oman

Even though only 4% of Oman's GNP is generated in the agricultural sector, 50% of the population derive their living from agriculture and fisheries. Cereal crops are grown for local consumption, while dates, limes and pomegranates are the main export crops. While in 1976 the agriculture and fisheries sector contributed only $53 million to GNP, in 1984 the contribution of the sector increased to $260 million.

Oman has a long tradition of cultivation with its ancient falaj system of irrigation, the traditional water distribution system used by Oman for hundred of years. The second five year development plan (1981–85) allocated $64.2 million for falaj maintenance and repair and the third five year plan is expected to continue this emphasis. The first plan's goal of self sufficiency in food has been dropped for the more practical aim of gradual growth in crop and livestock production.

Of Oman's 310 800 square kilometres, to date some 41 000 hectares of land have been cultivated. Further, development of land is limited due to lack of water and adequate manpower.

To tackle the problem of agricultural development and water conservation, the government has introduced a 'master plan' for development. According to the plan, priority is given to conserving water resources, redistributing lands, introducing new crops and insecticides as well as providing fertilizers for farmers, creating a food reserve and extending incentives for the private sector to increase its participation in the agriculture sector.

One of the main problems facing agriculture in Oman as in the other neighbouring countries is the dwindling water resources. If water is not replaced, farmers will face problems of salinity in coastal areas where sea water is slowly infiltrating fresh water supplies.

Two important features of the new agriculture policy involve the construction of recharge dams and repairs to the existing falaj. In the first instance, a series of recharge dams are to be built in many of the Sultanate's river valleys in order to save flood waters. Currently under construction is a five million cubic metre dam, the Wadi AlKhod, as well as a 1.5 million cubic metre catchment area at Wadi Hilti near Sohar and Soham.

The Ministry of Agriculture and Fisheries is also trying to repair as many as 5 000 falaj. The falaj conduct water either under or above ground from the river valleys to the land where it is needed. The falaj is very often the centre of village life as well as the basis of the country's irrigation system in all areas other than on the Musandam Peninsula in northern Oman and south in Dhofar province. By 1985, 5 000 falaj have been repaired and in operation.

Incentives to farmers include providing financial assistance through the Agricultural and Fisheries Development Bank which was established in 1980. Capitalized at $55 million, it has already distributed over $20 million in loans. The government is also providing farmers with equipment and technical assistance.

The fisheries sector in Oman is doing quite well. The country's present fishing haul is approximately 70 000 tons. The government is hoping to increase the present yield five times when the new storage, refrigeration and marketing facilities are completed.

INSURANCE: DECLINING GULF MARKETS

Falling oil revenues and the consequent shrinkage of business in the Gulf have had their effects on the formerly thriving insurance and reinsurance markets in the region. In the last two years it is estimated that the region's insurance market has dropped between 30% and 40%. However insurance companies are still optimistic. Some even see the current situation as a blessing in disguise because it has created an awareness among businessmen, importers, and even laymen about the advantages of having insurance coverage.

Insurers in the region have been in the habit of passing on all, or nearly all, of the risks they incur to insurers in London and the other international markets. Much of the bad business that has been passed on was accepted partly because of the poor loss record information on the area. However, as losses have accumulated, reinsurers have attempted to become more stringent about the terms under which they will accept business from the area.

The start up in July 1981 of Arab Insurance group (ARIG) with head quarters in Bahrain and paid up capital of $150 million was seen as a step towards breaking foreign domination of the region's reinsurance capacity. As an Arab based reinsurance company, it was hoped that ARIG would retain some of the premiums which had been flowing out of the region. In 1984 the company was deriving 32% of its income from the Arab world, and had had by then only a limited effect on the market. About 40% of ARIG's gross written premium came from facultative insurance.

During the boom years of the 70s, cargo-all-risk represented the largest sector of insurance business in the region, taking up 40% of the total value premiums which peaked in 1982 at $1500 million. In 1984–85 cargo-all-risk was estimated at about 20%, while cargo and marine hull made up 35% and fire cover at least 30% of total value. Motor insurance is less profitable in the region than elsewhere because of the high accident rate especially in Saudi Arabia and the high cost of repairs.

Medical insurance in the region has begun to pick up – companies are opting more often for providing group medical insurance for employees and their families. Workmen's compensation and life insurance are also picking up and the benefit market in general is thought to be one of the fastest growing in the region.

Shipping insurance, once a very profitable business, now seems riskier. The marine sector had suffered from the downturn in the region's oil exports and the decline in the number of cargo ships serving the Gulf. The situation is not helped by the proliferation of insurance companies trying to capture a portion of the dwindling business opportunities in this market. The fierce competition has reduced premium rates by 20% to 30% in 1984–85.

One sector that might generate more business is agriculture. The number of farms and agricultural products has been on the rise, and increasingly more of these businesses are seeking proper insurance.

Fire insurance has also been on the rise covering factories, houses, warehouses, personal belongings, vehicles and other valuable assets. Equally important is the increase in private political and war risk insurance, particularly since the start of the Iran-Iraq war in 1980. The main risks covered here include expropriation, inconvertibility, premature calling of bonds, payment problems that contractors are increasingly facing when working on governments' related projects, and of course, risk against acts of war by Iran and Iraq.

A novel concept in insurance was introduced to the region with the opening in 1980 of the Islamic Insurance Company in Khartum with a branch office in Jeddah. The basic difference between conventional and Islamic insurance is that the latter is operated on co-operative basis, with no profits returned to the parent company. In the five years since its inception the Islamic Insurance Company grew by around 500% and established branches and representative offices in various cities in the Gulf.

The Geneva based Islamic financial institution 'Dar al Maal Al Islami', established at the Islamic Takafol Company in Bahrain to provide insurance to all the Gulf countries in accordance with Islamic principles. Saudi Arabia also established in 1985 an Islamic Insurance Company called the National Company for Co-operative Insurance. The company which has the backing of the Saudi government is capitalized at $115 million. Islamic insurance will, therefore, present a major challenge to existing conventional insurance companies operating in the region.

Throughout the GCC region legislation is being introduced to regulate the insurance business as well as to ensure a greater local role. Kuwait, UAE, Qatar, Bahrain and Oman all have legislation to differing degrees. All insist on the local registration of insurance companies while Kuwait and Bahrain restrict the number of companies allowed to operate in their respective domestic markets. A new legislation in the UAE specifies a certain minimum capital of around $2.7 million for an insurance company to operate in the country. This makes it very difficult for all non-UAE companies to maintain profitable operations in the country. This follows a similar legislation introduced in Oman in 1982.

Other than Islamic insurance companies, no insurance companies are incorporated in Saudi Arabia. There is a multitude of agents, however, many of them of foreign companies and also of Saudi Companies registered offshore in Bahrain or elsewhere. All these companies compete for business in the Kingdom's insurance premium income market which in 1985 was estimated to worth over $1 billion.

Kuwait enjoys the most successful and dynamic insurance company sector in the Gulf, and to that effect, in the whole Arab world. This sector is highly developed and enjoys the support of the Kuwaiti government. In 1983–84, five Kuwaiti insurance companies figured among the ten most profitable insurance companies in the Arab world.

The Arab Commercial Enterprises Group of Companies (ACE) analysed the performance of the various Arab insurance companies and gave the following ranking by descending order of profits for the top 12 Gulf insurance companies.

ACE found that a dramatic drop in return on equity was encountered by the group as a whole. Most of the companies continued to be overcapitalized – for the premium levels written. ARIG and Abu Dhabi National Insurance Company were following the most conservative approach to the writing and retention of risk relative to their capital.

To conclude, the insurance sector in the Gulf region will continue

Rank 1982	Rank 1983	Company
2	1	Abu Dhabi National Insurance Co. – UAE
1	2	Kuwait Insurance Co. – Kuwait
4	3	Arab Insurance Group – Bahrain
5	4	Al Ahlia Insurance Co. – Kuwait
3	5	Gulf Insurance Co. – Kuwait
7	6	Qatar General Insurance Co. – Kuwait
6	7	Kuwait Reinsurance Co. – Kuwait
8	8	Qatar Insurance Co. – Qatar
9	9	Warba Insurance Co. – Kuwait
10	10	Saudi Arabia Insurance Co. – Bermuda
11	11	Oman National Insurance Co. – Oman
12	12	Oman Insurance Co. – Dubai

to attempt to survive the difficult times ahead, hopefully, without major disasters. Ignorance and undue risk are pitfalls that insurance companies cannot afford to live with. Companies that are long on management talent and expertise and short on adventurism will be able to survive the ruggedness of the market place in the second half of the 80s.

The following trends can be discerned in the Gulf insurance markets over the coming few years (Table 10.4):

1. Political insurance: the importance of this will increase as commercial contacts with the rest of the world expand.
2. Reinsurance: Gulf insurers will have to diversify their sources of reinsurance. This is because of increasing demand at a time when world reinsurance capacity is contracting for both facultative and treaty business; in addition, there is concern about the quality of reinsurers' security. To reduce their dependence on non-GCC markets, Gulf insurance companies are trying to maximise retention at national and regional levels, and create additional reinsurance capacity within local markets. The emergence of more national reinsurance companies – and joint ventures – is a strong possibility.
3. Policy conditions: these are likely to become more standardized as common legislation is introduced.
4. Banking: insurance and banking services may be combined in the same institutions, where laws allow, to provide a wider range of service – from guarantees and sureties to straightforward motor policies.

Table 10.4 Gulf national insurance companies: gross direct life and non-life premium, by class of business, 1984

		Non-Marine					Aviation Marine					Life	
Country	Fire/oil	Engin-eering	Motor	General accident	Misc	Total Non-marine	Aviation/marine	Cargo	Hull	Total Aviation/marine	Total Non-life	Total life	Total
Bahrain	11.55	5.54	11.85	–	2.65	31.59	1.63	4.62	12.49	18.74	50.33	–	50.33
Kuwait	28.76	22.67	49.09	18.39	11.87	130.78	(b)	54.76	(b)	54.76	185.54[a]	26.90	212.41
Oman	7.60	3.85	19.63	1.24	2.61	34.93	2.03	6.01	1.24	9.28	44.21	–	44.21
Qatar	14.85	(c)	11.25	0.59	13.11	39.80	(b)	13.00	(b)	13.00	52.80	–	52.80
Saudi Arabia	113.08	81.67	114.49	–	100.51	439.75	(b)	188.46	(b)	188.46	628.21[a]	–	628.21
UAE	23.98	14.66	17.32	13.32	4.00	73.28	7.99	9.33	42.63	59.95	133.23[a]	3.96	137.19

Note
[a] Estimated.
Combined: [b] Hull, cargo and aviation; [c] Engineering and miscellaneous.

Source
Arig statistics and research unit, 1986.

5. Islamic insurance: demand for insurance to conform to Islamic principles is growing in the Arab countries. Islamic insurance and reinsurance companies – known as co-operatives – are expected to expand in numbers and importance.

THE UPS AND DOWN OF GULF AVIATION

The boom days for airlines serving lucrative roots in the Gulf appear to be over and companies are fiercely competing for passengers in a shrinking market. The economic slowdown in the region, and the consequent readjustment of the countries' needs for expertise from industrial countries and labour from Asia, are major factors behind the decline. The Iran–Iraq war also had an adverse impact on the Gulf aviation market.

The Gulf aviation market reached a peak in the late 70s when the Gulf states were experiencing unprecedented boom conditions. In 1984, air transport in the region generated more than $7 billion. Of this Saudia, Kuwait Airways and Gulf Air got $2 billion, while the rest went to foreign airlines serving the six Gulf countries.

The most lucrative rout for airlines serving the region has been to and from the Indian subcontinent, carrying Indian, Pakistani and Sri Lankan workers to the Gulf to work on construction and other projects. However, with the completion of most of the infrastructural projects, the GCC countries started in 1983–84 to cut back on the number of workers from the subcontinent, as well as from the Philippines, South Korea, Taiwan and Thailand. This had noticeably affected airlines based in the region.

Other factors working against higher air traffic to and from the region are consumer spending patterns and the fact that the Gulf states are not noted tourist areas. Expatriates tend to see their assignment in the Gulf first and foremost as a way of saving money. Flying, unless on business or homeleave, is low on their list of priorities.

After several years of fast expansion in both passenger and freight traffic, the Gulf region showed a decline in the overall growth rate in 1984. For example, on the Middle East–Far East routes IATA statistics show that passenger traffic increased by 11% in 1984 compared to the 25% average growth rate recorded on these routes between 1978–83. On the Gulf–European routes passenger traffic

Table 10.5 Gulf Carriers Ranked by Size[a] (at 31 December 1984)

	Size of fleet	RTK million (MM) MM	RTK million (MM) % change 83/84	Passengers 000s	Passengers % change 83/84	Freight Tonnes 00s	Freight Tonnes % change 83/84	Net result $ MM
Saudia	76	1,883	6.5	11,366	1.8	164	6.3	105.5
Gulf Air	20	554	25.3	2,697	12.0	50	21.2	61.5
Kuwait Airways	21	528	7.1	1,498	−2.4	49	18.9	60.0

Note
[a] Ranked in order of size, measured in Revenue-Ton-Kilometres, RTK, 1984.

Source
IATA, World Air Transport Statistics, 1984.

growth in 1984 was around 6% down from the double digit growth rates recorded in the years before.

Freight figures were more encouraging. Traffic on Middle East–Far East routes increased by 36% in 1984, while that on Middle East–European routes was up 18%, against an average world wide increase of 14% for that year.

The region leading carrier for both passengers and freight was Saudia, with its fleet of 76 aircraft, the airline was ranked sixteenth in the world in terms of revenue–ton–kilometers (RTK the industry yardstick for comparing airline performance combining freight and passenger figures). Next came Gulf Air (37) followed by Kuwait Airways (39).

The three Gulf carriers recorded reasonable profits in 1984 (see Table 10.5). However, not much improvement in profits are forecasted for 1985 and 1986.

Only Kuwait Airways showed a decline of 2.4% in the number of passengers using the airline in 1984, in contrast to growth rates of up to 15% in previous years. This was especially due to the limitation placed on the number of entry visas issued to foreign visitors. The situation is not expected to improve in 1985 and 1986, and the number of passengers using Kuwait Airways is further forecast to drop by up to 10% in these two years.

Gulf Air continues to be profitable and it is believed to be the most efficiently run air carrier in the region. The company is going public and it is planning to offer its airline shares to citizens of the owner countries – Bahrain, UAE, Qatar and Oman. The airline joint ownership gives Gulf Air certain advantages. It has as a base a number of high density travel destinations. Doha, the capital of Qatar, for example, handles over a million arrivals a year in a country with a population of only 250 000. Dubai and Bahrain are international transit centres of major importance and carry many times that load.

If each of Gulfair's four owner states established its own airline, the profitability would quickly disappear into overhead and infrastructure. And Gulfair has been strengthening its advantage by using profits to boost the number of regional connecting flights around the Gulf, adding new international destinations, and offering a range of special family-price tickets and other concessions to its Gulf clientele.

In October 1985, the region witnessed the birth of a fourth airline – Emirates Airlines, which began service between Dubai, Karachi and Bombay. Dubai justified its move to set up its own airline as necessary to meet the air traffic requirements of the area and to boost the national economy. Dubai, which handles more international airlines than any other airport in the region, tends to be a haven for passengers seeking substantial discounts on fares. Ticket sales in Dubai alone were estimated at around $300 million a year in 1985.

Following Dubai's move, Gulf Air launched a plan to set up four specialized Arab Gulf air transport companies under the auspices of the Gulf Cooperation Council. One of the four companies would be an international passenger transport company merging the international wings of Gulf Air, Saudia and Kuwait Airways. The other three specialized companies would deal in regional passenger transport, freight, and an air taxi service. Gulf Air officials suggest that this approach would increase collective profits by rationalization and that undue competition would fragment profits by losing business to foreign airlines.

Perhaps the prospects for Gulf cooperation in the skies will be clearer in the coming few years. For the moment, air fares to the Gulf form almost any part of the world will remain high and thus leave room for the discounting that aviation officials in the region say they wish to stop. And whether the travelling public would be better served by what would in effect be a single monopoly airline or by several smaller airlines is a question that has yet to be answered.

BUSINESS DECLINE AFFECT HOTELS

The hotel industry in the Gulf has been noticeably affected by the slowdown of economic conditions in the region and the limit on the number of entry visas issued to foreign visitors. The industry depended largely on visiting businessmen who make up about 70% of those staying at five-star hotels. Tourism to the GCC countries from outside the region is rather limited. There is however a noticeable flow of tourists and vacationers from Saudi Arabia, Qatar and Kuwait to the lower Emirates of Bahrain and Dubai, considered to be the entertainment centres of the region.

The oversupply of hotel rooms is another factor for the declining profits of first class hotels in the region. The hotel sector began attracting investors since the late 1960s and responding to the economic boom conditions in the region governments issued permits to establish more hotels. But after the boom of the 70s the number of operating hotels began to exceed the region's needs, and this had led to a considerable surplus of rooms. Many hotels have been suffering a sharp decline in revenues.

There are as well many apartment buildings in the region that are operating like hotels but without a licence. These operations have also contributed to the decline in hotel revenues.

The average occupancy rates for five-star hotels over the past six years are estimated as follows:

	%
1978	91
1979	80
1980	82
1981	70
1982	58
1983	53
1984	47
1985	40 (estimated)

Turning to individual countries, the number of visitors to Bahrain is likely to increase once the causeway link to Saudi Arabia is opened towards the end of 1986. More than 154 000 Gulf nationals went to Bahrain for tourism in 1984, a figure which is expected to increase. On the other hand, efforts to boost 'stop over tourism' by passengers transiting through Bahrain Airport have proved unsuccessful. There are no international package tours. Average room occupancy rate in 1985 was 56.8% – 4.7% less than in 1984. Total revenues fell by 12.6% from 1984 to 1985.

Kuwait now has an overcapacity in international class hotels, and these are affected by high prices for food and drinks. The ban on alcohol means that the beverage industry is small, and prices for softdrinks tend to be high. Like other businesses in Kuwait, hotels are heavily dependent upon expatriate staff. Room occupancy rates have fallen since 1984 more than half to 25%.

In Saudi Arabia, while even four years ago finding hotel accommodation could be 'a nightmare' the report says, the situation today is much better with a good choice of accommodation in all main towns in the Kingdom. Even so, during the busy period – October–April – hotels tend to be heavily booked. The average room occupancy rate is 61% and has been going up recently.

The UAE, not having a tourism industry and suffering from the deterioration in business, saw a 12.1% decline in room occupancy rates, during 1984–85, to 51.5%. Total revenues fell 13.1%.

The service and efficiency of the top Gulf hotels compare favourably with the best hotels in the world. Unlike in many other countries, hotels in the Gulf are geared heavily toward businessmen rather than tourists, and thus face strong competitive demands to provide fast, 24-hour-a-day service plus other amenities, such as reliable telephone and telex services. It is worth noting that Gulf hotel prices, which have not increased in the last three years, are now relatively inexpensive compared to hotels in other parts of the world.

Hotel owners are alarmed about the deteriorating situation, and many are working hard, seeking a way out. They are urging the GCC governments to ease visa restrictions in order to allow more businessmen into the region, and to close down illegal hotel operations. They are also calling on the government to make it easier for expatriates who have a residence status in one of the GCC countries to travel to the other countries in the GCC region.

A drastic reduction in the number of foreigners residing in the region is forecast for the coming few years. However, as the cost of sending a visitor on several trips to the Gulf will be less than maintaining him full time there, companies looking to improve the efficiency of their operations will choose to operate from outside the region and increase their business trips there. The drop in hotel revenues due to the present economic slowdown is, therefore, expected to be partially offset by the changing business environment. Hotel occupancy is projected to continue to be depressed throughout the 80s before possibly picking up in the 90s.

SHIPPING SUFFERING A SLUMP

Activities at various Gulf ports continued to slow in the last few years reflecting declining economic growth, drop in oil exports, over capacity in the world shipping industry, fears about sending goods close to the Gulf war zone and unfair competition by foreign shipping firms.

The number of ships calling at the Dammam port in Saudi Arabia, for example fell by around 30% in the first 6 months of 1985 over the same period a year ago. Bahrain, Kuwait, Abu Dhabi and Dubai all recorded a noticeable drop in traffic at their respective ports. All kinds of vessels were effected with general freighters and bulk cement carriers showing the greatest decrease in port calls.

All construction materials have recorded a major drop in 1984–85. According to the Saudi Seaport Authority, imports of steel to the Kingdom were down by 25% in 1985, timber and construction materials were down by 21% and imports of heavy transport equipment decreased by 15%. Overall imports by the construction industry in the Kingdom were down by 35% from a year ago.

Consumer goods imported through Dammam fell by more than 46% during the first 6 months of 1985 compared to the same period a year ago. The corresponding drop in imports at Kuwait's port was 40%, Qatar 35% and the drop was around 30%, on the average, at the ports of the UAE. Only Oman witnessed a noticeable increase in the number of ships calling at its ports during 1984 and the first 6 months of 1985.

The Arabian Gulf is governed by an agreement among main nine shipping companies operating in the area. That resulted in maintaining the shipping rates at acceptable levels unlike the Red Sea, which is not governed by any agreement and that led to a 25% drop in shipping fares in 1984 alone.

Shipping companies in the Gulf are, therefore, struggling to keep their heads above water. The United Arab Shipping Company (UASC) which regards itself as the number one carrier in the Gulf and is among the top cargo carriers in the world exemplifies the difficulties facing Gulf shipping companies in general. Established in the mid-70s with an authorized capital of $1590 million, jointly owned by Saudi Arabia, Bahrain, Kuwait, Qatar and Iraq and with a massive fleet of 60 vessels, the company recorded losses of around $39 million in 1983 and $11.1 million in 1984. Results of 1985 and 1986 are not expected to be much better.

United Arab Shipping Company has just completed a major rationalization programme to meet the Middle East's changing trade needs. The cornerstone of the company's new strategy is the decision to terminate several key services at Fujairah, outside the Strait of Hormuz. The move, completed towards the end of last year, allows UASC greater flexibility so that transhipment-based services can be relayed over the port. UASC is also able to funnel boxes onto inbound ships to ensure maximum load factors once vessels have discharged some containers at Jeddah.

Meanwhile, UASC continues to expand its non-liner activities. In joint venture with National Shipping Company of Saudi Arabia (NSCSA) it is to operate a 41 000 dwt chemicals carrier, which will carry products for Jubail's Saudi Petrochemical Company (Sadaf). Delivery of the vessel, which is being built by South Korea's Daewoo Shipbuilding is scheduled for 1986.

Despite the general gloom, the future of some specialist operations appear to be more promising. Attention is drawn to the success of Kuwait Oil Tanker Company (KOTC) – a wholly owned subsidiary of Kuwait Petroleum Corporation (KPC) – which prudently moved into large-scale shipping of refined products as the rates for crude carriers declined. KOTC has pioneered the very-large-products-carrier (VLPC) concept to move cargoes to KPC's Rotterdam oil terminal. The 290 085 dwt Al-Funtas is already operating in a VLPC role, and two other large crude carriers are earmarked for conversion in 1987.

In addition, four liquefied petroleum gas (LPG) carriers each with a capacity of 72 000 cubic metres, trading between Kuwait/Turkey/Japan are on long term contracts until 1990. Three very large crude carriers (VLCCs) are deployed on Kuwait's shuttle service, carrying crude and refined products to clients' tankers off Fujairah, in the Gulf of Oman. The vessels, acquired in late 1984, give KPC security over its oil exports and some control of rates.

National carriers are getting special treatment from their respective governments, in an effort to boost their profitability and reduce competition from foreign shipping companies. A royal decree issued in early 1985 requiring all consignments for ministries, public establishments and contractors in Saudi Arabia to be carried by Saudi vessels whenever possible. Similar resolutions are expected to be put forth by the other GCC countries.

Over the last few years, a number of prominent shipping lines have disappeared from the Gulf trade. Others have developed joint service and slot-charter agreements with competitors in order to survive. The result has been fewer large vessels calling at Gulf ports.

Those deepsea lines which continue to serve Gulf have cut back on the number of ports on their direct sailing schedules, developing instead more mother ship/feeder vessel systems. For the ports, this has meant a battle to secure mother port status and the substantial transhipment traffic that tends to go with it, rather than settling for a second-tier role as a calling point for feeder vessels.

Efforts to alleviate competition between ports through political channels have yet to bear fruit. The GCC, for example, has in recent years tried to encourage member states to look at ways to reduce some of the more damaging competition.

The co-operation between the different Gulf states was needed before they all rushed ahead with their own major port developments. Now the facilities are established it would be asking a lot to expect anyone to step back and not try to sell them as hard as they can, particularly now the economic situation as a whole is not as bright as it was a few years ago.

Prominent in the field of Gulf transhipment operations is Port Rashid in Dubai, commonly referred to as Dubai port. Building on Dubai's longstanding tradition as a trading centre, about 70% of the port's annual cargo tonnage of more than 6 million tons involves transhipment traffic. In addition to the Gulf, Dubai serves as a transhipment point for traffic to and from the Indian subcontinent and the Far East.

Dubai port's chief rival in Bahrain's Mina Sulman, which handles over 100 000 TEUs a year. The port has about 600 metres of container berth, allowing it to handle two third-generation container ships at the same time, and is considering replacing the old finger pier which is used for conventional cargo.

It remains to be seen whether the new Bahrain–Saudi Arabia causeway, due to be opened this year, will boost Mina Sulman's transhipment role by attracting more Saudi traffic or threaten it by routing more freight through Saudi ports such as Dammam and Jubail.

After Mina Sulman and Dubai port comes Jebel Ali in Dubai, with about 70 berths supporting a major industrial zone of the same name; Mina Khalid in Sharjah, slowly recovering from the loss of its major customer, Hellenic Lines, a couple of years ago; and Mina Zayed in Abu Dhabi.

With the Iran–Iraq war showing no signs of ending, international shipping lines and some of the Gulf states have displayed renewed interest in using ports outside the Gulf itself. The boarding by Iranian military personnel of certain merchant vessels and the fact that vessels kept out of the Gulf war zone attract lower insurance premiums must have increased that interest. Ports that might benefit are Fujairah and Sharjah's Khor Fakkan in the Gulf of Oman.

To conclude the overcapacity in the world shipping industry is expected to prevail in the coming few years and possibly into the 90s. This will have a negative impact on the indigenous shipping activities in the Gulf. The problems in the region are further compounded by declining oil exports and the ongoing Iran–Iraq war. Until the Iraq and Iran markets for shipping services are opened again Gulf companies will have to turn to other markets to consolidate their activities. They need as well to introduce new services and find ways and means to trim costs. They should at least be able to cover their operating costs during the current slump of business activities so that when the regional economics start to ride the upward portion of the business cycle, Gulf shipping would be well positioned for a profitable take off.

11 Country Credit Analysis in the GCC Region

INTRODUCTION

In the last few years international business confidence in the GCC region has been somewhat shaken by the ongoing Iran–Iraq war, the decline in the region's oil revenues. The Manakh Stock Market Crisis in Kuwait, and the overall retrenchment of economic activities.

The international banking community and the Western media at large have been over-alarmed by what they perceive as destabilizing elements adversely affecting the stability and prosperity of the GCC countries. They now envisage the Gulf as a higher risk region. Our assessment of the situation is not that daunting. On the contrary, the outlook for internal stability of the GCC countries continues to be favourable. One can simulate various destabilizing scenarios but none of them appears to be imminent in the near future. Economically, even with the retrenchment of activities, the region still provides the largest concentration of commercial opportunities in the developing world, and the present transitory stage will eventually see the Gulf countries placing themselves on a more stable and normal growth path.

The rise of fundamentalism is often cited by the Western media as a major threat to the internal stability of the various GCC countries. The resurgence of fundamentalism came mainly as a response to the failure of the earlier secular Arab ideologies. It provides the new generation in search for traditional values, heritage and identity, a viable alternative which cannot be readily criticized by the authorities. The current regimes are not alien to this phenomenon, they too are conservative and adhere to traditional values, and the stability of the region has been the result of the strong religious elements that touch on every aspect of life in the GCC countries. A broad school of thought perceive fundamentalism as a passing phenomenon just as were the various nationalist ideologies of the 50s and 70s.

Far from being the fragile political structures which several western policy makers often characterize, the Gulf regimes are reinforced by social dynamics which make radical political change very difficult. The GCC states host a large community of expatriates who perceive these countries as their second home and are generally not susceptible to politicization. The most recent statistics show that the proportion of the labour force constituted by non nationals now stands at 90.3% for the United Arab Emirates, 84.5% for Qatar, 78.6% for Kuwait, 58.6% for Bahrain, 48.7% for Oman, and 46.6% for Saudi Arabia. The introduction of a substantial migrant labour community into the GCC countries, therefore, has created political dynamics in the Gulf fundamentally different from those which have followed from economic development elsewhere in the developing world.

A noticeable characteristic of the Gulf states is the predominance of commerce in the socio-economic structure of these countries. Some 21% of the United Arab Emirates' labour force is employed in commerce, as is some 19% of Kuwait's labour force, and some 16.5% of Saudia Arabia's labour force. These are substantially higher percentages than those which would hold for non-oil Arab economies. This has significant socio-political implications. The interests of the regimes and the interests of the import–export merchants tend to be closely intertwined. As the economic well-being of the merchants depends on the maintenance of a stable relationship between the Gulf states and the advanced capitalist world, the merchants effectively act as a 'liaison group' strengthening and protecting this relationship.

The development of an unusually large state administrative sector is another characteristic of the Gulf economies. Statistics reveal that the state administrative sector in the Gulf countries employs a considerably higher proportion of the total labour force than what is normally the case in non-oil producing Arab countries. That sector employs 55.9% of the total labour force in Kuwait, 29.3% of the labour force in the United Arab Emirates and 26.1% of the labour force in Saudi Arabia. The large state administrative sector, while creating a 'new middle class' whose values may be different from those of traditional Gulf society, also puts new instruments of management and control into the governments' hands. The impact of peasants and nomads on the political dynamics of the state loses significance.

The main destabilizing element in the region continues to be the ongoing Iran–Iraq war, the present economic slowdown and the repercussions of the Manakh Stock Market crisis in Kuwait.

THE SOCIO-POLITICAL EFFECTS OF THE RECESSION

The present economic slowdown has not yet reflected negatively on the internal socio-political stability of the region. Nevertheless, as the present recession becomes well entrenched, and as subsidies are slashed and taxes gradually raised, the high standard of living that people have been accustomed to is going to be harder to maintain. There is a growing fear that unfulfilled economic expectations could fuel feelings of resentment that has been subdued by economic prosperity up till now. The strains of the recession would gradually hit a wider spectrum of the social circles and outside powers could find certain sectors of the region's population a fertile soil for instigating internal trouble and disorder.

After more than a decade of booming business conditions, businessmen may find working in a 'normal' economy less pleasant than they expected. It may also be that young people just leaving university will be dissatisfied when they realize that they cannot earn the incomes that they had expected to get, or that their predecessors who left in the 70s used to earn.

Nevertheless, the region as a whole remains to be politically stable. It is still widely noticeable that people who used to be loyal, prosperous and conservative, albeit liable to complain about government policies in a general way, are still basically loyal and very much nationalistic. Perhaps they are a bit more disturbed now, but they are gradually learning to adapt to the new economic reality.

As a matter of fact, a fairly large segment of the population is not at all unhappy with the slowdown in economic activities of the region. Both the conservative sector of population and an increasing number of liberal intellectuals perceived the rapid pace of industrialization and modernization of recent years as being wasteful and has undermined the region's traditional Islamic values. Increasing competition is perceived as one way for the economy to gradually become more efficient. This could also be an opportunity to introduce a more rigorous work ethic and develop a more productive indigenous work force. Accordingly, lower oil revenues and slower economic growth is believed to give GCC governments the time needed to carry out reassessment of their economic, social and political development goals.

THE IRAN–IRAQ WAR

The most likely course of the war is a continuation of hostilities involving air and sea attacks on civilian targets as well as on tankers and oil terminals in the Gulf generating moderate disruptions of oil supplies. International pressure exercised on the warring countries may well guarantee that supply of oil from the Gulf will not be halted completely, nor for a long period of time. Piecemeal arms supplies to the two countries guarantees that the conflict will continue and that there will be no victorious party capable of imposing terms and spreading its influence in the region.

The fear of an Iranian victory enticed the USSR to move back towards Baghdad after maintaining an uneasy neutrality for the first three years of the war. This has been a vital change since USSR supply Iraq with two-thirds of its arms. The tilt by the US towards Iraq is less significant but it shows that USA is also worried of the consequences that an Iranian breakthrough in the war could have on the whole region.

The least likely end to the war is for either side to be victorious. It is more likely that the war would continue until economic and military attrition wear down the two warring countries and a sizeable part of the region's resources are exhausted. Many of Iran's leaders argue that Iran's superior resources could give it a decisive advantage in a long war. Iran can draw on thousands of volunteers from its large population of 44 million. Its estimated $5 to $10 billion annual income from oil revenues flowing at the rate of 1.2 mb/d plus barter deals seems to be just enough to fund the war expenses and pay the bill for essential imports for years to come.

Iraq seems to be near success in reversing the long term deterioration in its financial position brought about by the war. It is also preparing itself for a war that may go on for a long period of time. Iraq is planning to expand its oil exports from the mid-1985 level of around 1 mb/d (annual oil revenues of around $9.5 billion), to 1.5 mb/d by 1986 and up to 2 mb/d by 1987. Iraq could also count on continued aid and soft loans from the neighbouring Arab countries, however, at much smaller amounts than what it used to get before. The war between Iran and Iraq has curtailed significantly the oil production and export capacity of these two countries. This has eased considerably OPEC's difficult task of allocating quotas in recent years, when requirements for the cartel's crude oil were declining sharply. Because an end to the war would raise export potentials of the two countries, it could prove disruptive to the cartel's allocation process.

Iran was OPEC's second largest producer in 1978. However, after the war output fell from over 5 million b/d in 1978 to 1.4 million b/d in 1981. By late 1985, and during most of 1986, and after Iran's main oil terminal at Kharg Island became a war target for Iraq and was continuously raided by Iraqi planes, Iran's export capacity dropped further to 700 000 b/d.

It is impossible to assess precisely what Iran's production capacity would be if the war ended, given the lack of information of the damage of Iranian oil fields. A conservative estimate suggests that Iran's production capacity could increase by 1 mb/d within six months of a cease-fire and by 2 mb/d within a year.

Unlike Iran, oil field in Iraq have not been damaged seriously by the war. Nevertheless, production declined dramatically after 1980 due to Iran's destruction of Iraq's exporting terminals on the Persian Gulf. This was followed by Syria's closure of the pipeline to the Mediterranean. As a result, Iraqi production fell from roughly 3.5 mb/d in 1979 to 800 000 b/d in the early 80s. In 1985, it had recovered to 1.5 mb/d, following the expansion of a pipeline to the Mediterranean through Turkey and the launch of the 500 000 b/d of exports through the new pipeline link to the Yanbu terminal on the Red Sea.

In the 1983–86 period, Iraq has been trying to diversify and expand oil export outlets. Most important were the following

1. The construction of a pipeline linking Iraq's southern oil fields with Petroline, the trans-peninsular pipeline that terminates at Yanbu on the Red Sea. Initial capacity of the link is 500 000 b/d.
2. Another 500 000 b/d expansion of the Dortyol pipeline through Turkey has been agreed to and construction should be completed towards the end of 1986.
3. Within three months of a cease-fire, another 250 000 b/d would be available for loading at an installation that could quickly be constructed at Basra.

In addition, the pipeline through Syria – with a capacity of 1.4 b/d – remains operational and would be available within weeks of a political decision by Damascus to permit the line to reopen.

In summary, the combined exporting capacity of Iran and Iraq together could increase by some 1.25 mb/d within six months of a ceasefire and by almost 3 mb/d within a year. And if the Syrian pipeline were reopened, another 1.4 mb/d of capacity would become available.

Obviously, the end of the war would present OPEC with a difficult reallocation problem. The cartel is not likely to capture more than 18.4 mb/d of the world oil market in 1986–87, roughly comparable to the very depressed years of 1984 and 1985.

Nevertheless, the situation would not be hopeless for OPEC. Even though both Iran and Iraq would push aggressively for increased quotas to rebuild their war-torn economies, it should not be assumed that they would raise production to full capacity. The realities of the market-place should temper their expectations. After all, both countries wish to maximize oil revenues – not necessarily export volumes. They understand that unreasonable increases in their exports would lower oil prices and thus their revenues. In addition, an end to the war would permit a huge transfer of funds from fighting a war to rebuilding the economy.

Finally, two other moderating factors are that Iran has been a strong advocate of production constraints to raise prices, and Iraq owes a heavy political debt to its Arab neighbors in the Gulf.

Given these realities, a combined production increase of some 0.8 mb/d for Iran and Iraq would prove acceptable to these countries. Most of the increase would be assigned to Iraq, (0.5 mb/d), since its exports have been most seriously curtailed by the war. Indeed, even without an end to the war, Iraq's exports will be increasing significantly, in line with the expected increase in pipeline capacity.

The bulk of the quota reductions necessary to accommodate the Iraqi and Iranian increases may end up being made by the Gulf countries. These countries are more financially able to accept meaningful reductions. Moreover, the cutback burden for Saudi Arabia and Kuwait would be eased by eliminating the need to produce 350 000 b/d on account for Iraq.

While an end of the Iran–Iraq war could enhance political stability in the region, the expected decline in the Gulf countries oil revenues – to accommodate larger production quotas by Iran and Iraq – would further accentuate the current depressionary trends in the region.

THE MANAKH STOCK MARKET CRISIS

The Build Up of the Crisis

In August 1982, Souk Al Monakh, the unofficial Kuwait Stock market, came crashing down leaving shock waves still reverberating through Kuwait's and the entire Gulf's financial system.

The whole problem arose because the bulk of the trading on the unofficial stock exchange took place on the basis of undue speculation. While the official stock exchange dealt with the stocks of all Kuwaiti-incorporated companies, the Al-Manakh market traded in the stocks of companies registered elsewhere in the Gulf area. As such, there was no direct government control on the activities of the Manakh market.

In an attempt to slow down expansion of the official stock market the Kuwaiti government restricted the licensing of new Kuwaiti companies. This restriction was maintained for longer than necessary, but while it lasted Kuwaiti entrepreneurs wishing to establish new companies – whether to make cement or invest in real estate – went offshore to the UAE or Bahrain to register the company. An additional attraction of going offshore was the opportunity it offered of avoiding restrictions imposed by Kuwaiti law. The shares in these companies were thus called Gulf securities and were traded over the counter in Souk Al Manakh in Kuwait.

The greatest innovation of Souk Al Manakh was the reliance on post-dated cheques for trading. Shares were brought and sold forward and paid for by post-dated cheques. The mechanism was something like this: A stock trading, for example, at $10 would attract a buyer who would offer to buy the stock, delivery after one year, at $20, expecting the price to double within one year. He then went to a third person who, hoping for continued market upturn, bought it for $30 with the same delivery period. As this trade went on, prices kept ballooning. In the meantime, the second seller, who had a cheque for $30 on hand and a liability of $20, went to someone else and had it discounted for $25. With that much solid cash on hand, he went back to the first seller and proposed to take his $20 cheque back and in return for a payment of $15 right away. The first seller was only too happy to agree because he made straight $5 profit on the deal, while the second seller ended up with a clean $10 gain, with no liability, out of nothing.

As people made their piles, the spot values of shares naturally increased and forward prices skyrocketed as well. In the end, share values on the market went out of all proportions, with absolutely no underlying economic reason for that increase. This created a situation where a large number of people had a large number of both future deliveries and future settlements, and sort of formed an inverse pyramid. If any one element in that pyramid broke loose, the whole structure would follow suit.

Finally, that was exactly what had happened. A lot of the payments became due almost simultaneously in the summer of 1982. Transactions no longer matched, and the process stopped. One default led to another and the whole market collapsed with traders having commitments of over $90 billion.

The crisis badly tarnished the image of Kuwait's financial sector. The government stepped in to protect smaller investors, and worked out a viable formula for the repayment of obligations and a number of people were declared bankrupt.

In 1983, a decree was issued indicating that the premium on post-dated cheques can be no more than 25% of the value of shares sold at the time of transactions (law 100/83).

The simultaneous admission to full listing of eight selected Gulf companies represented the first step towards the formation of a unified market. This was carried a stage further in November 1984 when the Manakh market was closed and all trading in unlisted companies transferred to the new stock exchange building.

The Lingering Impact of the Manakh Crisis

Shares of Kuwaiti companies traded on the official stock exchange were adversely affected as well by the crisis. The all-share price index of officially traded Kuwaiti shares plummeted in 1984 by 50% from the artificial price support levels prevailing at the start of the year. In 1985, the price index declined further more by around 39%. Gulf shares, previously dealt in on the Souk Al-Manakh, fell by a similar amount in 1984 and the decline was around 24%. Since no transactions were recorded in the shares of 18 of the 47 listed companies, subsequent to the withdrawal of the government support operation for share prices, the actual decline in realizeable values of all the stock shares certainly exceeded these figures. It is estimated that the decline in 1984 could have reached 70%.

It became obvious that the collapse in prices would have a profound effect on the book values of the portfolios of those companies that held shares among their assets. It would also change the collateral value of the shares pledged to banks by companies and individuals alike. The focus of concern about the effect of the débâcle has shifted from the fate of individual share traders to the fate of the corporate sector and, more particularly, the banks and financial companies that form its heart.

Largely due to the fall in share prices, borrowers either lacked the liquidity, or refused to liquidate foreign assets to repay their loans and/or to provide additional collateral as the need arose. Likewise, it became difficult, not to mention costly, for a bank to foreclose and sell off whatever collateral it has because selling in a thin share and real-estate market would only accelerate the downward pressure of prices and make the collateral worth even less.

In an effort to stabilize share prices the government spent around $2.5 billion during 1984 and ended up having majority shareholding in most quoted Kuwaiti companies. However, when the government stopped purchasing shares, stock prices resumed their downward slide. The support price mechanism was considered to be against the spirit of the officially recognized free enterprise system. Besides, unless the government starts selling back its stock holdings to the private sector, there would be an extreme shortage of tradeable stock in the market.

The total cost of the crash to the government has been much greater than that. It has spent about $2.9 billion on its small shareholder fund. The fund was set up to bail out those with claims of less than $6.7 million, then reduced to $1.7 million. It has also sunk around $1.3 billion into the commercial banks to bolster their reserves, and has provided at least $1 billion to Kuwait Foreign Trading Contrasting and Investment Company (KFTCIC) and the Kuwait Investment Company (KIC) to provide collateral for debt settlements. The total direct cost of the Manakh crisis by the end of 1985 came to around $8 billion of public funds.

The Government's attempt to bail out companies facing difficulties (e.g. the exchange company of Jawad & Haidar Y. Abdulhassan) with public funds has added fuel to the fire of the debate in the assembly over whether to allow more public funds to be used in the effort to prop up mismanaged enterprises or simply allow these institutions to go into gradual liquidation on their own.

The effect of the crash on the banks have been substantial. Of the $16.5 billion in private sector debts to banks in 1985, it was estimated that non-performing and doubtful loans stood at around $5 to $6 billion or 40% of all domestic loan commitment. The growing number of doubtful loans threatened to deprive banks of substantial interest income. The estimated bank reserves both hidden and published amounted to around $5 billion in 1984. Even though, not all these reserves are available in readily realizable form some could still be used to smooth the effect of loan provisions in the coming few years.

Two majority state-owned companies, the Kuwait Foreign Trading, Contracting and Investment Co. (KFTCIC), over 90% Government-held, and the Kuwait Investment Company. (KIC), over 60% government-held, recorded financial losses because of the collapse of Souk Al Manakh. They were subsequently transformed by the Government into funding vehicles for assisting investors with liquidity problems. KIC's losses increased to $107 million in 1984 from $64 million in 1983. KIC, in fact, wrote off its losses against its reserves resulting in a reduction of shareholders' equity by 44% to $197 million in 1984 from $350 million in 1982, the year of the crisis.

The near future is likely to see the liquidation of several unviable Gulf and closed shareholding companies, and mergers between others. However, there are limits to the financial collapse which the Kuwait Government would be willing to allow when the country's international reputation is at stake.

It is important to differentiate between two 'tiers' of Kuwait's financial institutions. The first tier comprises the big commercial banks and investment companies which have unconditional and guaranteed government support through access to the Central Bank's discount window, swap and loan facilities. Their credit standing is, in a sense, as good as the state itself, because at least for first-tier firms in a state-supervised capitalist economy like Kuwait's, the line demarcating sovereign and private risk is a blurred one.

It is the second tier of the financial institutions, the investment companies and money changes, whose status with government support in times of need is not very clear. Here it is commonly believed that government intervention would be considered on a case by case basis, depending on what the government perceive as the potential damage to the financial system in case of a crisis.

Solving the Problem of Bank Loans

A wide ranging programme to solve the problem of non-performing bank loans has been put forward by the Central Bank of Kuwait in July 1985. The programme calls on the government to make an unlimited financial commitment to support the banking and finance sector, with the possibility that some of the public funds used may not be recovered.

According to the central bank estimates, $1650 million was needed to overcome the bank indebtedness problem, a further $330 was required to support investment companies and money changers. The central bank also wanted all the government's deposits with local banks to be placed under its control. This would give the central bank the flexibility to provide additional cash support, and to place the funds at different interest rates, according to the needs of individual commercial banks. By the end of 1985, the Kuwaiti government had placed deposits worth $10 billion with commercial and specialized banks in the country since 1982.

The programme was considered as a general framework within which the central bank can try to clear bank indebtedness, support the banks' financial positions, and evaluate investment and money changing companies. The viable ones will then be supported and the others liquidated. In October 1985, Kuwaiti authorities suspended trading in shares of Gulf companies presumably until a comprehensive review of the financial status of these companies is completed.

To reduce to a minimum the amount of government financial support needed, the programme intended to encourage banks to write off losses over an appropriate length of time in order to reduce their immediate burdens. The conditions for support was made such that only banks in real need would be tempted to apply. This entailed tightening up supervision of a bank's credit policies, the settlements reached on non-performing loans, and even the administrative expenses of banks seeking support. Public funds could be safeguarded by demanding a share of future profits when a supported bank's position improves.

To conclude, no upward momentum in share prices is likely to be sustainable until all losses due to the crisis are absorbed and all drawbacks that led to the debacle are eliminated. Of the limitations that were still outstanding in 1985: lack of understanding of accepted investment criteria, scarcity of readily available investment analysis and advice and the use of misleading statements in company reports.

The Ministry of Commerce in Kuwait suggested that companies affected by the sharp declines in the market values of their cross shareholding can spread their losses equally over three year period 1985–87 provided no dividends were paid. The years 1985, 1986 and 1987, are expected, therefore, to be lean years for the major financial institutions in Kuwait. Besides, an extended period of time will be required to build up confidence which is currently at very low levels.

COUNTRY CREDIT ANALYSIS IN THE GCC REGION

Country credit analysis seeks to identify those cases where countries are unable to obtain enough foreign currency to meet their external commitments. The analysis also include the evaluation whether certain events, both internal (e.g. economic mismanagement), or external (e.g. country involved in a war), could create debt servicing difficulties or repayment problems.

The chain of events that could lead to a default may be as follows:

Inept economic management ⟶ large budget deficit ⟶ inflation ⟶ fall in domestic savings ⟶ over borrowing from abroad ⟶ debt servicing problems ⟶ default.

The GCC countries are characterized by having low to moderate political risk, very good access to international financial markets, low levels of external debt, and good economic growth prospects. Only Oman and Bahrain among the GCC countries had some long-term debt outstanding in 1985, however, their debt is quite manageable, while the external debt of the other GCC countries was mostly trade related and short term. The six GCC countries have continuously been given high credit rating by major international financial journals.

In 1984, Bahrain's short-term (bank claims and non-bank trade related credit) dropped sharply by around 37% while that of Oman, recorded an increase of 60%. The other GCC countries (Saudi Arabia, Kuwait, Qatar and UAE) have been net exporters of capital, and had little or no external long-term public debt outstanding. Their combined external short-term indebtedness was around $20 billion by the end of 1984. However, their sizeable international reserves always provided ample coverage for their imports and their outstanding short term debts.

The GCC countries' use of supplier credits declined considerably in 1984–85 while use of bank facility has increased. The overall short-term debt structure of these countries have changed with the completion of large infrastructural and industrial projects. With an estimated 25% decline in trade, the region is seen to be shifting from supplier to buyer credits to finance its external short-term transactions.

QUALIFYING COUNTRY RISK ANALYSIS

The following sections summarize the suggested technique for constructing indices aimed at quantifying country risk analysis in the GCC region. The indices are simply weighted averages of scores, varying from 0 to 100, of specific variables.

$$I = \Sigma W_i C_i$$
I = index
W = weights
C_i = score on individual variable
$\Sigma_w = 1$ (sum of the weights should add to one)

The indices are designed to answer two fundamental questions: (1) "Are the country's liquid assets sufficient to cover its immediate needs?"; and (2) "Is the economy sound, well-managed, and capable of generating external revenue in the future?". Accordingly, two indices are constructed for each GCC country: (a) a liquidity index, which measures the adequacy of the country's international assets to meet its current international obligations, principally to pay for imports and to service international debt; and (b) a structural index, which tests for the underlying soundness of the economy. A country is assigned numerical scores for each index: 100 represents the highest score (or the lowest risk), and 0 the lowest score (or the highest risk).

The first step in constructing an index is to choose the indicators to be included. Variables are restricted to those that bear a close and demonstrable relationship to payments difficulties in a large sample of countries (see following sections). Further, only data that are readily available from standard sources such as World Bank, IMF or BIS are utilized.

The information sources that are most easily available for a wide sampling of countries on a uniform basis are: (1) the International

Monetary Fund, International Financial Statistics (IFS); (2) the World Bank's World Debt Tables (WDT); and (3) the data from the Bank for International Settlements (BIS) on the positions in foreign currencies of the banks of the major industrial countries; the assets of these banks *vis-à-vis* a given country closely approximates the debts of the country to the commercial banks of the major industrial countries.

Weighting is based upon the variable's ability to explain payment problems. For example, it may be decided to assign a weight of five for the increase in consumer prices in the most recent year. The inflation rates of all countries in the sample group are arranged from the highest to the lowest and scores are assigned on the basis of where any inflation rate falls in comparison to the inflation rates of all countries. For instance, an inflation rate of 5-7% may yield a score of 60, while a rate of 2-4.9% yields 80. The score is then multiplied by the weight assigned to that indicator and the final index number for a country is then the sum of all its weighted scores.

LIQUIDITY INDEX

The liquidity index is relatively simple to construct, since it involves matching a country's current foreign exchange income or assets to its obligations. The indicators used and the weights assigned to these indicators are shown in Table 11.1. The liquidity indicators include:

Table 11.1 Indicators used in liquidity index

Indicator	Weights (%)
1. Reserves/average monthly imports	40
2. Debt service/export earnings	30
3. Percentage change in short-term debt	10
4. Late payment experience	10
5. IMF credit/quota	10
	100

1. The ratio of foreign reserves to average monthly imports, or what it commonly referred to as foreign reserves in months of import coverage. This ratio indicates how long imports could be main-

tained if revenues suddenly become unavailable (e.g. a halt of oil exports from the Gulf).
2. The current capacity to service debt from exports as represented by the ratio of debt service (interest plus principal repayment) due within a given year to total exports plus net invisibles. That is how much of the country's foreign earnings go for servicing debt.
3. Percentage change in short-term debt which indicates improvement or deterioration in trade and bank related debt situation.
4. Late payment experience which is a clear sign of mismanagement and/or insufficient liquidity. (Any late payment to any creditor automatically results in a score of 0 on this indicator.)
5. Use of IMF credit facilities, which indicates the degree to which a country's financial situation has forced it to use Fund credit and to submit to requirements imposed by an international financial institution.

STRUCTURAL INDEX

The structural index is intended to point out more fundamental problems in the economy and the likelihood of future payments problems, and hence the conceptual underpinnings of the structural index deserve some elaboration. Detailed analysis by country specialists suggests that those countries which experience payments difficulties have certain definable economic traits in common. Specifically, these countries usually pursue improper management policies including expansionary monetary policies where budget deficits are normally financed by the creation of new money leading as a result to high rates of inflation. The governments of these countries typically pursue protectionist industrialization policies and often refuse to make needed exchange rate adjustments. As a result, the country's agriculture and industry tend to be uncompetitive internationally, which makes it very difficult to expand export earnings.

Several quantitative studies employing various forms of correlation analysis have succeeded in relating a sampling of macroeconomic variables to debt rescheduling or payments delay. The economic variables most closely correlated with payments difficulties were found to be inflation, normally generated by excessive money supply growth, high levels of external debt, and overvalued exchange rates. Conversely, the rate of export growth, the rate of real GDP growth, and investment as a share of national income were negatively corre-

Table 11.2 Indicators used in structural index

Indicator	Weight (%)
1. Percentage change in consumer prices (inflation)	10
2. Debt/Export and Invisibles	30
3. Debt/Gross Domestic Product (most recent year)	10
4. Political and social factors	50
	100

lated with payments problems. The suggested approach to building structural index is to select those variables chosen for the Gulf countries that are closely related to payments difficulties, and assign weights on the basis of each indicator's weight as predictor of payment difficulties. The variables and their assigned weights are shown in Table 11.2.

Debt related indicators are clearly very important. More weight is given in the structural index to debt as a percent of export earnings because exports are the principal means of repaying debt. Export earnings include merchandise exports plus such invisibles as income from foreign investment and tourism, shipping receipts, and net transfers.

Political and social factors are among the most important elements in a country risk evaluation. However, the analysis of political factors is difficult due to their subjective nature and their dependence on the analyst's judgement of political affairs.

To come up with a rating for a country's political stability the analyst needs to assign numerical scores to non-numerical events. If a country is perceived to be politically and socially stable it would be given a high percentage score that corresponds to its low risk. The percentage score declines with the increase in political risk as perceived by the analyst.

The six GCC countries are characterized by having low to moderate political risk. The ratings used takes into consideration a set of factors, both external and internal, believed to influence the stability of the respective countries. Given the present political set-up and the well organized internal security forces, the six countries should be able to survive short unexpected political upheavals. Militarily, these countries are less powerful than their neighbours. However, under the GCC military umbrella, they should be able to defend their boarders in case of outside aggression. A score of 80 is given for Saudi Arabia and Oman and a score of 75 for the remaining four Gulf countries.

International reserves of the GCC countries provide a useful cushion in case of a sudden disruption of oil revenues. Most of the countries have more than 4 months of import coverage, and if foreign assets are also considered, Saudi Arabia would have the equivalent of 33 months of imports at the 1983 level, Qatar 26 months, UAE 23 months, and Kuwait more than 100 months. Even though a good part of the GCC's foreign assets may not be readily transferable to cash nevertheless, at least part of these assets could be leveraged and/or turned into liquid assets within a reasonably short period of time.

The debt/exports ratio and the debt service ratio of Bahrain and Oman are quite low in comparison with the other indebted less developed countries. The incidence of debt rescheduling has been considerably higher for countries with debt/exports ratio that exceeded 200% and with debt service ratio of more than 40%. These threshold levels are considerably higher than the estimated ratios of either Oman or Bahrain (Table 11.3).

Liquidity index = 0.4 (score of Reserves in Months of Import Coverage)
+ 0.3 (score of Debt Service Ratio)
+ 0.1 (score of Change in Short-term Debt)
+ 0.1 (score of Late Payment Experience)
+ 0.1 (score of IMF Credi Qota)

The liquidity indices for the various GCC countries are:

Saudi Arabia	= 0.4 (100) + 0.3 (100) + 0.1 (90) + 0.1 (90) + 0.1 (100) = 89
Kuwait	= 0.4 (100) + 0.3 (100) + 0.1 (40) + 0.1 (90) + 0.1 (100) = 84
UAE	= 0.4 (2) + 0.3 (100) + 0.1 (45) + 0.1 (90) + 0.1 (100) = 72.5
Bahrain	= 0.4 (85) + 0.3 (85) + 0.1 (90) + 0.1 (90) + 0.1 (100) = 78.5
Qatar	= 0.4 (80) + 0.3 (100) + 0.1 (85) + 0.1 (90) + 0.1 (100) = 80.5

Table 11.3 Basic indicators and country credit rating in the GCC region ($ million where appropriate)

Countries (ranked according to regional credit rating)	Institutional investor Rank (global) 1986	Credit rating (max. 100) 1986	Long term external debt 1985	Bank and trade related debt 1985	Current account balances 1985	Inflation rate % 1985	Population (million) 1985	Gross Domestic Product 1985	Int. reserves including gold* 1985
S. Arabia	24	64.9	—	13 416	−20 000	1.1	10.4	93 653	100 000
Kuwait	26	62.3	—	8 749	2 759	1.3	1.8	22 458	70 000
UAE	28	58.6	—	8 667	3 808	2.0	1.2	28 781	18 000
Qatar	36	54.2	—	628	−192	1.8	0.28	6 705	15 000
Bahrain	30	56.1	350	553	50	1.5	0.4	5 013	1 368
Oman	35	52.7	1476	1 593	−64	2.5	1.13	8 625	617

Note
* Gold valued at $300 per ounce. For Saudi Arabia, Kuwait, Qatar and UAE this column represents net foreign assets.

Country Credit Analysis

Countries (ranked according to regional credit rating)	Liquidity indicators			Structural indicators				Liquidity index (maximum =100)	Structural index (maximum =100)
	Debt service ratio	Int. reserves in months of import coverage	% Change in short term debt	Political & social factors (lowest risk = score of 100)	Ratio of long-term debt to exports & invisibles	Ratio of long-term debt to GDP			
	1985	1985	1985 (2nd half)	1985	1985	1985		1985	1985
Saudi Arabia	—	11.6	+2.3	80	—	—		89.0	89.0
Kuwait	—	7.7	+8.9	75	—	—		84.0	86.5
UAE	—	3.3	−7.8	75	—	—		72.5	86.5
Qatar	—	4.3	+21.5	15	—	—		80.5	86.5
Bahrain	4	5.0	+8.0	75	13	10		78.5	79.5
Oman	6	3.9	+11.9	80	37	18		68.5	80.0

Oman   = 0.4 (75) + 0.3 (85) + 0.1 (30) +
                    0.1 (90) + 0.1 (100) = 68.5

Structural index = 0.1 (Inflation rate)
                   +0.3 (Debt/Exports and invisibles)
                   +0.1 (Debt/GDP)
                   +0.5 (Political and social factors)

The structural indices for the various GCC countries are:

Saudi Arabia   = 0.1 (90) + 0.3 (100) + 0.1 (100) +
                 0.5 (80) = 89.0
Kuwait   = 0.1 (90) + 0.3 (100) + 0.1 (100) +
                 0.5 (75) = 86.5
UAE   = 0.1 (90) + 0.3 (100) + 0.1 (100) +
                 0.5 (75) = 86.5
Bahrain   = 0.1 (90) + 0.3 (85) + 0.1 (75) +
                 0.5 (75) = 79.5
Qatar   = 0.1 (90) + 0.3 (100) + 0.1 (100) +
                 0.5 (75) = 86.5
Oman   = 0.1 (85) + 0.3 (85) + 0.1 (85) +
                 0.5 (75) = 80.0

Based on the aforementioned indices, the six GCC countries were found to have an overall very good credit rating with Saudi Arabia heading the list followed respectively by Kuwait, UAE, Qatar, Bahrain and Oman. The data available show that the six countries were both liquid and solvent. Their economies appeared to be well managed and the sovereign risk involved in lending to these countries was rather low.

Statistical Appendix

CONTENTS

A1 Total population and agricultural population
A2 Average birth and death rates and life expectancy
A3 Population and percentages of urban and rural population for years 1984, 1985 and 2000
A4 Distribution of population by age (1984 and 1985)
A5 Proven oil reserves (1980–84)
A6 Natural gas proven reserves (1980–84)
A7 Overall capacity of oil refineries
A8 Gross Domestic Product at current price: distribution by sector (1980)
A9 Gross Domestic Product at current price: distribution by sector (1981)
A10 Gross Domestic Product at current price: distribution by sector (1982)
A11 Gross Domestic Product at current price: distribution by sector (1983)
A12 Gross Domestic Product at current price: distribution by sector (1984)
A13 Expenditure on Gross Domestic Product at current prices (1984)
A14 Expenditure on Gross Domestic Product at current prices (1983)
A15 Expenditure on Gross Domestic Product at current prices (1982)
A16 Expenditure on Gross Domestic Product at current prices (1981)
A17 Expenditure on Gross Domestic Product at current prices (1980)
A18 Extracting industries value added at current prices
A19 Extracting industries contribution to GDP
A20 Other industries value added at current prices
A21 Other industries contribution to GDP
A22 Government revenues and percentages to GDP
A23 Surplus or deficit in government budget and % to GDP
A24 Government expenditures and percentages to GDP

Statistical Appendix

A25 Classification of current expenditures
A26 Saudi Arabian budget for the years 1981/82–1985/86
A27 Sectoral appropriations
A28 Saudi Arabia: main budget allocations
A29 Kuwait: budget 1984/85–1985/86
A30 Kuwait's budget for the years 1981/82–1985/86
A31 Qatar's budget 1984/85–1985/86
A32 Qatar's budget for the years 1981/82–1985/86
A33 Oman's budget for the years 1983–85
A34 Bahrain's budget 1982–85
A35 UAE's budget for 1981/82–1985/86
A36 Monetary authorities structure of deposits (1980–84)
A37 Structure of domestic liquidity (1981–84)
A38 Changes in factors affecting domestic liquidity (1982–84)
A39 Ratio of changes in factors affecting domestic liquidity (1982–84)
A40 Commercial banks: structure of deposits and percentages to GDP (1980–84)
A41 Commercial banks: credit structure and % of total credit to GDP (1980–84)
A42 Balance of payments (1979–83)
A43 Exports and imports of agricultural products
A44 International reserves: 1980–84

Table A1 *Total population and agricultural population* (000s)

Country	Year	Total	Agriculture	total	Agriculture	%
UAE	1970	223				
	1980	980				
	1984	1 255				
Saudi Arabia	1970	5 745	3 794	1 575	1 040	66.0
	1980	9 229	5 551	2 383	1 433	60.1
	1984	10 824	6 243	2 744	1 583	57.7
Oman	1970	654				
	1980	978				
	1984	1 181				
Qatar	1970	111				
	1980	246				
	1984	291				
Kuwait	1970	744	13	241	4	1.8
	1980	1 372	23	360	6	1.7
	1984	1 703	28	430	7	1.7
Bahrain	1970	220				
	1980	347				
	1984	414				

Source
FAO, United Nations, June 1985.

Table A2 Average birth and death rates and life expectancy: average of two periods (1980–85) and (1995–2000)

Country	1980–85 Birth (000s)	Death (000s)	Natural growth (000s)	Life expectancy	1995–2000 Birth (000s)	Death (000s)	Natural growth (000s)	Life expectancy
UAE	27.0	4.0	23.0	70.6	20.3	4.3	16.0	73.7
Saudi Arabia	43.0	12.1	30.9	56.0	37.8	7.3	30.5	64.7
Oman	47.3	15.9	31.4	49.7	39.3	10.9	28.4	57.2
Qatar	30.1	4.6	25.5	70.6	31.2	4.7	26.5	73.7
Kuwait	36.8	3.5	33.3	71.2	28.0	3.2	24.8	74.8
Bahrain	32.3	5.3	27.0	68.2	29.2	4.5	24.6	69.8

Source
United Nations, *Estimation & Projection of World Population* (New York, 1984).

Table A3 Population (000s) and percentage of urban and rural population for years 1984, 1985 and 2000

Country	% Population	1984 % Urban	% Rural	Population	1985 % Urban	% Rural	Population	2000 % Urban	% Rural
UAE	1 255	78.0	22.0	1 312	77.7	22.2	1 916	77.8	22.2
Saudi Arabia	10 824	72.0	28	11 240	73.0	27.0	8 864	81.8	18.2
Oman	1 181	9.0	81.0	1 228	8.8	91.2	1 909	15.1	84.9
Qatar	291	88.0	12.0	301	88.0	12.0	469	91.3	8.7
Kuwait	1 703	93.0	7.0	1 785	93.7	6.3	2 969	97.2	2.8
Bahrain	414	81.0	19.0	431	81.7	18.3	688	85.3	14.7

Source
United Nations, *Estimated Projection of World Population* (New York, 1984).

Table A4 Distribution of population by age (1984 and 1985)

Country	0–14 years 1984 Total (000s)	%	1985 Total (000s)	%	15–65 years 1984 Total (000s)	%	1985 Total (000s)	%	over 65 years 1984 Total (000s)	%	1985 Total (000s)	%
UAE	376	30.0	403	30.7	853	68.0	877	66.8	25	2.0	32	2.4
Saudi Arabia	4 654	43.0	4 850	43.1	5 845	54.0	6 086	54.1	325	3.0	304	2.7
Oman	519	44.0	542	44.2	638	54.0	655	53.4	24	2.0	30	2.5
Qatar	100	34.0	102	33.8	183	63.0	191	63.6	9	3.0	8	2.6
Kuwait	698	41.0	734	41.1	988	58.0	1 025	57.4	17	1.0	26	1.5
Bahrain	141	34.0	143	33.3	265	64.0	279	64.7	8	2.0	9	2.0

Source
United Nations, *Estimated Projection of World Population* (New York, 1985).

Statistical Appendix

Table A5 Proven oil reserves (1980–84)
(billion barrels)

Country	1980	1981	1982	1983	1984	% change (1984–83)
UAE	30.4	32.2	32.4	32.3	32.5	0.6
Saudi Arabia	167.5	164.8	168.3	168.9	171.7	1.7
Oman	2.3	2.6	2.7	2.8	3.5	25.0
Qatar	3.6	3.4	3.4	3.3	3.4	3.0
Kuwait	67.9	67.7	67.2	66.8	92.7	38.8
Bahrain	0.2	0.2	0.2	0.2	0.2	–

Source
Arab Oil Producing & Exporting Countries.

Table A6 Natural gas proven reserves (1980–84)
(billion cubic metres)

Country	1980	1981	1982	1983	1984	% change
UAE	588	658	810	884	906	2.5
Saudi Arabia	3 183	3 346	3 433	3 426	3 610	5.4
Oman	56	76	76	80	209	161.3
Qatar	1 699	1 699	1 756	4 249	4 249	–
Kuwait	940	981	966	879	1 038	18.1

Source
Arab Oil Producing & Exporting Countries.

Table A7 Overall capacity of oil refineries
(000 b/d)

Country	1982	1983	1984
UAE	135	135	195
Saudi Arabia	750	920	1 170
Oman	50	50	50
Qatar	13	13	63
Kuwait	560	560	560
Bahrain	255	255	255

Source
Arab Oil Producing & Exporting Countries.

Table A8 Gross Domestic Product at current price: distribution by sector (1980) in (US$ million):

Country	Agriculture	Extractive	Other	Electricity	Construction	Commerce	Finance
UAE	223.1	19 088.0	1 130.4	349.8	2 652.5	2 452.9	194.2
Saudi Arabia	1 397.3	71 716.4	5 799.9	81.4	12 958.1	5 338.5	1 375.1
Oman	152.3	3 722.9	38.8	46.3	341.1	545.2	30.4
Qatar	41.0	5 263.5	257.9	17.5	425.6	353.6	49.8
Kuwait	64.0	18 726.6	1 613.3	92.5	813.8	1 731.3	678.8
Bahrain	39.5	1 152.5	556.9	32.1	259.7	432.7	376.2

Transportation	Housing	Government services	Other services	GDP at factor prices	Indirect taxes (net)	GDP at market prices
1 006.4	1 080.5	1 615.4	273.5	30 066.7	−441.5	29 625.2
4 734.0	3 295.2	7 029.1	1 581.3	115 306.3	666.4	115 972.7
110.9	309.5	563.4	97.6	5 933.5	24.9	5 958.4
109.1	305.5	920.9	62.4	7 806.8	23.8	7 830.6
459.8	805.3	2 053.5	270.8	27 309.7	239.7	27 549.4
298.2	178.3	366.9	91.0	3 602.0	182.0	3 784.0

Source
Arab Fund for Economic & Social Developments, Economic Accounts for the Arab World, March 1985.

Table A9 Gross Domestic Product at current price: distribution by sector (1981) in (US$ million):

Country	Agriculture	Extractive	Other	Electricity	Construction	Commerce	Finance
UAE	282.2	19 087.7	2 200.2	421.4	2 853.4	2 955.3	574.5
Saudi Arabia	1 647.3	101 310.5	7 611.9	118.0	14 884.4	6 499.1	1 994.0
Oman	179.8	4 329.8	69.5	54.1	419.5	727.6	31.0
Qatar	47.2	5 542.1	409.6	22.8	448.3	510.4	60.4
Kuwait	99.7	14 793.9	1 208.4	98.7	943.6	1 813.3	833.4
Bahrain	48.4	1 153.7	621.8	41.2	302.1	443.4	562.0

Transportation	Housing	Government services	Other services	GDP at factor prices	Indirect taxes (net)	GDP at market prices
1 348.4	1 259.1	2 427.1	383.5	33 792.3	-464.5	33 329.3
5 062.1	3 539.6	8 840.8	1 627.2	153 134.9	767.2	153 902.1
155.8	378.7	754.2	123.9	7 191.2	32.7	7 223.9
112.4	340.9	1 061.7	76.4	8 632.2	28.3	8 660.5
522.0	878.7	2 430.7	294.2	23 916.6	257.2	24 173.8
365.4	234.6	418.1	105.3	4 076.3	219.7	4 296.0

Source
Arab Fund for Economic & Social Developments, Economic Accounts for the Arab World, March 1985.

Table A10 Gross Domestic Product at current price: distribution by sector (1982) (US$ million):

Country	Agriculture	Extractive	Other	Electricity	Construction	Commerce	Finance
UAE	311.6	15 331.0	2 570.4	504.2	2 769.8	2 972.8	680.5
Saudi Arabia	1 966.4	94 910.5	6 530.9	125.1	16 975.2	7 312.9	2 722.8
Oman	191.4	4 124.8	103.9	61.7	491.6	867.1	53.9
Qatar	52.2	4 120.8	382.1	24.4	502.4	487.6	87.6
Kuwait	107.7	9 610.7	1 297.1	104.6	983.1	1 889.7	1 000.4
Bahrain	50.3	1 081.7	506.1	50.3	360.9	520.5	769.7

Transportation	Housing	Government services	Other services	GDP at factor prices	Indirect taxes (net)	GDP at market prices
1 488.7	1 807.1	2 623.8	444.8	31 504.7	−483.5	31.021.2
5 797.6	3 665.1	10 609.0	1 988.0	152 353.3	741.8	153 095.1
187.9	397.5	883.0	150.3	7 470.5	42.6	7 513.1
125.8	390.1	1 298.5	95.0	7 566.5	29.4	7 595.9
596.8	972.6	2 723.4	322.4	19 608.5	287.3	19 895.8
437.8	247.7	488.8	102.9	4 491.8	151.9	4 643.7

Source
Arab Fund for Economic & Social Developments, Economic Accounts for the Arab World, March 1985.

Table A11 Gross Domestic Product at current price (US$ million): distribution by sector (1983)

Country	Agriculture	Extractive	Other	Electricity	Construction	Commerce	Finance
UAE	307.8	12 341.1	2 463.9	538.3	2 996.5	2 706.6	672.6
Saudi Arabia	2 525.5	56 346.4	6 939.0	246.0	15 892.3	8 130.1	3 620.3
Oman	233.1	4 008.7	183.0	69.5	542.6	914.0	60.2
Qatar	54.9	2 943.1	381.6	29.7	457.7	428.3	86.3
Kuwait	116.7	10 615.2	1 375.8	117.0	991.5	1 825.2	1 094.5
Bahrain	51.1	929.5	548.1	58.5	446.5	550.0	773.7

Transportation	Housing	Government services	Other services	GDP at factor prices	Indirect taxes (net)	GDP at market prices
1 392.0	1 705.3	2 766.3	465.8	28 356.2	−813.7	27 542.5
6 220.2	3 853.3	13 484.5	2 433.8	119 199.4	767.2	119 966.6
211.1	441.2	1 042.3	168.2	7 811.1	62.8	7 873.9
137.1	339.3	1 422.7	105.2	6 385.9	32.7	6 418.6
655.3	1 049.9	2 895.3	340.7	21 077.1	258.7	21 335.8
517.7	316.8	539.6	114.4	4 751.6	94.4	4 846.0

Source
Arab Fund for Economic & Social Developments, Economic Accounts for the Arab World, March 1985.

Table A12 Gross Domestic Product at current price (US$ million): distribution by sector (1984)

Country	Agriculture	Extractive	Other	Electricity	Construction	Commerce	Finance
UAE	312.4	12 526.3	2 501.0	546.2	3 041.4	2 747.2	682.6
Saudi Arabia	3 224.0	35 714.7	8 091.3	0.0	16 761.8	8 982.9	4 781.7
Oman	263.5	4 407.9	239.7	82.8	588.0	999.7	67.2
Qatar	57.7	3 090.4	401.1	31.0	480.5	449.7	90.7
Kuwait	124.2	11 535.1	1 416.5	127.6	1 020.5	1 879.2	1 111.9
Bahrain	53.7	1 004.0	591.8	62.0	466.8	567.0	797.9

Transportation	Housing	Government services	Other services	GDP at factor prices	Indirect taxes (net)	GDP at market prices
1 412.7	1 730.9	2 807.7	472.9	28 781.3	−825.7	27 955.6
6 627.7	4 025.7	17 025.7	2 960.1	108 195.6	706.1	108 901.7
230.7	508.1	1 130.0	179.5	8 624.7	72.4	8 697.1
143.9	356.3	1 493.8	110.0	6 705.5	35.7	6 741.2
698.3	1 134.2	3 058.1	352.0	22 457.6	274.2	22 731.8
559.3	334.0	556.1	120.5	5 013.4	99.7	5 113.1

Source
Arab Fund for Economic & Social Developments, Economic Accounts for the Arab World, March 1985.

Table A13 Expenditure on Gross Domestic Product at current prices (US$ million): 1984

Country	Gross capital formation	Private consumption	Government consumption	Exports goods & services	Imports goods & services	Gross Domestic Product
UAE	7 442.2	8 063.2	5 627.9	15 834.9	9 012.5	27 955.7
Saudi Arabia	38 117.0	41 055.6	32 696.1	48 017.1	50 984.3	108 901.5
Oman	2 232.2	2 932.8	2 514.5	4 416.6	3 326.6	8 769.5
Qatar	1 815.8	1 433.9	1 766.3	4 274.3	2 549.2	6 741.1
Kuwait	4 220.8	11 311.7	4 298.6	12 868.9	9 967.9	22 731.8
Bahrain	2 287.3	1 558.5	851.1	3 973.4	3 557.2	5 113.1

Source
Arab Fund for Economic & Social Development (Kuwait, 1985).

Table A14 Expenditure on Gross Domestic Product at current prices (US$ million): 1983

Country	Gross capital formation	Private consumption	Government consumption	Exports goods & services	Imports goods & services	Gross Domestic Product
UAE	7 332.0	7 423.6	5 544.3	15 585.7	8 343.2	27 542.4
Saudi Arabia	37 744.0	40 170.3	31 999.3	64 669.4	54 616.7	119 966.6
Oman	2 100.8	2 671.1	2 257.7	4 248.1	3 341.1	7 936.6
Qatar	1 764.9	1 362.0	1 679.0	3 889.8	2 277.3	6 418.4
Kuwait	4 810.2	10 954.5	4 157.6	12 052.8	10 639.2	21 335.9
Bahrain	2 167.8	1 476.9	806.9	3 763.9	3 369.4	4 846.1

Source
Arab Fund for Economic & Social Development (Kuwait, 1985).

Table A15 Expenditure on Gross Domestic Product at current prices (US$ million): 1982

Country	Gross Capital formation	Private consumption	Government consumption	Exports goods & services	Imports goods & services	Gross Domestic Product
UAE	9 012.4	9 102.4	5 181.1	19 650.8	10 172.4	31 021.2
Saudi Arabia	37 627.8	36 912.4	29 781.6	103 553.5	54 780.2	153 095.1
Oman	2 009.3	2 531.3	2 070.6	4 310.5	3 374.1	7 555.6
Qatar	2 089.4	1 611.9	1 987.6	4 602.0	2 695.1	7 595.9
Kuwait	4 911.8	10 327.0	4 125.4	11 779.3	11 247.8	19 295.7
Bahrain	2 235.9	1 589.6	767.0	4 098.7	4 047.6	4 643.6

Source
Arab Fund for Economic & Social Development (Kuwait, 1985).

Table A16 Expenditure on Gross Domestic Product at current prices (US$ million): 1981

Country	Gross Capital formation	Private consumption	Government consumption	Exports goods & services	Imports goods & services	Gross Domestic Product
UAE	8 709.9	6 410.0	4 353.3	24 563.6	10 708.3	33 328.5
Saudi Arabia	33 348.0	33 969.4	24 216.6	108 917.7	46 549.7	153 902.0
Oman	1 666.5	1 992.8	1 900.4	4 694.0	2 997.1	7 256.6
Qatar	1 537.2	1 478.7	2 236.9	5 897.3	2 489.6	8 660.5
Kuwait	4 168.3	8 771.1	3 535.1	17 343.4	9 644.0	24 173.9
Bahrain	1 874.0	1 510.7	596.5	4 652.4	4 377.5	4 296.1

Source
Arab Fund for Economic & Social Development (Kuwait, 1985).

Table A17 Expenditure on Gross Domestic Product at current prices (US$ million): 1980

Country	Gross Capital formation	Private consumption	Government consumption	Exports goods & services	Imports goods & services	Gross Domestic Product
UAE	8 403.4	5 116.3	3 234.6	23 086.8	10 215.8	29 625.3
Saudi Arabia	26 307.1	25 234.6	26 514.7	77 700.9	39 784.6	115 972.7
Oman	1 333.6	1 656.1	1 445.3	3 748.1	2 199.8	5 983.3
Qatar	1 335.5	1 224.5	1 537.6	5 778.2	2 045.2	7 830.6
Kuwait	3 639.4	8 124.4	3 171.0	22 436.3	9 821.6	27 549.5
Bahrain	1 713.1	1 324.4	491.9	3 916.2	3 661.5	3 784.1

Source
Arab Fund for Economic & Social Development (Kuwait, 1985)

Table A18 Extracting industries value added at current prices (US$ million)

Country	1980	1981	1982	1983	1984
UAE	19 088.0	19 087.7	15 331.0	12 341.1	12 526.3
Saudi Arabia	71 716.4	101 310.5	94 910.5	56 346.4	35 714.7
Oman	3 722.9	4 329.8	4 124.8	4 008.7	4 407.9
Qatar	5 263.5	5 542.1	4 120.8	2 943.1	3 090.4
Kuwait	18 726.6	14 793.9	9 610.7	10 615.2	11 535.1
Bahrain	1 152.5	1 153.7	1 081.7	929.5	1 004.0

Source
Arab Fund, Economic Accounts for the Arab World, March 1985.

Table A19 Extracting industries contribution to GDP (%) at current prices

Country	1980	1982	1983	1984
UAE	63.5	48.7	43.5	43.5
Saudi Arabia	62.2	62.3	47.3	33.0
Oman	62.5	54.9	50.9	51.1
Qatar	67.4	54.5	46.1	46.1
Kuwait	68.6	49.0	50.4	51.4
Bahrain	32.0	24.1	19.6	20.0

Source
Arab Fund, Economic Accounts for the Arab World, March 1985.

Table A20 Other industries value added at current prices (US$ million)

Country	1980	1981	1982	1983	1984
UAE	1 130.4	2 200.2	2 570.4	2 463.9	2 501.0
Saudi Arabia	5 799.9	7 611.9	6 530.9	6 939.0	8 091.3
Oman	38.8	69.5	103.9	183.0	239.7
Qatar	257.9	409.6	382.1	381.6	401.1
Kuwait	1 613.3	1 208.4	1 297.1	1 375.8	1 416.5
Bahrain	556.9	621.8	506.1	548.1	591.8

Source
Arab Fund, Economic Accounts for the Arab World, March 1985.

Table A21 Other industries contribution to GDP (%) at current prices

Country	1980	1982	1983	1984
UAE	3.8	8.2	8.7	8.7
Saudi Arabia	5.0	4.3	5.8	7.5
Oman	0.7	1.4	2.3	2.8
Qatar	3.3	5.0	6.0	6.0
Kuwait	5.9	6.6	6.4	6.4
Bahrain	15.5	11.3	11.5	11.8

Source
Arab Fund, Economic Accounts for the Arab World, March 1985.

Statistical Appendix

Table A22 Government revenues and percentages to GDP (million Arab dinars)

Country	Revenues 1980	1981	1982	1983	1984	% to Gross Domestic Product 1980	1981	1982	1983	1984
UAE	3 227.67	3 756.69	3 087.83	2 481.64	2 769.07	42.53	41.51	34.38	29.77	31.88
Saudi Arabia	26 799.93	30 755.05	21 686.74	17 217.34	19 776.99	90.23	70.63	46.91	46.02	56.76
Oman	710.94	1 073.95	1 040.31	1 177.77	1 315.85	49.02	55.33	47.83	43.95	43.92
Qatar	1 330.88	1 494.42	1 363.10	914.89	1 069.92	65.75	60.44	56.98	45.70	36.59
Kuwait	6 067.08	4 410.06	4 429.35	4 494.15	4 697.54	86.98	64.22	73.37	63.39	68.74
Bahrain	309.30	406.44	446.55	402.05	471.56	31.99	33.62	31.95	26.20	30.40

Source
Budgets of Arab countries: 1980–82 – actual data; 1983 – preliminary data and 1984 – budget estimates.

Table A23 Surplus or deficit in government budget and % to GDP (million Arab dinars)

Country	Surplus or deficit 1980	1981	1982	1983	1984	% to Gross Domestic Product 1980	1981	1982	1983	1984
UAE	659.90	384.83	274.65–	431.61–	290.04–	8.69	4.25	3.06–	5.17–	3.33–
Saudi Arabia	8 587.60	6 966.41	111.88	2 927.04–	4 239.91–	28.91	16.01	0.24	7.82–	12.16–
Oman	54.65	153.37	110.84–	218.74–	341.91–	3.76	7.90	5.09–	8.16–	11.41–
Qatar	322.78	47.52–	60.35–	48.49–	445.12–	15.94	1.92–	2.52–	2.42–	15.22–
Kuwait	2 866.50	574.12	749.92	525.26	294.82	41.09	8.36	12.42	7.40	4.31
Bahrain	93.63	147.74	71.23–	85.25–	0.00	9.68	12.22	5.09–	5.55–	0.00

Source
Budgets of Arab countries: 1980–82 – actual data; 1983 – preliminary data and 1984 – budget estimates.

Table A24 Government expenditures and percentages to Gross Domestic Product (million Arab dinars)

Country	Expenditures					% to GDP				
	1980	1981	1982	1983	1984	1980	1981	1982	1983	1984
UAE	2 567.77	3 371.86	3 362.47	2 913.25	3 059.11	33.84	37.25	37.55	34.95	35.22
Saudi Arabia	18 212.33	23 788.64	21 574.86	20 144.38	24 016.90	61.31	54.67	46.67	53.85	68.93
Oman	656.29	920.57	1 151.15	1 396.51	1 657.77	45.25	47.43	52.93	52.11	55.34
Qatar	1 008.10	1 541.94	1 423.45	963.38	1 515.04	49.81	62.36	59.50	48.13	51.81
Kuwait	3 200.53	3 835.94	3 679.43	3 968.89	4 402.73	45.88	55.86	60.95	55.98	64.42
Bahrain	215.67	258.71	517.77	487.30	471.56	22.30	21.40	37.05	31.76	30.40

Source
Budgets of Arab countries: 1980–82 – actual budgets; 1983 – preliminary data and 1984 – budget projections.

Table A25 Classification of current expenditures (% of total)

Country	Expenditure on defence (%) 1980	1981	1982	1983	1984	Expenditure on government services (%) 1980	1981	1982	1983	1984	Expenditure on economic program (%) 1980	1981	1982	1983	1984
UAE	47.11	47.98	49.25	51.36	51.36	15.72	22.42	22.42	22.42	22.42	16.27	14.44	14.44	14.39	14.40
Saudi Arabia	11.79	11.70	11.70	12.38	12.38	32.77	30.21	30.21	31.89	31.89	6.87	9.75	9.75	10.42	10.42
Oman	59.99	60.90	65.41	60.35	59.59	9.54	7.72	7.99	7.60	7.99	13.58	13.67	13.67	10.43	13.27
Qatar	28.73	34.67	35.49	41.66	30.48	15.29	11.60	18.80	17.10	14.04	6.68	6.47	7.99	7.99	7.35
Kuwait	14.43	16.53	22.03	22.17	22.17	33.4	23.46	28.23	29.45	27.39	17.30	24.77	14.50	13.36	15.43
Bahrain	26.72	29.54	28.19	28.44	28.40	17.27	17.04	15.52	16.34	15.96	14.09	13.62	12.03	12.26	11.62

Country	Expenditures on social services (%) 1980	1981	1982	1983	1984	Other expenditures (%) 1980	1981	1982	1983	1984
UAE	11.51	9.92	9.92	9.00	8.99	9.37	5.21	3.95	2.80	2.81
Saudi Arabia	37.88	37.44	37.44	30.75	30.75	10.66	10.88	10.88	14.53	14.53
Oman	9.03	9.63	8.99	8.55	8.98	7.84	8.05	3.92	13.04	10.14
Qatar	33.88	36.55	27.19	27.00	29.99	15.40	10.69	10.50	6.23	18.13
Kuwait	34.80	35.21	35.22	34.99	34.99	0.00	0.00	0.00	0.00	0.00
Bahrain	27.71	27.03	24.10	26.05	25.49	14.19	12.76	20.14	16.88	18.50

Source
Budgets of Arab countries: 1980–82 – actual budgets; 1983 – preliminary budget and 1984 – budget projections.

Table A26 Saudi Arabia budgets for the years 1981/82–1985/86 ($ million)

	1981/82	1982/83	1983/84	1984/85	1985/86
Total revenues	107 761	71 690	64 378	60 225	55 400
Total Expenditures	83 352	70 974	74 392	73 136	55 400
Surplus or (deficit)	24 409	716	(10 014)	(12 911)	–

Table A27 Sectorial appropriations ($ million)

Sector	1985/86 Appropriations	1984/85 Appropriations	Percentage
Manpower development	29 950	27 947	−16.7
Social development	14 830	18 085	−21.9
Infrastructure	6 670	9 830	−47.4
Municipal services	11 800	17 460	−46.8
Transport & communications	16 500	23 630	−43.2
Economic resources	14 434	17 560	−21.7
Defence and security	64 580	79 900	−23.7
Domestic subsidies	8 344	10 525	−26.1
Lending institutions	9 300	16 000	−72.0
Administration	6 200	–	–
Other spending	23 310	–	–

Table A28 Saudi Arabia: main budget allocations (SR million)

	1984/85 Administrative	1984/85 O & M and construction	1985/86 Administrative	1985/86 O & M and construction
Human Resources				
Education ministry	8 692	1 735	9 250	1 285
Women's education	5 198	718	5 022	930
King Saud University	1 383	615	1 588	3 337
King Abdel-Aziz University	789	585	962	543
University of Petroleum & Minerals	339	182	400	290
King Faisal University	374	76	444	162
Imam Mohammea Ibn-Saud Univ.	635	453	743	532
Islamic University	211	51	250	75
Umm Al-Qura University	388	64	423	90
SANCST	132	265	150	160
Gotevot	567	355	650	660
Health & Social Development				
Health Ministry	5 495	3 320	6 265	5 470
Information Ministry	565	397	680	520
Labour & Social Affairs Min.	2 092	146	2 106	250
Youth Welfare	454	1 524	490	2 250
Transport & Communications				
Transport Ministry	224	4 489	280	6 870
PTT Ministry	597	3 704	1 440	5 000
Civil Aviation	197	3 896	310	5 350
Seaports Authority	280	1 700	355	2 870
Saudi Railroad Organization	93	770	166	500
Economic Resources				
Agriculture & Water Ministry	481	1 544	910	2 030
Saline Water Conversion Corp.	51	1 928	58	2 745
Petroleum & Mineral Res. Min.	194	397	310	620
Industry & Electricity Min.	116	5 230	3 880	5 500
Grain Silos Corporation	73	1 862	92	1 940
Infrastructure				
Public Works & Housing Min.	121	1 803	150	2 100
Royal Commission for Jubail & Yanbu	67	4 358	82	6 970
Municipal Services				
Municipalities and Rural Settlements	2 330	7 094	2 593	11 080
Water and Sewage Dept.	319	2 146	340	3 060

Table A29 Kuwait: Budget 1984/85–1985/86 (KD million)

	1985/86	1984/85	% Change
Expenditure			
General	3 420.1	3 578.5	−4.4
Reserve fund for future generations	311.6	322.7	−3.4
Increase in KFAED capital	30.0	30.0	–
TOTAL	3 761.7	3 931.2	−4.3
Revenue			
Oil	2 801.9	2 912.5	−3.8
Other	314.1	314.5	−0.1
TOTAL	3 116.0	3 227.0	−3.4
Deficit	645.7	704.2	−8.3

Note

Exchange rate $1=KD 0.301

Table A30 Kuwait's budget for the years 1981/1982–1985/1986 ($ million)

	1981/82	1982/83	1983/84	1984/85	1985/86
Total revenues*	15 454	11 074	10 359	10 646	10 352
Total expenditure	13 464	10 752	12 681	12 969	12 497
Surplus or deficit	2 011	322	(2 322)	(2 323)	(2 145)

Note

*Does not include Income from Foreign Investments.

Table A 31 Qatar's budget 1984/85–1985/86 (QR million)

	1985/86	1984/85	% Change
Total spending, of which	17 048.0	16 951.2	+ 0.6
Foreign commitments	1 441.0	–	–
State projects	3 800.00	4 069.00	−6.6
Other capital spending	1 341.0	1 186.0	+13.1
Total revenues	9 737.0	11 970.9	−18.7
Deficit	7 311.0	4 980.3	46.8

Note

$1 = QR 3.6401.

Table A32 Qatar's budget for the years 1981/82–1985/86 ($ million)

	1981/82	1982/83	1983/84	1984/85	1985/86
Total revenues	5 170	4 514	2 400	3 280	2 650
Total Expenditure	4 069	4 166	3 900	4 644	4 694
Surplus or (deficit)	1 101	348	(1 500)	(1 364)	(2 044)

Table A33 Oman's budgets for the years 1983–85 (RO million)

	1983	1984	1985
Revenue sources			
1. Net oil revenue	1 181	1 100	1 292
2. Other revenue	130	170	212
3. Aid	10	5	67
4. Development loans	122	166	148
5. Drawing from reserve fund	–	120	–
Total revenue	1 443	1 561	1 719
Applications			
1. Defence & Security			
a) recurrent expenditure	486	514	562
b) capital expenditure	126	163	155
2. Civil Purposes			
a) current expenditure	383	477	55
b) development	362	360	370
3. Financial dev. institutions			
a) Oman Bank for Agriculture & Fisheries.	4	5	5
b) Oman Housing Bank	4	4	4
c) Oman Development Bank	4	4	4
4. Aid to private sector	19	9	9
5. Govt. share in PDO expenditure			
a) recurrent	62	59	64
b) development	135	100	105
6. Repayment of loans	35	50	57
7. Investment or Loans	30	20	28
Total applications	1 650	1 765	1 918
Deficit	(207)	(204)	(199)

Note

$1 = RO 0.3368

Table A34 Bahrain's budget 1982–85 (BD million)

	1982	1983	1984	1985*	1985**
Total Revenues	556.1	484.8	548.8	575.0	549.6
(a) Oil revenue	401.9	328.6	355.4	361.4	n.a.
(b) Non-oil revenue	154.2	156.2	193.4	213.6	n.a.
Total Expenditure	472.6	535.4	538.6	575.0	549.6
(a) Recurrent	298.3	309.9	325.0	364.5	339.1
(b) Capital	174.3	222.0	210.0	210.5	210.5
(c) Others (including university college expenditure)	–	3.5	3.6	n.a.	n.a.

Notes

* Original estimates.
**Revised estimates.

Table A35 UAE's budget for 1981/82–1985/86 ($ million)

	1981/84	1982/83	1983/84	1984/85	1985/86
Total revenues	6 318	4 372	3 526	3 502	3 537
Total expenditure	5 621	5 245	5 014	4 696	4 531
Surplus or (deficit)	697	(873)	(1 488)	(1 194)	(994)

Table A36 Monetary authorities structure of deposits (%) (1980–84)

Country	Govt	1980 Public Enterprises	Commercial banks	Other institutions	Govt	1981 Public enterprises	Commercial banks	Other institutions
UAE	62.60	0.26	36.40	0.74	72.22	0.00	27.21	0.57
Saudi Arabia	0.00	0.00	0.00	0.00	0.00	0.00	0.00	0.00
Oman	0.00	0.00	0.00	0.00	0.00	0.00	0.00	0.00
Qatar	0.00	0.00	100.00	0.00	0.00	0.00	0.00	0.00
Kuwait	0.00	0.00	0.00	0.00	0.00	0.00	0.00	0.00
Bahrain	0.00	0.00	0.00	0.00	0.00	0.00	0.00	0.00

Table A 36 Monetary authorities structure of deposits (%) (1980–84)

Govt	1982 Public Enterprises	Commercial banks	Other institutions	Govt	1983 Public enterprises	Commercial banks	Other institutions	Govt	1984 Public enterprises	Commercial banks	Other institutions
70.72	1.38	27.44	0.46	27.93	0.59	71.48	0.00	28.49	0.25	71.26	0.00
0.00	0.00	0.00	0.00	0.00	0.00	0.00	0.00	0.00	0.00	0.00	0.00
100.00	0.00	0.00	0.00	100.00	0.00	0.00	0.00	100.00	0.00	0.00	0.00
0.00	0.00	100.00	0.00	0.00	0.00	100.00	0.00	0.00	0.00	100.00	0.00
0.00	0.00	0.00	0.00	0.00	0.00	0.00	0.00	0.00	0.00	0.00	0.00
0.00	0.00	0.00	0.00	0.00	0.00	0.00	0.00	0.00	0.00	0.00	0.00

Statistical Appendix

Table A37 Structure of domestic liquidity (%) 1981–1984

Country	Money	1981 Quasi money	Domestic liquidity	Money	1982 Quasi money	Domestic liquidity	Money	1983 Quasi money	Domestic liquidity	Money	1984 Quasi money	Domestic liquidity
UAE	30.8	69.2	100.0	28.9	71.1	100.0	25.1	74.9	100.0	19.6	80.4	100.0
Saudi Arabia	70.9	29.1	100.0	67.7	32.3	100.0	65.2	34.8	100.0	60.8	39.2	100.0
Oman	47.2	52.8	100.0	42.7	57.3	100.0	39.7	60.3	100.0	36.7	63.3	100.0
Qatar	45.5	54.5	100.0	44.3	55.7	100.0	42.7	57.3	100.0	40.8	59.2	100.0
Bahrain	34.1	65.9	100.0	34.2	65.8	100.0	29.7	70.3	100.0	28.9	71.1	100.0

Source
Arab Monetary Fund, International Financial Statistics June & July 1985

Table A38 Changes in Factors affecting Domestic Liquidity (%): (1982–84)

	Net foreign assets 1982	1983	1984	Domestic credit total 1982	1983	1984	government net 1982	1983	1984	Public enterprise net 1982	1983	1984	Private enterprise net 1982	1983	1984	Others net 1982	1983	1984
UAE	15.2	5.7	–50.8	16.7	19.1	0.3	29.0	75.0	24.2	–8.6	13.7	–32.3	–7.2	6.3	8.6	17.0	–9.3	–41.9
Saudi Arabia	11.4	3.7	–3.6	–2.6	19.9	11.5	4.4	–3.8	8.7	—	—	—	16.0	13.3	5.0	29.8	–6.5	4.5
Oman	23.2	24.7	15.3	34.2	1.1	15.7	2.7	47.3	–24.3	—	—	—	12.7	24.3	20.8	27.9	–15.5	–16.4
Qatar	3.4	18.9	–19.7	32.2	8.5	5.1	–12.5	3.9	–7.7	—	—	—	23.7	8.6	3.4	–20.4	–29.0	10.2
Kuwait	13.9	6.4	–3.1	17.7	17.4	3.2	3.3	5.4	15.4	—	—	—	23.7	12.2	6.1	49.4	–14.7	–6.2
Bahrain	1.4	5.6	0.8	607.4	27.9	31.1	–16.4	4.9	–23.2	—	—	—	11.7	11.4	5.5	9.9	13.9	–18.4

Statistical Appendix

Table A39 Ratio of changes in factors affecting domestic liquidity to changes in domestic liquidity (%): 1982–84

Country	Net foreign assets 1982	1983	1984	Domestic credit total 1982	1983	1984	government net 1982	1983	1984	Public enterprise net 1982	1983	1984	Private enterprise net 1982	1983	1984	Others net 1982	1983	1984
UAE	63	46	−141	91	204	1	45	132	4	2	−4	−4	48	76	9	54	−58	−42
Saudi Arabia	265	280	−205	−38	−276	358	71	−93	327	—	—	—	33	183	31	127	−104	53
Oman	88	121	101	43	2	29	5	82	67	—	—	—	38	84	96	31	−23	−30
Qatar	16	1 240	−180	108	573	58	−10	33	−14	—	—	—	98	606	44	−24	−567	22
Kuwait	94	85	−78	147	292	129	112	−41	191	—	—	—	259	251	320	141	−107	−107
Bahrain	22	73	42	−268	69	401	−153	30	−618	—	—	—	115	99	217	190	−42	−259

Table A.40 Commercial banks: structure of deposits & percentages to GDP (1980–84)

Country	1980 Demand deposits	Time deposits	Govt deposits	% Total to GDP	1981 Demand deposits	Time deposits	Govt deposits	% Total to GDP
UAE	20.80	64.54	14.67	41.30	20.62	66.95	12.54	37.58
Saudi Arabia	60.16	33.41	6.44	24.54	54.16	37.37	8.47	32.17
Oman	19.05	54.17	26.78	35.21	21.62	53.32	25.07	38.07
Qatar	28.97	59.34	11.70	32.21	34.29	57.90	7.81	33.08
Kuwait	16.94	77.11	5.95	64.97	26.85	68.78	4.38	55.53
Bahrain	24.32	60.25	15.43	60.67	25.50	66.26	8.24	71.40

1982 Demand deposits	Time deposits	Govt deposits	% Total to GDP	1983 Demand deposits	Time deposits	Govt deposits	% Total to GDP	1984 Demand deposits	Time deposits	Govt deposits	% Total to GDP
19.59	69.40	11.01	31.36	16.98	73.98	9.04	30.37	12.41	79.04	8.55	42.73
50.57	41.01	8.42	25.28	47.62	43.31	9.07	20.19	–	–	–	–
19.38	62.18	18.43	27.49	17.19	62.87	19.95	31.33				
33.66	60.77	5.56	27.42	32.46	61.76	5.78	24.97	30.83	63.46	5.71	30.20
21.37	69.33	9.30	56.82	19.11	72.63	8.26	64.81	13.82	77.60	8.58	78.92
25.56	66.78	7.66	54.02	19.97	67.12	12.91	54.96	16.27	58.44	24.29	56.89

Table A41 Commercial banks:
credit structure and % of total credit
to GDP
(1980–84)

Country	1980 Public government	Private enterprises	Enterprises	% Credit to GDP	1981 Govt	Public enterprises	Private enterprises	% Credit to GDP
UAE	7.97	5.00	87.03	47.67	7.14	4.58	88.28	42.35
Saudi Arabia	0.00	0.00	100.00	16.52	0.00	0.00	100.00	17.33
Oman	1.12	0.00	98.88	32.07	0.18	0.00	99.82	28.60
Qatar	0.00	0.00	100.00	23.51	0.00	0.00	100.00	21.20
Kuwait	0.00	0.00	100.00	62.75	0.00	0.00	100.00	51.29
Bahrain	5.88	0.00	94.12	50.90	2.75	0.00	97.25	49.22

1982 Govt	Public enterprises	Private enterprises	% Credit to GDP	1983 Govt	Public enterprises	Private enterprises	% Credit to GDP	1984 government	Public enterprises	Private enterprises	% Credit to GDP
9.79	4.95	85.26	33.86	10.53	5.13	84.35	32.76	11.28	1.72	87.00	34.13
0.00	0.00	100.00	13.00	0.00	0.00	100.00	10.91	–	–	–	–
2.23	0.00	97.77	19.72	3.52	0.00	96.48	20.49	2.88	0.00	97.12	23.44
0.00	0.00	100.00	19.47	0.00	0.00	100.00	19.20	0.00	0.00	100.00	21.15
0.00	0.00	100.00	57.40	0.00	0.00	100.00	70.03	0.00	0.00	100.00	87.82
4.21	0.00	95.79	39.96	3.72	0.00	96.28	39.20	12.04	0.00	87.96	41.82

Table A42 Balance of payments 1979–83 (million Arab Dinars):

	UAE	Saudi Arabia	Oman	Qatar	Kuwait	Bahrain
Exports						
1979	3 880.00	14 582.33	588.00	1 002.18	4 673.00	588.67
1980	5 683.33	25 794.67	960.00	1 455.83	5 394.00	906.67
1981	6 153.33	31 411.33	1 327.33	1 652.00	4 433.33	1 180.83
1982	5 503.33	22 072.33	1 335.33	1 360.00	3 273.00	1 144.13
1983	4 800.00	14 150.00	1 326.33	962.00	3 465.00	997.50
Imports						
1979	1 570.00	6 070.67	347.33	367.77	1 256.67	540.33
1980	1 940.00	7 232.00	479.33	368.74	1 730.00	773.67
1981	2 433.33	9 599.00	728.00	429.10	1 994.67	1 006.17
1982	2 460.00	10 402.00	855.33	587.87	2 345.00	982.07
1983	2 466.67	10 431.33	838.67	556.90	2 177.00	937.93
Trade balance						
1979	2 310.00	8 511.67	240.67	634.40	3 416.33	48.33
1980	3 743.33	18 562.67	480.67	1 087.07	3 664.00	133.00
1981	3 720.00	21 812.33	599.33	1 222.90	2 438.67	174.63
1982	3 043.33	11 670.33	480.33	772.93	928.00	162.03
1983	2 333.33	3 718.67	487.67	406.00	1 288.00	59.53
Other goods & services						
1979	136.67–	4 265.67–	99.00–	148.19–	580.67	15.33–
1980	90.00–	5 894.67–	114.00–	312.71–	1 094.33	42.33–
1981	223.33–	8 197.00–	179.67–	237.17–	1 893.33	11.07–
1982	73.33–	10 429.33–	178.67–	139.50–	925.00	15.67
1983	233.33–	7 833.67–	259.67–	110.37–	635.67	32.00
Unilateral transfers						
1979	750.00–	1 772.00–	26.33–	71.12–	332.33–	46.67–
1980	1 016.67–	2 065.00–	67.00–	80.40–	404.67–	26.00–
1981	953.33–	2 773.67–	86.67–	312.10–	442.00–	42.93–
1982	853.33–	1 573.33–	193.67–	301.87–	459.33–	42.80–
1983	700.00–	1 632.67–	201.67–	252.87–	494.00–	41.40–
Current account						
1979	1 423.33	2 474.00	115.33	415.09	3 664.67	13.67–
1980	2 636.67	10 603.00	299.67	693.98	4 353.67	64.67
1981	2 543.33	10 842.00	332.67	673.63	3 890.00	142.77
1982	2 116.67	332.00–	108.00	331.57	1 399.67	134.90
1983	1 400.00	5 747.67–	26.67	42.80	1 429.33	50.17

Table A43 Exports and imports of agricultural products (US$ million)

Country	Exports 1979	1980	1981	1982	1983	Imports 1979	1980	1981	1982	1983
UAE	180.0	188.5	217.9	129.9	79.2	932.3	878.0	1 000.1	823.7	792.6
Saudi Arabia	49.9	98.5	113.3	101.1	54.3	3 576.4	4 844.5	5 760.9	5 994.2	5 252.7
Oman	41.9	29.7	45.4	34.8	39.9	217.5	315.4	382.3	421.1	446.5
Qatar	–	–	–	–	–	169.4	213.8	217.4	180.6	170.9
Kuwait	106.7	135.0	197.5	135.1	122.3	892.9	1 131.4	1 227.8	1 180.2	1 165.1
Bahrain	10.7	22.2	5.3	24.3	26.3	224.9	262.4	249.2	236.4	243.9

Source
Food & Agriculture Organisation (FAO) *Yearbook on Trade.*

Table A44 *International Reserves (million Arab dinars): 1980–84*

Country	1980	1981	1982	1983	1984
UAE	526.67	917.00	669.67	659.67	696.67
Saudi Arabia	6 125.33	9 231.67	8 929.00	8 688.00	8 416.00
Oman	152.00	213.00	263.67	242.67	306.00
Qatar	89.67	104.67	116.67	122.33	120.33
Kuwait	1 026.67	1 165.00	1 786.67	1 653.00	1 561.00
Bahrain	249.33	442.33	464.00	454.00	443.00

Index

Abdulhassan, Jawad & Haidar Y. (company), 213
Abu Dhabi: share dealing in, 84; steel plant in, 150; shipping traffic, 201, 204; *see also* United Arab Emirates
Abu Dhabi National Insurance Company, 193–4
administrative sector, 206
advertising, 51–4
agriculture, 182–91, 232–6; insurance, 192; exports and imports, 255
air lines and aviation, 196–8
Al Ain, 187
Algeria, 32
Al-Mal (bank), 94–5
Al-Manakh, *see* Souk Al-Manakh
Al Rajhi Company (Al Rajhi Banking Investment Corporation), 82
aluminium, 153–4
ammonia, 141, 147, 152
Arab Banking Corporation (ABC), Bahrain, 92, 94
Arab Commercial Enterprises Group (ACE), 193
Arab Company for Trading of Securities (ACTS), 78–9
Arab Insurance Group (ARIG), 191, 193
Australia, 63
aviation, *see* air lines and aviation

Bahrain: in GCC, 1; GDP rates, 1, 232–42; banks and banking in, 6–7, 90–2, 97, 104, 252–3; balance of payments, 9, 177, 254; imports, 10, 90, 177, 254–5; administrative spending, 12; budgets, 13, 248; foreign workers in, 48, 206; TV sets in, 53; advertising in, 53; car sales, 58; food market, 63; proposed stock exchange, 82–3, 86; as regional financial centre, 86–7; construction in, 106, 111, 112, 117, 232–6; finances Saudi construction projects, 117; cement production, 147–50; steel project, 150; fertilizer production, 152; aluminium production, 153–4; light industries, 154; dairying, 156; currency exchange, 159–61; foreign assets, 164, 256; current account balance, 166, 177; oil production and reserves, 177, 231; agriculture in, 183–4, 232–6, 255; insurance in, 193–5; and Gulf Air, 198; tourism, 199–200; shipping, 201–2, 204; long-term debt, 216, 223; liquidity and other indicators, 221–4, 250–1; population, 227–30; structure of deposits, 249; international reserves, 256
Bahrain Monetary Agency, 97
balance of payments, 8–9, 88, 254
banks and banking: difficulties, 6–8; Islamic legal constraints on, 7, 14, 42, 90, 101; outflow of funds, 15; credit facilities to production projects, 34; development of, 66, 88; and investment policy, 69–70, 102–3; and instruments for investment, 71–2, 101, 102–3; adjustments to change, 88–9, 97–9, 104–5; and business opportunities, 89–91, 97–102; reserves, 91; internationalization, 91–6; participation in syndicated loans, 92–3; lending by region, 95; foreign competition, 96; regulating and monitoring of, 96–7; private, 103–4; mergers and closures, 104; financing of construction projects, 111,

257

114–16, 118–19; and agriculture, 184–5, 191; and Al-Manakh crisis, 215–16; structure of deposits and credit, 252–3
Basmah (company), 131
Britain, *see* United Kingdom
budgets: reduced expenditure, 8–9, 45; deficits, 11, 70; financing, 11–15; tables, 244–8

capital: outflow, 15; markets, 72–4; and industrial development, 124; export of, 216; deposit structure, 249
cars (automobiles), 57–60
cement industry, 147–50
China: livestock from, 63
coal, 24, 27–8, 31–2
commercial vehicles, 57–60
Committee on Natural Resources (United Nations), 28
communication products, 55–7
computers, 55–7
conservation: effect on oil production, 29
construction: decline in, 5, 7, 106, 109–11; international contractors, 111–13, 118; financing, 113–20; tables, 232–6
consumer goods and spending, 18, 45, 47–53
co-operatives (food), 63
country credit, 216–17, 222–3
country risk, 217–19
credit ratings, 217–18, 221–4
currency: proposed single regional, 85; *see also* exchange rates
current accounts, 166–77

dairy industries, 156, 184–7
Dammam, Saudi Arabia, 201
Dar al Maal Al Islami, 192
dates (fruit), 184–7
devaluation, 14
dollar: exchange rates, 159–64
Dortyol pipeline, 209
Dubai: food co-operatives, 63; steel plant in, 150–1; aluminium production, 153–4; insurance in, 194; international air traffic, 198; tourism, 199; shipping, 201, 204

Ecuador, 28
education, 42, 45, 106
electronics and electrical appliances, 54–5
Emirates Airlines, 198
employment: pattern of, 35, 42; *see also* labour
energy resources (non-oil), 24–5, 27–8, 31–2
engineering, 40, 132
Engineering News Record, 111–12
ethylene, 140–2, 144–5, 146
Eurocurrency, 92–3, 102–3
European Economic Community, 144
exchange rates, 159–64
expatriate labour, *see* labour
extracting industries, *see* minerals

fertilizers, 151–3, 188, 190
fisheries and fishing, 186–91
food products, 156
foodstuffs, 62–4, 182
foreign assets and investments, 164–6, 256
France, 46, 61, 112, 160
Fujairah (port), 202, 204
fundamentalism (Islamic), 205
furniture, 60–2

gas, natural: as energy source, 31–2, 152; industries, 123–4, 142–3; and fertilizers, 151–3; Saudi supply, 180; reserves, 231
Germany, West: imports from, 9–10, 45–6, 90, 164, 169; car and truck sales, 57–8; furniture sales, 61; currency value, 159, 162, 164; Gulf investments in, 164–5
Greece, 147
Gross Domestic Product (GDP): growth rates, 1, 107; and private sector, 5; related to oil demand, 23–5; non-oil contributions to, 35; industrial contribution, 121; and external sector, 163; in

Index

structural index, 220; tables of, 232–9
guarantees and warranties, 55
Gulf Air, 196–7
Gulf Co-operation Council: adjustment to slow development, 1–2; lower oil revenues, 2, 20–1; population, 2, 48, 227–31; diversified industrial base, 2, 33; development plans, 2–3, 34–44, 45, 68, 121; private sector involvement, 4–6, 19, 34, 38–41; budgetary expenditure, 8–9, 11, 45, 70; imports, 10–11, 45, 164; external debt, 14; socio-political stability, 16–17, 38, 44, 205–7; social and cultural effects of boom, 17–18, 47; outlook, 18–19, 33–44; and expected oil boost, 19, 32; oil production and quotas, 20–2, 209; oil reserves, 28; and world oil demand, 32, 33–4; growth rates, 34, 67; investment opportunities, 38–41, 44; free enterprise encouraged, 38; Unified Economic Agreement, 39; manufacturing potential, 39–40; expatriate labour, 46–7; consumer markets, 47, 48–65; racial groups, 51; vehicle sales, 57–60; furniture sales, 60–2; high per-capita income, 64; co-operation in, 66; investment policy, 68–70; financial integration in, 85–7; construction in, 106, 109, 111, 113, 117; industrialization, 121–32, 157; common economic agreements, 124; joint ventures, 132–3, 139–40; petrochemicals industry, 140–7; cement production, 148; fertilizer production, 151; and aluminium industry, 153; and light industries, 155–6; exchange rates, 161–4; foreign assets, 164–5; current account balances, 177, 180; agriculture, 182–91; insurance in, 193; and air transport, 198; and hotel business, 200; shipping, 203; fundamentalism in, 205; effects of recession in, 207; country credit and risk, 216–18; liquidity and structural indices, 218–21; *see also* individual countries
Gulf International Bank, 94, 103
Gulf Investment Corporation, Kuwait, 69
Gulf Organization for Industrial Consulting, 38, 133, 147–51

Hormuz, Strait of, 16
hotel industry, 199–201
housing, 232–6
hydro power, 31

IBM corporation, 56
imports, 10–11, 45–6, 125
India, 163
Indonesia, 28, 32
Industrial Bank of Kuwait, 78
Industrial Development Fund, 43
industrialization and industries: development of, 35–7, 39–40, 121–4; and investment, 43; and comparative advantage, 123–4; factors hindering, 125–6; new, 126–32, 134–7; small and medium, 134–7, 154–6
insurance, 191–6, 203
interest: religious prohibitions on, 7, 14
International Energy Authority, 29
International Finance Corporation, 85
International Labour Organization, 48
International Monetary Fund (IMF): Special Drawing Rights, 159–60; Saudi loans to, 165
investment: in Gulf region, 38–41, 44, 66–9, 72–4; risks and constraints, 41–4; instruments for, 43, 70–1; banking, 102–3; outlets for small and medium industries, 134–7; joint ventures, 132–3, 138–40; *see also* banks and banking; capital

Iran: oil production, 20, 22, 209; oil exports, 32, 210
Iran–Iraq war (Gulf war): effect on Gulf economies, 1, 15–16, 41, 73, 205–6, 208–11; ending forecast, 19; and oil markets, 22, 209–11; and insurance, 192, 203; effect on aviation, 196; effect on shipping, 203–4; course of, 208
Iraq: oil production, 20, 22, 208–9; oil reserves, 28; oil exports, 32, 208, 212; cement production, 147, 149; shipping, 202
iron, 150–1; see also steel
irrigation, 164, 189–90
Islamic Insurance Company, 192
Italy, 9, 46, 60–1

Japan: exports to Gulf countries, 9–10, 45–6, 65, 90, 164, 169; electronic and electrical appliances, 54; car and truck sales, 57–8; furniture sales, 61; construction work, 115; cement supply, 148; currency value, 159, 162, 164; external sector, 163; Gulf investments in, 166
Jebel Ali, Dubai, 204
Jeddah, 4
joint stock companies, 12, 14, 35, 82, 75

Kharg Island, 209
Khor Fakhan, Sharjah, 204
Korea, South, 111–12, 147, 202
Kuwait: in GCC, 1; stock market, 1, 7, 19, 43, 66, 72–8, 211–15; GDP rates, 1, 232–42; decline in property values, 4; share price index, 4–5; banks in, 6, 66, 91, 97–8, 252–3; budgetary economies, 8, 70; balance of payments, 9, 254; imports, 10, 254–5; budgets, 11, 13, 246; capital investment, 15; oil reserves, 28, 231; oil production and earnings, 32, 172, 231; development plan and industrialization, 34–6; foreign labour in, 46, 206; TV sets in, 53; advertising in, 53; car sales in, 58; furniture sales in, 60–1; food market, 63; financial investment in, 69; listed companies, 74, 75; brokers, 77; ATMS in, 103; construction in, 106, 109–11, 117, 232–6; petro-chemical industry, 146; cement production, 147–50; steel project, 150; fertilizer production, 151; light industries, 154; dairying, 156; currency exchange, 159, 161–2; foreign assets, 165, 256; current account balance, 167; agriculture in, 183, 232–6, 255; insurance in, 193–5; hotels, 200; shipping, 201–2; administrative sector, 206; Central Bank, 205; exports capital, 216; liquidity and other indicators, 221–4, 250–1; population, 227–30; structure of deposits, 249; international reserves, 256
Kuwait Airways, 196–8
Kuwait Foreign Trading, Contracting and Investment Company (KFTCIC), 77, 95, 213–14
Kuwait International Investment Company, 77, 94
Kuwait Investment Company (KIC), 77, 95, 213–14
Kuwait Oil Tanker Company (KOTC), 202
Kuwait Petroleum Corporation (KPC), 202
Kuwait Supply Company, 63

labour: foreign (expatriate) force, 35, 46–8, 125–6, 206; nationals, 42, 126; agricultural, 187; flying by airlines, 196
law: Islamic and western, 42
Libya, 32, 166
liquidity index, 218–19, 221, 223, 250–1

Index

machinery, 156
Manakh, Al-, *see* Souk Al-Manakh
methanol, 142, 145, 147, 152
Mexico, 26–7, 32
Middle East Bank, Bahrain, 92
Middle East Executive Report, 52
Mina Khalid, Sharjah, 204
Mina Sulman, Bahrain, 204
Mina Zayed, Abu Dhabi, 204
minerals, 40, 131; extraction, 239–42
money supply, 162

Nasheshibi, Hikmat: 'Arab to Arab Eurobonds Can Work', 95
National Bank of Abu Dhabi, 84, 94
National Cash Register (NCR) Corporation, 56
National Commercial Bank, Saudi Arabia, 95
National Company for Co-operative Insurance, Saudi Arabia, 193
National Industrialization Company (NIC), Saudi Arabia: stock floated, 14, 71, 81–2, 180; and petrochemical joint ventures, 144; and food production, 155
National Marine Dredging Company, 84
National Shipping Company of Saudi Arabia (NSCSA), 202
Nestlé company, 131
net back deals (oil prices), 21
newspapers and magazines, 54
New Zealand, 63
Nigeria, 32
nitrogen, 151
nuclear power, 24–5, 27–8, 31–2

OECD (Organization for Economic Co-operation and Development): oil demand in, 19, 23–5, 30; alternative energy sources, 27; and Gulf trade imbalance, 43; report on petrochemicals, 143
oil: OPEC increase, 1; lower revenues, 2, 9, 11, 43, 88, 211; changing demand, 19, 23–7, 29–30; production quotas, 20–2, 30–1, 179–81, 209; net back pricing deals, 21; non-OPEC producers, 21, 25–7, 29–31; structural market changes, 22–6; prices, 22–3, 43; and Iran–Iraq war, 22, 209–11; energy alternatives to, 24–5, 27–8, 31–2; reserves, 28, 231; efficiency improvements, 29–30; refining and associated industries, 123–4, 126–30; servicing industries, 131; dollar pricing, 162, 164; shipping, 202; pipelines, 209–10
Oil Producing and Exporting Countries, *see* OPEC
Oman: in GCC, 1; GDP rates, 1, 232–42; balance of payments, 9, 172, 254; imports, 10, 254–5; budgets, 11, 13, 70, 247; foreign workers in, 46–8, 206; TV sets in, 53; no commercial TV, 53; car sales in, 58; furniture sales in, 61; interest in stock exchange, 85; construction in, 111, 117, 232–6; mineral resources, 131; cement industry, 148; steel project, 150; exchange rates, 161; consumer prices, 164; foreign assets, 165, 256; current account balance, 167, 172, 178; oil production and reserves, 174, 231; agriculture in, 182–4, 190–1, 232–6, 255; insurance in, 193–5; and Gulf Air, 198; long-term debt, 216, 223; liquidity and other indicators, 222–4, 250–1; population, 227–30; structure of deposits, 249; banks in, 252–3; international reserves, 256
OPEC (Oil Producing and Exporting Countries): and world demand for oil, 1–2, 30–2; crude oil production and quotas, 20–2, 30–1, 177, 180–1, 209; benchmark price, 21; and structural market changes, 22–3; oil reserves, 28–9; foreign assets, 164; and Iran–Iraq war, 209–11; *see also* oil

Pampers nappies, 131
Perez de Cuellar, Javier, 28
petrochemicals, 39, 43, 123–4, 126–31, 140–7, 155, 180
Petromin (company), 82
Port Rashid (Dubai port), 204
price increases, 65, 163–4
private sector: increased involvement in economy, 4–6, 19, 34, 38–41, 44; constraints on, 41–4; and financial development, 68–70; in Saudi economy, 180
profit margins, 5
property values (real estate), 4
public debt instruments, 14

Qatar: in GCC, 1; GDP rates, 1, 232–42; budgetary economies, 8, 70; balance of payments, 9, 174, 254; imports, 10, 254–5; budgets, 11, 13, 246–7; foreign workers in, 48, 206; TV sets in, 53; advertising in, 53; food market, 63; lacks stock exchange, 85; banks, 91, 252–3; construction in, 107, 110, 117, 232–6; petrochemical industry, 146; cement production and imports, 147–50; steel production, 150–1; fertilizer production, 151–3; light industries, 154; currency exchange, 159–61; foreign assets, 165, 256; current account balance, 166, 176; agriculture in, 182–3, 232–6, 257; insurance in, 193–5; and Gulf Air, 198; shipping, 201–2; exports capital, 216; liquidity and other indicators, 221–4, 250–1; oil reserves and production, 231; structure of deposits, 249; international reserves, 256

Ras Al Khaimah, 151, 187
riba (ban on interest), 7, 14
Rostow, Walt Whitman, 33
Russia, *see* Union of Soviet Socialist Republics

Saudi Arabia: in GCC, 1; GDP rates, 1, 232–42; oil revenues, 2, 21, 169; banking reserves, 4; share price decline, 5; private sector in, 5; bank earnings, 6–7; budgets, 8, 11, 13, 70, 180, 244–5; balance of payments, 9, 179, 254; imports, 10, 45, 201, 254–5; administrative spending economies, 12, 206; joint stock companies, 12, 14; overseas investment, 15; oil production, 20–1, 32, 169, 177, 180–1, 231; oil reserves, 28, 231; development plan and industrialization, 34–5, 37, 121–2, 180; low interest loans to industry, 38; local employment policy, 42; imports reduced, 45; foreign workers in, 46, 48, 206; population, 48, 227–30; customs duties and tariffs, 49, 62; TV sets in, 53; advertising in, 53; computers in, 56; car sales in, 58, 60; furniture sales in, 60, 62; foodstuffs in, 62–4; agriculture, 64; banking practice in, 69, 90, 98, 101–2, 115–16, 252–3; stock market and supervision, 78, 80–2; construction in, 106–11, 149, 232–6; mineral resources, 131; joint ventures, 132–3, 138–40; petrochemical industry, 140–7, 180; main spending sectors, 141; cement production and imports, 147–50; steel production, 150–1; fertilizer production, 151; and aluminium production, 153; light industries, 154–6; currency and exchange rates, 159–61; consumer prices, 163–4; foreign assets, 164–5, 169, 256; loans to IMF, 165; current account balance, 166–9, 181; liquid assets, 180; natural gas in, 180; economic policy response to deficit, 177, 180–1; agriculture in, 182–7, 232–6, 255; insurance in, 192–5; hotels, 202; shipping,

201–3; exports capital, 216; liquidity and other indicators, 222–3, 250–1; structure of deposits, 249; international reserves, 256
Saudi Arabia Basic Industries Company (SABIC): share prices, 5, 81; stock floated, 14, 71, 81–2, 121, 180; and petrochemicals, 141, 144, 146; and iron and steel, 150–1; and fertilizers, 151; liquidity index, 221
Saudi Arabia Monetary Agency: and investment policy, 69, 71; and stock market, 80–1; banking control, 97, 102; and exchange rate, 160
Saudi Industrial Development Fund, 133, 155
Saudi International Bank, 94
Saudi Petrochemical Company (Sadaf), 202
Saudi Share Registration Company, 80
Saudia (national airline), 82, 196–8
share prices, 4–5, 72–3, 76–7, 79, 83; *see also* stock markets
Sharia law, 7, 90
Sharjah, 204
sheep: import of live, 63
shipping, 201–4
Sony company, 55
Souk Al-Manakh, Kuwait: stock market crisis, 1, 7, 19, 73, 74, 77–8, 80, 83–4, 90–1, 205–6; collapse described, 211–15
Spain, 147
Special Drawing Rights (IMF), 159–60
steel industry, 130, 131, 150–1, 201
stock markets, 43, 66, 72–8, 80–6, 121; *see also* Souk Al-Manakh
structural index, 219–21, 223
subsidies, 12, 43, 185, 188–9, 207
Switzerland, 164–5
Syria, 209–10

tariffs (customs): increased, 12, 39, 43, 65; on consumer goods, 48, 62; on cement, 149
taxation, 11, 71, 132–3, 207
television sets, 47, 53
Texaco, 31–2
tourism, 199
tractors, 59
trade fairs, 54
Turkey, 112, 209

Umm Al Quwain, 84, 148
Unified Economic Agreement (GCC), 39
Union of Soviet Socialist Republics (USSR), 208
United Arab Emirates: in GCC, 1; GDP rates, 1, 232–42; banks and banking in, 6, 69, 71, 96–7, 101, 252–3; budgets, 8, 11, 13, 248; balance of payments, 9, 172, 254; imports, 10, 254; capital outflow from, 15; oil reserves, 28, 231; oil production and exports, 32, 231; foreign workers in, 46, 48, 51, 206; racial composition, 51; TV sets in, 53; advertising in, 53; car sales in, 58; furniture sales in, 60; food imports, 63; proposed stock exchange, 84, 121; construction in, 106–13, 117, 232–6; mineral resources, 131; petrochemical industry, 147; cement production, 147–50; steel production, 150–1; fertilizer production, 151–3; aluminium production, 153; currency exchange, 159–61; consumer prices, 163; foreign assets, 165, 256; current account balance, 167, 176; agriculture in, 183, 187–9, 232–6; insurance in, 193, 195; and Gulf Air, 198; hotels, 200; shipping decline, 201; administrative sector in, 206; exports capital, 216; liquidity and other indicators, 221–4, 250–1; population, 227–30; structure of deposits, 249; international reserves, 256
United Arab Shipping Company

(UASC), 201
United Kingdom (Britain): imports from, 9–10, 45–6, 90; oil production, 25–7; oil supply, 32; furniture sales, 61; currency value and exchange rate, 159, 162; external sector, 163; Gulf investments in, 164–6
United Nations *see* Committee on Natural Resources
United States of America: imports from, 9–10, 45–6, 90; Gulf investments in, 23, 165–6; oil reserves and production, 27, 31; car sales, 57–8; dollar exchange rates, 159, 166, external sector, 163

urea, 152
usury, 7, 14

vehicles, 57–60
Venezuela, 28
video entertainment, 53–4

water, *see* irrigation
wheat production, 185–6
Whitaker, Peter, 52
women: and consumer marketing, 52
Wusail project, Qatar, 110

Yanbu oil terminal, 209

DATE DUE